Developments in Landscape Management and Urban Planning, 2

DESIGN FOR DIVERSITY

TITLES PUBLISHED THUS FAR IN THIS SERIES

1. R.J.A. Goodland and H.S. Irwin
Amazon Jungle: Green Hell to Red Desert?

2. B.B. Greenbie[*]
Design for Diversity

3. K. McCoy
Landscape Planning for a New Australian Town

---

[*] (See p. iv)

To VLASTA

who shares my territory
and makes it home

Contents

THE DISTEMIC WORLD:

Photo of the planet Earth from Apollo 11, July 1969, 98,000 miles in space. (U.S. Aeronantics and Space Administratim).

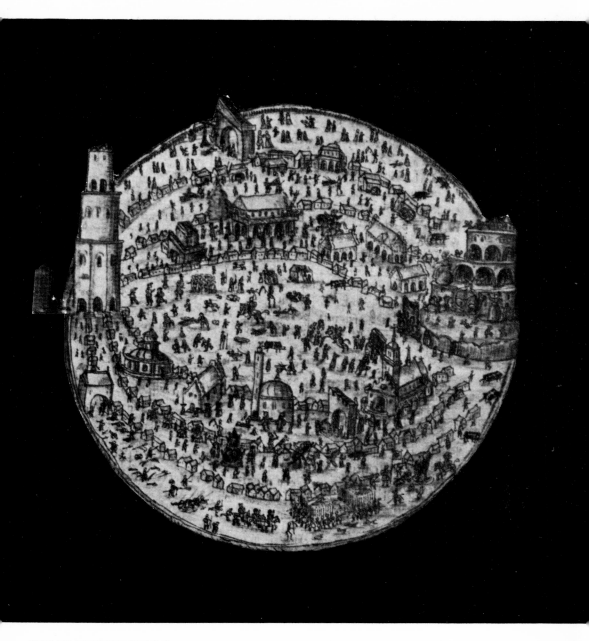

THE PROXEMIC WORLD:

Sketch from "The Labyrinth of the World and the Paradise of the Heart" by the Czech philosopher J. A. Comenius, 1623. (State Library, Prague, Czechoslovakia).

That each shall in his house abide,
Therefore was the world so wide.
Emerson

Preface

It has been observed that more knowledge has been generated since World War Two than in the entire previous history of human thought. This is attributed not only to the explosive development of information processing technology, but also the increasing specialization of knowledge. But as with so many technological accomplishments which foster human hubris, breakthroughs become breakdowns when technical systems collide with biological ones. For all practical purposes the ultimate information processing mechanism is a biological organism, the human brain. If the purpose of knowledge is to enable our species to adapt to our social-physical environment in a manner that will assure our survival, then there is indeed some question whether we have in the last two generations learned more than our ancestors knew. In fact there is a real question whether we "know" more, in this sense, than do much more primitive creatures.

Probably in no other field of intellectual activity has the gap between objective information and subjective understanding become so wide as in the design and management of the natural habitat of industrial mankind, the urbanized landscape. While specialized science continually extends its knowledge of human and non-human nature, less and less of this knowledge is available in a form that enables ordinary people to come to terms with each other and the environment. When scientific information becomes so specialized that only scientists can use it, society effectively becomes unscientific.

Growing awareness of this problem has prompted academic and research institutions, funding agencies, and many scientists, to place increasing emphasis on interdisciplinary work. There are two ways in which interdisciplinary research can come about. In one, a number of specialists come together to attempt to synthesize and coordinate their various activities and viewpoints. This is the most fashionable approach at the moment. The other is for a single mind, or a group of minds with similar perspectives, to attempt to synthesize information from a variety of fields.

One profession has, from its inception, tended to follow the latter course: the so-called *generalist* in urban and regional planning. The traditional format for such planning, the *comprehensive plan*, has been a mechanism for relating various classes and systems of information about human beings and their habitats. The essence of such a plan, theoretically, lies not in the independent facts involved, but in their relationships. Since no one can be an expert about everything, the generalist planner is stuck with the problem of using information as intelligently as possible from a variety of sources with which he has little first hand knowledge. However, the irony of this situation is that generalized planning itself tends to become a speciality, with its own techniques and dogmas which isolate the comprehensive planner from all that he purports to comprehend.

Since the amount of complexity that even the most able and disciplined mind can manage is very limited relative to all that needs to be dealt with, comprehensive planners unfortunately tend to rely on very limited sets of data and concepts. Like physicians and engineers, planners deal with matters that have important consequences for others. Quite understandably they like to play it safe with "the facts," even when those facts have proved to be something less than adequate in leading to solutions to problems; as long as such data do not clearly cause people harm they are more likely to be trusted than less familiar kinds of information which might have unpredictable results.

During the formative years of the profession, at least in the United States, an attempt was made to extend the comprehensive planner's field of view and freedom of vision by keeping him out of politics, securely perched on olympian planning commissions where he could look at the environment rationally, free from the conflicts among vested interests centered in the city hall. With a marked decline of faith in human rationality that has followed World War II, the planning pendulum has swung the other way, toward passionate, political advocacy. Now to the fear of empirically uncertain information has been added the fear of politically (i.e., ideologically) unpopular information. Irrational attitudes have quite properly now been included in the data base, but unfortunately destructive irrational objectives are also taken as desirable goals. One purpose of this book is to offer a planning paradigm which on the one hand accepts the important role of irrational behavior in human affairs, but on the other attempts to deal *rationally* with the irrational.

In my view, the one great gain (despite the intellectual dangers) in the shift of planning from objectivity to political relevance, is the inclusion in interdisciplinary problem-solving of the non-professional public who must live with the solutions that emerge, whether good or bad. The citizens of free societies, or those which seek to be free, cannot leave planning to the experts, any more than they can leave war to generals, law-making to lawyers, or, as noted, science to scientists. Thus, while this book is written from the perspective of a professional planner and physical designer, it is not addressed to my professional and academic colleagues alone. It has been written for all who share my own perplexity and concern with the future of our species, which obviously includes many many times the number of people who are likely to read it. It is also offered both as response and thanks to the many minds from several fields of knowledge who provided what facts it contains, and who contributed to my own insight regarding the relationships among them.

In this book I have attempted to extend the planner's generalist approach to include a field of specialized knowledge that has been largely outside the frame of reference for this profession — and even, in many quarters, formally taboo. I have attempted to compare some relatively recent scientific theories and findings regarding the behavior of other animals with conceptually similar research regarding our own species. But because of the impassioned confusions that have been evoked by other attempts to do this, I must stress at the outset that the primary subject of the book is only one animal, *Homo sapiens.* I am not a zoologist.

The subjects I will examine involve four distinct disciplines with entanglements in a number of others. I have not attempted a comprehensive survey of them, but rather I have quite deliberately concentrated on the work of a few scientists who have generalized between non-human and human behavior, and whose theories appeared to me to be most directly applicable to my own professional interests, the planning and design of satisfactory human habitats. I have taken for granted that the intelligent reader will realize that there are considerable differences of opinion in these matters, and I have not felt it necessary to reiterate that fact at every stage of the discussion or to examine all the other points of view that might be brought to bear on it. I have been quite selective in comparing my main subject, ethological theory, with concepts from psychology, anthropology, and sociology, and make no claim that my choices in regard to any of these disciplines are representative of the thinking in those fields. The selection in each case was based on my perception of remarkable similarities in observations that have been drawn from very different theoretical bases.

If similar conclusions emerge from the insights and observations of researchers working independently, with different paradigms, on a great variety of subjects, using widely disparate techniques, it is reasonable for both the professional generalist and the citizen generalist to assume that something significant has been turned up, even if all the facts are not established conclusively to anyone's satisfaction. One such conclusion is that there is a strong propensity among most, if not all, animals, including us humans, to organize in discrete groups in space — a complex and highly variable propensity which has been loosely called territorial behavior.

My interest in this question was sparked by the popular and highly controversial writings on the subject that appeared in the mid-sixties by such luminaries as Robert Ardrey and Konrad Lorenz, and by less spectacular but equally influential scholars like Edward T. Hall. It occurred to me that if there is such a thing as a *territorial imperative*, we who spend our working lives putting up walls and drawing boundaries around human activities might do well to find out as much as possible about it. The result of my own investigation of this subject is that I have produced a book, not primarily about *physical form*, which is my real business and remains my chief interest, but *social structure*.

It is a characteristic of human exploration that we often set out, like Columbus, to find one thing and discover another. This in itself may be one of the differences between us and other animals. In any case, it is somewhat to my own surprise that I have arrived, not at a physical plan, but a social theory. I had no clear theory to start with, nor did any of my own colleagues with whom I discussed a much-discussed subject at the time. Theory as such was not my ultimate objective. I view all theories, including the ones presented here, as tools to do something with, or, more correctly, to obtain information to do something with, to be used when useful, to be sharpened or reshaped as need be, and to be put aside or discarded when they fail to solve a problem.

One of the great difficulties with multi-disciplinary teamwork, despite its many advantages, derives from the difficulties of blending different theoretical systems. I suspect one has to stand almost entirely outside theory in order to fully appreciate the similarities in phenomena which so often wear the disguises of the diverse perceptual systems of their investigators. I believe this is a justification for the individual generalist, especially the generalist who steps outside his own field of specialization, where he too will tend to be limited perceptually by the boundaries of accepted theory. On the other hand, since conclusions derived in this manner cannot be judged against the collective wisdom of the specialized discipline, they can only be assessed in terms of the objectives and biases of the individual who has drawn them. I have therefore adopted a frankly personal style in presenting this material.

In respect to this, the book contains a few philosophical passages which some who have read the manuscript have objected to. Planners tend to be moralists, which is perhaps inevitable, since only those with a large measure of irrational idealism would attempt the improbable mission of putting the messy human world in order. I am probably no exception, but this is reflexive, rather than intentional, since the book itself is an attempt to deal with the culturally relative nature of most moral attitudes. For those who like their "facts" straight, without dilution by rhetoric, or who object to my inferences, I simply ask tolerance, and suggest that they skip to the substantive parts which I hope are presented meaningfully enough to make it worth while to look for them.

I have tried to be as careful as possible in distinguishing ideas which are my own from those of others. Yet it is always difficult and often impossible to separate one's thoughts from the words and activities of people who have stimulated them. To the innumerable persons who have contributed to my own insights, directly and through print, I wish to express my gratitude and to apologize in advance for any flaws in fact or interpretation which may have occurred through an attempt to translate various scientific thought-systems into those of the applied arts.

Barrie B. Greenbie
Amherst, Mass.
December 1974

*The research on which this book was based was supported in part by Grant A71-I-26 from the National Foundation on Arts and Humanities, National Endowment for the Arts

ELSEVIER SCIENTIFIC PUBLISHING COMPANY
335 Jan van Galenstraat
P.O. Box 211, Amsterdam, The Netherlands

AMERICAN ELSEVIER PUBLISHING COMPANY, INC.
52 Vanderbilt Avenue
New York, N.Y. 10017

ISBN 0-444-41329-4

Printed in The Netherlands

Developments in Landscape Management and Urban Planning, 2

DESIGN FOR DIVERSITY

Planning for Natural Man in the Neo-technic Environment:
An Ethological Approach

BARRIE B. GREENBIE

Department of Landscape Architecture and Regional Planning, University of
Massachusetts, Amherst, Mass. (U.S.A.)

ELSEVIER SCIENTIFIC PUBLISHING COMPANY
Amsterdam — Oxford — New York   1976

Acknowledgements

Some of the information and much of the conceptual framework are the result of personal interviews. The travel in connection with these interviews was supported in part by a grant from the National Endowment for the Arts, and this assistance is gratefully acknowledged.

I would particularly like to thank an American pioneer researcher in human ethology, A.H. Esser, who has been of great help to me. He has played a major role in developing communications between environmental designers and behavioral scientists. I am indebted to him directly and indirectly for an important part of the background information presented in this book, especially that which originated in the 1968 American Association for the Advancement of Science Symposium which he organized, and which will undoubtedly prove to be a major landmark in late 20th century efforts to introduce ethological concepts into the study of man—environment relations.

I am also indebted to the other scientists whose work I have leaned on heavily. Paul Leyhausen, Fred Fischer, and Irenaeus Eibl-Eibesfeldt were not only extremely generous with their own professional time, but they and their families were most hospitable to my wife and me personally during a research visit to Europe.

V.O. Wynne-Edwards was not in Scotland during the only time I could arrange to be there, but he graciously arranged for me to meet his colleagues George M. Dunnet, Ian J. Patterson, Robert Moss, and William Bourne, who were most generous with their time and ideas. Detlev Ploog of the Max Planck Institute for Psychiatry was very helpful and gracious, as were his associates, Peter Gottwald and John Ellring; they all made our stay in Munich productive and enjoyable. Three fellow-planners in Holland, Meto Vroom and W.J.G. Van Mourik of the Agricultural University of Wageningen, and C.R. Walter, were, together with their wives, exceedingly hospitable to us during our stay in The Netherlands, and they provided us with insights into the social and spatial structure of that country. Professor Vroom, who had recently returned from the U.S., also gave me his interesting insights into my own country. Several informative hours at the Technical University of Delft were spent with Derk de Jonge and his associate, H. van Hoogdalem. Architect Michael Kuhn served as my intellectual and geographical guide through Israel; he and Mrs. Kuhn extended warm personal hospitality. Professor David Amiran of The Hebrew University provided a most interesting analysis of Jerusalem. Hans W. Lissman and his wife Corrine combined a warm personal welcome in Cambridge, England with informative discussions together with

Dr. Lissman's colleagues at the Maddingly Animal Behaviour Laboratory. (I deeply regret having missed Robert Hinde there.) H. Hediger granted me an interesting interview in the company of Dr. Fischer, along with a tour of the famous Zurich Zoo. John Hutt took time out of a busy schedule at short notice for a most stimulating discussion in Oxford, England.

In the U.S., John Cassel of the University of North Carolina School of Public Health provided insights on which I have leaned heavily, as did Edward T. Hall, whose theory of proxemics is such an integral part of the design for diversity which I have offered in this book. John B. Calhoun and Paul D. MacLean, of the National Institute of Mental Health, likewise have provided an important part of the information and theory concerning human behavior on which this work is based. Dr. Calhoun invited me to spend a day in his laboratory, with his assistant Harley Marsden, despite the fact that my visit came at a most hectic time for them.

Dr. MacLean introduced me to his monkeys and showed me the workings of their (and our) brains, and then compounded his theoretical contributions with a thoughtful reading of my manuscript. An anthropologist whose writings are well known in the general subject area of this study, Lionel Tiger, was most courteous and stimulating in the early stages when I was developing my material. A geographer, Emmanuel Meier, provided helpful criticism and the introduction to Professor Amiran.

My Amherst colleague, R.W. Wilkie, a geographer and something more, provided valuable criticism of the manuscript, as well as important input into the theory it describes, as did another Amherst associate, sociologist Milton Gordon. Within my professional home territory, that of urban—regional planning, I wish to thank David Ranney, who prompted me to undertake this study in the first place, and Leo Jakobson, whose encouragement and critical comments were most helpful. I also must acknowledge a very special debt to ecologist Hugh H. Iltis for most valuable suggestions and his inimitable kind of moral support. From an editorial point of view, I am deeply indebted to Ellen Graham and to Ada Reif Esser for detailed criticisms which greatly improved the manuscript. I am also indebted to Antonin Mestan and to Kenneth Craik for thoughtful comments which led me to make important clarifications. My thanks as well to students and colleagues who read the manuscript in various stages of maturation, and to those scientists presented in its pages who read the parts dealing with their work. I must also thank my department colleagues at the University of Massachusetts, particularly Ervin Zube and Paul Procopio, who helped to assure me time for the writing of this book in the early stages.

Regarding material support, in addition to the grant from the National Endowment for the Arts, this work was also supported by a grant from my wife, who among other things made up for lost income in the initial phases. It is customary to acknowledge the distaff contribution to a work of this kind, but I must also gratefully acknowledge professional as well as personal help from Vlasta Koran Greenbie. As a research librarian, she provided bibliographic assistance indispensable in charting a course through unfamiliar academic territory, and she further served as my translator in foreign cultural territories. She was also, as wives are wont to be, my best and toughest critic.

However, I must take full responsibility for the conclusions and ideas expressed here. Except for specific quotations, my acknowledgements of assistance should not suggest that my views are necessarily shared by any of the individuals named, or, of course, by the National Endowment for the Arts.

My thanks also to Linda Mitton, Susan Zimnoski, and especially Ruth Laliberte, for patiently typing and re-typing the manuscript in various versions.

A portion of Chapter 1 and most of Chapter 7 have previously appeared in an article in the Journal of the American Institute of Planners (Greenbie, 1974), and permission to re-use this material is acknowledged.

PART ONE
THE CONCEPTUAL FRAMEWORK

Chapter 1

Introduction

In the year 1972 Americans watching the daily news on television might have seen in half an hour four life scenarios projected on their screens — and on their consiciousness of the environment. In the first, soldiers push through the burning debris of a village shattered by bombs and artillery fire in Vietnam. In the second, an uninhabitable housing project is deliberately dynamited by the same agency that hopefully constructed it a few years before. In the third scene, armed men surround a hijacked airliner. In the fourth scene, angry men and women wave placards at a school bus into which children are being herded by police.

Among the many meanings that such scenes have for the millions of people who are affected, directly or indirectly, by the events depicted, there are certain common elements that have particular significance for those to whom this book is addressed, urban designers and planners, and their clients, the residents of the urbanizing world. One of the common elements is *power*, the power to make decisions which have unintended consequences and which are made at a remote distance from those who are affected by them. Another is *territory*, which may be defined as the social organization of physical space. Still another is the social organization of symbolic systems which can be considered *conceptual territory*, and which has such a large influence on the way we organize ourselves in relation to each other and to physical space.

This book is an attempt to look into some of the complex processes which tie these elements together, and to the dangerous misalignments of people, space and mythology which can lead to a war one side could neither win nor comprehend, to the construction and eventual destruction of an expensive building no one will live in, to an airplane trip the passengers didn't want to be on and could not get off, and to conflicting programs for initiating children into cultures their parents cannot share.

Of the scenes described, the one that is most relevant to the subject to be discussed is the second, the uninhabitable habitation designed in good faith for health and welfare, and built in fact for misery, crime, and fear. How can this be?

In the early nineteen sixties, some years before the first rumblings of the big ghetto riots which shook our urban foundations like an earthquake, Jane Jacobs (1961) drew widespread attention to the idea that, in the large scale reshaping of American cities called "urban renewal," vital social structures were being demolished along with obsolete bricks and beams. She described then what life was like in the "Pruitt-Igoes" of New York, those publicly sponsored catacombs of fear and loneliness, and contrasted them (too romantically, perhaps) with streets where the relationship of scale to the human psyche made life both possible and interesting, if not always happy. Her brilliant insights were wrapped in theories of density and city structure which many planners of the time found outrageous, and which probably to most of us are at least questionable to this day. It is a peculiarity of the intellectual tribes and clans of our species that we mark our territories with theories, an attack on which will be reflexively interpreted as an assault on the territory itself. Jane Jacobs' important perceptions and her not insignificant array of facts were submerged in the counter-attack on her theories. Meanwhile, the bulldozers rolled on. At about the same time, sociologist Herbert Gans, who later did much to balance out Jacobs' viewpoint (Gans, 1968), published a thoughtful study of an ethnic neighborhood in Boston (Gans, 1962) that substantiated Jacobs' best perceptions. As that book was pondered by assorted theoreticians, its locale, an "urban village" which was the West End of Boston, fell to the wrecking ball.

The most succinct and crucial of Jane Jacobs' formulations of the processes that lead to the "Death and Life of Great American Cities" were two. The first was that a city cannot be viewed as merely a larger village, that it is qualitatively a different kind of entity, and that the chief difference between a metropolis and a small town is that public spaces of the former must be kept habitable for people who do not know each other personally. The first requirement of this is that safe streets must be kept full of people, and in order to keep streets well-populated urban environments, they must be kept continuously interesting and therefore diverse. Her second key formulation was that the healthy city does contain within itself some of the characteristics of the small town in that it is built up of discrete social and physical clusters to which a significant number of people feel identity, and for which they feel responsibility. She delineated a number of such areas, and for the process of organic self-renewal, which even minimum assistance to such areas brought forth, she coined the term *unslumming*.

In the decade that followed, a wide range of social studies focussed on the complexities of modern urban community structure, generating continuing debate on all sides. But Jane Jacobs touched the imaginations and evoked the hostility of working architects and planners perhaps more than any other writer at that time. Meanwhile, the bulldozers pushed on through our urban tissue, systematically transplanting people, structures, and functions into alien ecological relationships in which apparently few of them could thrive. In the middle of all this, a dramatist-turned-anthropologist named Robert Ardrey (1966) churned up another kind of controversy by drawing attention to new theories that the *territorial imperative* was a basic instinct which man shared with other animals.

Late in 1972, the year of the Pruitt-Igoe immolation, an architect scientist named Oscar Newman defined the parameters of *defensible space* with an empirical study which suggested a relationship between human territoriality and a major symptom of urban disease, crime. Newman has been criticized, largely on the methodological grounds that this theory is not derived from his data, but no one, to my knowledge, has disproved his conclusions, and his work has focussed on a long-neglected aspect of social-physical space:

> The time has come to go back to first principles, to reexamine human habitat as it has evolved, to become attuned again to all the subtle devices invented over time and forgotten in our need and haste to house the many. . . For one group to be able to set the norms of behavior and the nature of activity possible within a particular place, it is necessary that it have clear, unquestionable control over what can occur there. Design can make it possible for both inhabitant and stranger to perceive that an area is under the undisputed influence of a particular group, that they dictate the activity taking place within it, and who its users are to be. . .
>
> *Defensible space* is a model for residential environments which inhibits crime by creating the physical expression of a social fabric that defends itself. . . .When people begin to protect themselves as individuals and not as a community, the battle against crime is effectively lost. . . "Policing" is not intended to evoke a paranoid vision but refers to the oldest concept in the Western political tradition: the responsibility of each citizen to insure the functioning of the polis. (Newman, 1972, p. 3.)

Now that the arrogance of well-intentioned ignorance has helped sections of our large cities to become virtually uninhabitable, we are faced with propositions that may, if the increasingly sophisticated knowledge of human behavior is not immediately put to work, extend the same disastrous policies to the suburbs. Suburbs, whatever else they may or may not be, have tended to be relatively stable communities. We may assume that is one reason why they are being looked to by reformers who have given up on the central city. A number of campaigns are underway to relocate core city poor through a legal assault on what is called "exclusionary zoning," but it is not their "exclusionary" nature as such that is causing the trouble; it is rather the unworkable and unbalanced distribution of populations in relation to resources — economic, natural, and cultural — that has resulted from a false view of what it is appropriate to exclude and what it is not. A restructuring of the way residential communities are organized around centers of transportation, commerce and available space, with due regard to the ecosystem is essential, but exclusion pro or con is not an adequate definition of the problem.

The attack on zoning as exclusionary is dangerous, in my opinion, because it is an assault on one of the few remaining means of defining social territory, without any alternative being offered. Zoning in the United States originated in an attempt to bring form to an increasingly formless urban environment. It did so precisely because the forces which shaped earlier communities were no longer operative. In general, it has proved to be a crude and blunt instrument, mangling the physical environment and permitting no subtleties, either in human or non-human relationships. But the fact that it has proved to be a poor solution on the one hand, and that it has led to a new problem of community structure on the other, does not mean that it can be breached like a castle wall without recognizing and respecting the more constructive purposes it was designed to accomplish in the first place.

A viewpoint dear to many planners is that the ideal community will contain a "mix" of socio-economic, racial, religious, and whatever groups of people. Jane Jacobs and others have made an excellent case for diversity of all kinds, and there is good reason to believe that under proper conditions social heterogeneity on some levels is a prerequisite for cross-cultural cooperation. In fact, the achievement of such conditions is the primary objective of this book, as the title suggests; but rarely are plans for social mixing accompanied by consideration in careful detail of who is to be mixed with whom, how, where, and under what conditions. If a chemist advanced the proposition that a "mix" per se is good, we would call him mad! If a cook advanced such a notion, we would go elsewhere to eat. Yet there is much clear evidence that some people mix well and some do not, that the same people can mix safely and happily under some conditions but not under others, and above all, that he who would intrude one group into another's territory should be prepared to guarantee the safety of both if his egalitarian predictions prove false. As with other animals, there is good reason to believe that indiscriminate mixing of incompatible human beings is likely to be as destructive as mixing incompatible chemicals. As we shall see later on, this does not necessarily lead to violence. It may merely lead to disease.

The modern suburb in North America may be seen as an attempt to combine two incompatible types of social organization — the ancient village where people unite in common space for common interests and are more or less bound by both, and the egalitarian outlook of the frontier, where everybody has more or less equal claim to space and each other's company, and where social strata are themselves viewed as a violation of cultural norms, because people have not lived together long enough to develop a natural dominance hierarchy based on close personal acquaintance and psychological assessment of individual capacities.

The popular American model of the suburb has been that of the colonial town, similar to what Donaldson has identified as the agrarian myth of Thomas Jefferson, "whose utopia could be represented as a band of yeomen farmers conducting the business of their community at an open town meeting." (Donaldson, 1969, p. 8.) Such established pre-suburban old towns contained a real measure of individual and class diversity precisely because that diversity contained important common features. Everyone, or almost everyone, knew everybody else, and shared not only a common geographical space, but a common conceptual territory as well. The modern zoned subdivision attempts to cope with the fact that our socially, economically, and physically mobile middle classes inhabit disparate conceptual territories, constantly being reformed by the media, and carried by continually shifting groups to new places. Under such conditions social status tends to be based, not on personal qualities, but on the rather arbitrary structuring of visible externalities. Thus, it is not how a person thinks or behaves that binds him to a community, but how his house is arranged on the lot, what sort of car is parked in the yard, what value is publicly recorded in the assessor's office, how much he earns, and where. This can and does often lead to an internal conformity in taste, opinion, and style, but whether it does so more than any other society is highly debatable. The emphasis on physical externalities may, however, permit a remarkable degree of conceptual privacy for those who want it, since philosophical theories, cultural interests, and psychological states are not considered a matter of public consequence. This can, and I believe does, offer protection of a sort against a more degrading and dangerous kind of conformity — that of thought control imposed by religious and political orthodoxies. The current social ferment in industrial societies, which has so often been generated within "suburbia" itself, seems to me to be evidence of this.

Of course, conceptual freedom is a matter of high priority only to those whose physical wants are reasonably well met. It is likely to be a matter of less interest to those whose daily lives are completely engrossed in a struggle for survival, and for whom crowding provides little opportunity for such privacy in any case. Mechanisms which directly or indirectly protect this sort of freedom, however important to a society as a whole, may well be considered a device to push their problem aside. Nevertheless, the evidence is strong that community identity in a discrete space is considerably more, not less, important to the poor, who do not have the conceptual (e.g., educational) resources to compensate for loss of geographical territory by substituting conceptual territories based on arts, hobbies, or professional activities.

The idea that human societies form nucleations as other natural phenomena do is hardly new. Geographers have long noted the tendencies of urban communities to grow around centers, and to establish linkages, giving rise to various location theories usually based on efficiency (Morrill, 1970), and variants such as Christaller's "central place theory" (Johnson, 1970). Planners have attempted to apply Keppler's laws of interacting bodies to the relationships of urban centers in a "gravity model." In the 1920's Burgess developed a model of city growth in concentric rings which was basically centripetal, anticipating the current suburban explosion. Hoyt (1939) modified this by finding the rings divided into wedge-shaped segments. McKenzie had proposed a model for sociology under the discipline of "human ecology" in which he drew on analogies from plant and animal studies (Hawley, 1968). This movement has been summarized by Michelson (1970), who shows that as it developed it tended to lean on economic explanations for human behavior, rather than on physical ones.

A biological model of urban growth was provided by Geddes (1915) and by Saarinen (1943). These saw human settlements as cells surrounding a nucleus, differentiating into larger and more complex organisms in a hierarchy of discrete units; they both recognized undifferentiated sprawl as a symptom of decay and disease. But these were largely spatial. What is urgently needed today is the inclusion into our concept of the urban environment of functional and behavioral hierarchies which correspond more closely to the ecologist's view of the natural world, the ecosystem. We are suffering, not only from physical sprawl, but also from social sprawl. And unfortunately this tendency has been fostered, particularly in this country, by a mechanistic view of "equality" which applies to human relationships the standardizing processes that facilitate mass production and mass consumption. It is also facilitated by setting up a false dualism between "physical" planning and "social" planning. As Michelson has suggested, social function cannot be isolated from physical form. Nor, as Rapoport has shown (1969), can physical form be usefully considered independent of the cultural relationships of its creators and users. Yet, much planning today still ignores basic biological as well as cultural realities.

Frightened at last as we are by our deteriorating physical environment, both planners and the public have begun to listen to the natural ecologist's view of the intricate interrelationships that make up what Charles Darwin called the "web of life." It has taken a hundred years for scientific man to come to terms with the concept of evolution: we are biological beings inexorably linked to the natural processes that brought forth the long chain of evolving life which preceded us on this planet. Until very recently, however, our acceptance of human evolution has been largely on the physical level, except for the brief and ignominious era of so-called "Social Darwinism." Only in the last two or three decades have biologists turned their attention systematically to the evolution of behavior. They are turning up increasingly hard evidence that not only in our bodies but in our minds, our hearts, and perhaps even in what we perceive as our souls, we are a species of animal. We are an animal with unique power to alter many aspects of our external environments, and, to a limited extent, to alter ourselves in the process. But we do not have the power to override the processes that brought us, along with all other living things, into being. If we originated in the same processes that brought forth other animals, we may well consider their behavior in attempting to understand and constructively direct our own.

Recently in the U.S.A. there has been a renewed interest in ethnic groups as a fundamental component of our culture (Novak, 1972). Levine and Campbell (1972) have examined ethnocentrism, the self-referencing tendency of each group to measure other cultures by its own. Glazer and Moynihan (1970), having originally predicted (1963) that diversity based on ethnicity would more and more be defined by race and religion, revised this estimate after the turbulent events of the 1960's increased the role of race and decreased that of religion. With the growing public awareness of the plight of urban black communities, the cultural life of racial ghettos has been investigated by a large number of social scientists (see Rainwater, 1966, 1971; Rossi, 1973; Rossi and Boesel, 1971). Among these, Suttles (1968, 1972) has been particularly concerned with the question of "neighborhood identity." In many cases ethnic homogeneity appears to be strongly related to community stability; in fact the anxieties attributed to the mobile middle classes, including the revolt of their young, may be due to the fact that such groups have renounced the security of small group identity. There is a large amount of literature on this subject and in a single volume it is difficult not to oversimplify. But at least for many Americans, where the melting pot has actually melted anything, it appears to have produced a very brittle alloy.

Perhaps the most thorough attempt to develop a theory of ethnicity under conditions of cultural pluralism as it has emerged in the United States is that of Milton Gordon (1964). Gordon has, among other things, distinguished between *assimilation* and a partial degree of it which he called *acculturation*. In the latter, ethnic groups adopt the prevailing cultural attitudes as their own, participating in the larger society on the level of secondary relationships, while retaining their ancestral identity in modified form for primary group associations. I shall return to the theories of Gordon and Suttles in a later chapter.

The egalitarian myths of our North American culture which have so often led us to ignore and even condemn social distinctions officially, while furtively ghettoizing them, undoubtedly have contributed to reluctance on the part of even those social scientists who study group and class structure to accept comparisons with the territorial behavior of other animals. Territory as a phenomenon is most often interpreted negatively, that is, to keep something out, rather than positively to protect something within. Egalitarians are quite ready to accept as characteristic, or even innate, the obvious propensity of human beings to cooperate, but they reject such universality for personal or small group territory, often on the implicit assumption that this is antithetical to cooperation. On the other hand, ethological studies of animal behavior in space strongly suggest that social cooperation and territory are correlates, that territory defines the space in which specific kinds of social relationships take place and which necessarily implies that contradictory social relationships must be excluded. Many ideological egalitarians show a tendency to confuse *equality* with *sameness*. But any meaningful concept of equality implies difference. The formula $X = X$ is nonsense. The relationship

$X = Y$ is predicated on the assumption that there is something about X which is unlike Y, but which has eqal value in some particular context. Equality as the context in which diversity can flourish requires an equitable distribution of territories, rather than their obliteration.

To accuse egalitarians in general of such simple-mindedness is undoubtedly unfair to the many humanists who are quite aware of differences, and who seek a framework of social justice which can accomodate them. Herbert Gans, who has been particularly sensitive to variations in outlook among ethnic groups in our culture, calls himself an egalitarian and asks simply for "more equality," not absolute identity (Gans, 1973). Others hedge the issue by calling for "equality of opportunity," and certainly that widely-accepted view of the subject allows for differences in individual capacities. But it does not allow adequately for differences in both individual and group aspirations. The question always arises, opportunity for what? On the level of basic necessities, such as food, clothing, shelter, air and water, human beings are generally equal both in need and aspiration. But the farther above the level of mere survival a society rises, the more social differences begin to matter. At least insofar as egalitarian ideologies emerge in political rhetoric and public policy, the "public good" is most often viewed in monolithic terms.

I shall return to this question in a later chapter. For the present I would simply note that, ironically, one of the most persistent arguments against the concept that we share innate behavioral characteristics with simple animals is that it denies the diversity of human cultures. This argument is heard much more from students of human behavior than from biologists whose task is to come to terms with the incredible diversity of nature itself. Diversity seems to be the common characteristic of the universe; and yet, no matter how complex phenomena appear, and how infinitely varying their manifestations, there is always some area of commonality present in order for us to perceive diversity. We cannot consider variety without considering that which is being varied.

Both the rediscovery of ethnic America and the increasing interest in biological behavior, if applied carefully and creatively, may help us to correct some of the mistakes that have contributed heavily to social as well as physical decay in our urban environments. Some corrections have already occurred. Current housing policy in Washington is to refrain from putting low-income families with children into high-rise buildings, and new public housing is beginning to show a more humane scale. Defensible space does appear to work on the level of the familiar community.

But this new awareness is no panacea for human happiness. It will solve only one part of a comprehensive problem. Industrialized human beings cannot survive in a social environment constructed entirely of tribal villages. Our entire technological world is based on forms of super-communication which are cross-cultural and in many cases accultural. For instance, an airplane pilot from the U.S. and one from Japan will have very different requirements in the design of a home. But they will agree quite readily on the design of an airport. The survival of civilization defined by any standard which can be applied to contemporary society requires that cultural groups, as well as individuals, cooperate on an unprecedented scale. It is to this other aspect of urban design, the opposite and complement of defensible space, that this book is primarily addressed.

Partly, no doubt, because of the urgency of the problems caused by failure to understand innate behavior, and partly because of some characteristics of behavior which later chapters will try to explore, most studies of human territoriality have dealt largely with *personal space*, the title of Robert Sommer's book on the subject (1969). My primary concern in this book is the relationships between human territorial groups, rather than within them. Edward T. Hall, who has pioneered in viewing use of space as a cultural phenomenon (1966, 1968, 1974), uses the term *proxemics* to describe the highly-varied spatial relationships and perceptions of diverse societies. While this concept is not the sort on which one can put arbitrary limits, it does tend to be considerably less explicit in spaces larger than those in which people can communicate sensually. To maintain continuity with Hall's concept, I will use the word *distemics* to describe those spatial relationships which transcend cultural group boundaries, and which rely primarily on communication by means of abstract symbols and instruments, what Hall himself calls *extensions* (which of course are also involved in proxemics). Behaviorally, these extensions appear in the barter of goods of one sort or another and the symbolic representations of goods which eventually became money, as well as all manifestations of technology. In neo-technic societies, such communication also requires those technical extensions, which A.H. Esser (1971a) calls *prostheses*, artificial aids to the biological senses, such as printed words or radio transmissions. I will come back to Hall's concept and my own extension of it later as a central part of my design for diversity.

For the present, let us return to the television scenes with which the chapter opened. In the Vietnam war we had, superimposed on the ancient territorial battles of tribal man, the actions of modern people who have no territorial interest at all in that region, except for the extension of a symbolic world, a cultural value system, that fits neither our "allies" nor our "enemies." We may safely conclude that such a war can never be won by outsiders, because, among other things, such alien symbolic systems cannot be fitted to that particular piece of space and the people who inhabit it. Whatever "honor" or "dishonor" Americans may have incurred as a result of that war is largely irrelevant to the people and customs over which it was fought, though the physical consequences are not. In the Pruitt-Igoe fiasco, an abstract concept of shelter has led to the construction of habitats so out of phase with human psyche that physical environments shared with rats under leaky roofs offer a preferable choice. In the political hijacking, we have a brutal confrontation between tribal loyalties and prosthetic cooperative systems. To the political hijacker his own group is all that demands moral responsibility, and in its interests a vast network of people, symbols and machines can be brought to a halt by a few dedicated individuals. To call such acts "immoral" is effectively meaningless: such men can be murderers abroad and heroes at home, and so it was in Vietnam, and so it will always be as long as small group identity is the only identity and thus overrides global necessities. In the bussing controversy, abstract concepts of justice, equality, and education come into violent collision with ancient territorial breeding impulses. All of these situations pertain to conflicting ways in which human beings lay claim to and use space and to the problems of designing physical relationships which can safely accommodate cultural and conceptual diversity.

The cultural lag in applying new knowledge to policy is at least partly due to conceptual conflicts among the decision-makers themselves, by the difficulties of translating the thought systems of the various sciences that initiate theory and draw forth information about the environment into thought systems that can be used by those who act directly on it. Every scientific or academic discipline, as well as every practicing profession, is at least partly a cultural group entity in its own right, with its own symbolic communication system, its kinships, and its territorial alliances. In simpler times, individuals who organized knowledge also organized objects, spaces, people, and events. The scientist, artist, and political leader could be the same person. Today, the management and governance of all but the most "underdeveloped" societies requires a complex hierarchy of sub-associations which appear to have some of the same difficulties intellectually as subcultures have behaviorally in communicating adequately across their respective boundaries.

Since this book will examine a number of such intellectual "subcultures," or disciplines, it may be well to start designing for diversity by recognizing certain differences between the designer, or architect, and the planner. The planner begins with one or more theories (in my view the more the better, provided he can tie them together adequately), and shapes them in forms which permit their constructive application to practice. He differs from the scientist, generally speaking, in that knowledge is not his objective but his starting point. But, like the scientist, the planner deals with generalities and abstractions, with forms which are yet to become embodiments in particular points of space and time. Despite a current cliché of the profession, "planning for people," planners are inevitably asked to manage, not people, but populations. It is the designer who plans for people, that is, for particular persons in particular places and particular points in time. To the designers most theories, being generalities, are irrelevant, and to many they are an anathema. To the most creative planners, all theories are interesting and most theories are useful, because most human thought is based on some response to some aspect of reality. But to be meaningful to those for whom both planning and design are directed, eventually information must be applied in a specific time—space context. At some point, all data, whether gathered from animals in Africa or the man next door, must be put to the test of use. At that point, what is generally true is only of limited help.

For example, in discussing a neglected aspect of "Women's Liberation," Levitt (1971) points out that whatever the majority of women may want, a particular woman should not be required to want it. This is true for all minorities, and in the last analysis we are all a minority of one. What is generally true for everybody is of only partial interest to the individual in his private life. One objective of this book will be to suggest the boundaries at which both planners and designers should leave people alone.

For the planner, there is a further impediment to the use of scientific knowledge. Planners deal with the future, and nothing whatsoever about the future is subject to verification by any means, scientific or otherwise. The planner deals with probabilities; scientific investigation can help to establish what has happened in the past and what is happening now, and therefore offers some clues to what is most likely to happen next. But it offers no certainties. And even when the planner has established, with the help of scientists and all the apparatus of science, including statistical techniques and computers, as accurately as possible what is happening now, he must combine probability with purpose in an attempt to influence events as he, and his clientele, wish them to be. This requires the intuition of the artist, broadly defined. Planning is the exercise of informed judgment, and judgment originates in mental regions which science has not yet penetrated as deeply as space or the oceans, and B.F. Skinner (1971) notwithstanding it most likely never will. Consciousness, like other forms of life, constantly evolves.

In the next chapter, I will sketch briefly my impressions of the development of the new science of *ethology*, the study of animal behavior in the natural environment, which seems to me to have unique applicability to the study of the natural habitat of *Homo sapiens*, the city.

In Part Two, I will look in detail at some of the theories and observations of three prominent ethologists, whose related but diverse ideas seem to me to have most direct bearing on the current human condition, making no claim to a comprehensive view of their work, which can only be obtained from the originals. In Part Three, I will examine the work of four researchers, all of them (among other things) medical doctors who have used ethological techniques or conceptual references in examining the behavior of human beings. In neither case is a full survey of the respective fields attempted, which would require several volumes. In Part Four, I will attempt to weave the theories and insights of these people together, to combine them with other theories, observations, and aspects of the human environment here and abroad, and arrive at some formulations of my own which I hope will help to establish a paradigm that may make it easier to shape the urban environment in a form which allows full room for our primitive emotional needs within a framework of rational interdependence of man and man, and man and nature.

Some of the theories I will draw on are among the most controversial in our time. Since anyone daring to enter this arena with a discernible idea on the subject will inevitably commit himself to controversy, it might as well be faced head on. It is a subject which should remain controversial; in science, as in politics, to which science is becoming ever more closely related, public debate is the only assurance of liberty, if not of ultimate truth. Furthermore, controversy is interesting; it is, as I think the following pages will demonstrate, the very essence of life. One hypothesis I have drawn from my studies is that intellectual combat is the most human, and usually the most humane, expression of the primitive urge toward territorial aggressiveness. But while it would be fatuous to break into print in this area without being prepared for controversy, theoretical battle is not my mission. I come as a wayfarer through strange conceptual countries, seeking not conquest in ideas, but trade.

Chapter 2

Ethology: a science for planning and design

> ...*every behavior selected for study, every observation and interpretation, requires subjective processing by an introspective observer. Logically, there is no way of circumventing this or the more disturbing conclusion that the cold, hard facts of science, like the firm pavement under foot, are all derivations of a soft brain.*
>
> Paul D. MacLean

One of the manifestations of *future shock*, the term Alvin Toffler (1970) has coined for the rapid environmental changes to which neo-technic man is increasingly subjected, is the speed with which new words come and go in the living language. A decade ago the word *ecology* had a rather specific meaning as the name of a science concerned with the relationships of living things to their environment. Today it is a household word which means something that everybody is supposed to be in favor of, even though not all are very clear on what it is. In this chapter I would like to look at a new science with a confusingly similar name, *ethology*, a science concerned with the relationships of that class of living things called animals to each other within their environment.

When I first came across this word less than a decade ago, I looked in a widely-used "collegiate" dictionary which happened to be close at hand and I coudn't find it. In the larger dictionaries, I found it had very different meanings, depending on whether the copyright date was before or after about 1960. The difference in meanings is in itself interesting evidence of the evolution of ideas and of scientific knowledge.

The current Random House "Dictionary of the English Language" (1966) defines ethology as "the scientific study of animal behavior, especially in relation to habitat." This describes ethology as the term is used by scientists at the present time. The early ethologists, in this sense of the word, were literally bird-watchers, many of them amateurs.

Lorenz, whose work began to appear in the 1930's, is universally credited (Ardrey, 1966; Fletcher, 1957; Huxley in "Foreword" to Lorenz, 1952; Eibl-Eibesfeldt, 1968) with being the first to formulate a new scientific discipline called *comparative ethology*. He shares this credit and the Nobel Prize with N. Tinbergen, who wrote the first authoritative text in ethology (1951). Both Lorenz (1952, 1966) and Tinbergen (1951, 1953) placed the question of instinct back in the psychological limelight, after its eclipse by the Behaviorists (Watson, 1925), so that acceptance of some role for instinct has become associated with an ethological approach to behavior, in both men and other animals. But this is not, in my opinion, the most important distinguishing characteristic of that science.

The characteristic that most distinguishes ethology from much experimental science is that it practices direct observation of behavior of animals in the natural habitat, or within environments which simulate as closely as possible the original habitat, and that it attempts to correlate all expressions of behavior simultaneously, without giving unequal weight to any one phenomenon. By contrast, the favorite devices of empirical investigators are to isolate, insofar as possible, a particular phenomenon for investigation, and set the subject up in the controlled environment of a laboratory where extraneous or presumed irrelevant information may be screened out, and where as many variables as possible may be held constant. In ethology there are virtually no independent variables; everything that subject animals do is recorded over time to ascertain underlying patterns of meaning.

The key to ethological method is this record, called an *ethogram*, which is prepared in exhaustive detail with every effort being made to avoid prejudging or weighing any evidence. This requires vast patience and a willingness to refrain from influencing events. It is similar to the methods of personality investigation known as *gestalt* psychology. Ethologists may disagree about the care, accuracy, and objectivity of each other's ethograms, but will agree that everything starts there. All science includes observation, of course; the difference between ethological field technique and experiment is in the scope and the type and amount of control that is exercised over what is being observed. Laboratory science will generally tend to develop from hunch to hypothesis to experimental verification and thence to a theory which will explain the sustained hypothesis or relate it to other hypotheses. Ethology will proceed from observation to perception of a pattern to a theory which will account for the pattern or relate it to others.

These are not incompatible, of course, but are complementary. Quite obviously a great deal of ethological theory developed from field observation can be subjected to test in the laboratory, and of course many scientists are doing just that; probably all ethologists do it to some extent. For instance, Harlow's laboratory studies of emotional deprivation in monkeys (1962) can be related very fruitfully to field studies of primate behavior. The observations of Jane Goodall (1971) of the prolonged close personal relationships between chimpanzee mothers and babies in the wild and the interests of all members of the troop in newborn infants correlate very well with Harlow's finding that infant monkeys deprived of association with the mother will develop into behaviorally crippled, while physically healthy, adults. Such deprivation would be difficult to note under natural conditions, because in the first place it would not be likely to occur, and, in the second place if it did, the infant would not be likely to survive long enough for the consequences to be determined. On the other hand, Calhoun (1971) has been studying the effects of overpopulation on mice by eliminating in his laboratory disease and predation which in the natural habitat would prevent the overpopulation from taking place. Except for that, he records what the overpopulated mice do "naturally." The line of demarcation between the ethological and experimental approach is not firm nor impenetrable, but there do tend to be important differences in point of view between the various investigators on each side.

In explaining their objectives in turning to ethology, a husband—wife team of experimental psychologists, S.J. and C. Hutt (1970, p. 16), described the differences between these scientific methods this way:

> The ethological approach differs from that of experimental psychology and other branches of behavioral sciences in that it insists upon an *ethogram* as the legitimate point of departure of any experimental study. *Before attempting to modify behavior, the ethologist demands to know what behavior there is to modify.* (My italics.) Before reaching conclusions about the effects of external physical stimuli, he seeks to know the endogenously generated patterns of behavior shown by an organism. Psychologists seem constrained to stimulate their subjects of study. Ethologists generally prefer to leave them alone. Until we know what an animal will do in the absence of a particular stimulus, we are in no position to make assertions regarding the effect of the stimulus. . .
> Ethologists proceed from naturalistic observations; they are interested in questions of *why* and *how* animals do what they do. Methods serve these ends and therefore are not of primary consideration. Psychologists are much more concerned with methodology, usually dictated by theoretical tenets or the requirements of statistical propriety. Consequently, what ethologists find out is interesting and significant even if methodologically circumspect, whereas what psychologists find is technically exemplary even if its validity and significance are sometimes obscure.

A number of new concepts have found their way into the laboratory for empirical examination which would probably never have been postulated to begin with if they had not first been observed by field ethologists. Among these are concepts which relate to phenomena that have long been observed, but for which no adequate mechanism has been postulated. Freud and others earlier noted that events in the life of the human infant seem to have a peculiarly tenacious hold on the later mind of the adult. Lorenz observed that the first thing that the infant chick sees when it breaks out of the egg, will be identified as "mother." By removing the actual mother and exposing the chick to another bird, animal, or object, a chick could be induced to identify that as its parent. In one case he had ducklings following an orange balloon with utter devotion; on other occasions birds were induced to follow Lorenz himself with equal passion. This phenomenon, first described in 1873 (Eibl-Eibesfeldt, 1968), is called *imprinting*. It has been investigated particularly by Lorenz. Its precise relevance to similar infant—mother attachments in more complex animals, including man, has obvious implications for education and mental health. Harlow (1959), in a famous series of experiments, raised infant monkeys in a laboratory which identified models made of cloth and chicken wire as mothers.

Another important ethological concept is that of *displacement*: this phenomenon occurs when an animal is engaged in aggressive behavior which would presumably be dangerous to the animal if carried to its logical conclusion. Instead of continuing with its attack on another animal, it suddenly stops and engages in irrelevant and seemingly senseless behavior, such as furiously pulling up grass, in the case of some birds. Lorenz views this as a sort of safety valve in which aggressive energy is sidetracked into harmless forms; it is central to his concept of the way aggression is restrained among non-human animals. According to him, most animals simply have no choice in the matter; they must behave that way. Tinbergen has recorded this sort of behavior, along with other rituals, in a wide variety of forms in birds and fishes. In mankind, its equivalent can be seen in banging a fist on the table (instead of an opponent's nose).

Because of the breadth of phenomena which comes under the ethologist's field of observation, this new science has attracted members from a wide range of disciplines. Biologists, naturalists, and particularly zoologists make up the largest part of its population. But ethology has attracted many anthropologists, some sociologists, and even a classics scholar (Havelock, 1971). It appears to draw psychiatrists and clinical psychologists rather than experimental psychologists, so many of whom lean to the anti-evolutionary attitudes of the "behaviorists." The field also continues to attract gifted amateurs from non-science professions. Israel has an ethologically-oriented architect, Michael Kuhn; Wynne-Edwards' Culterty Field Station in Scotland utilizes the service of an Aberdeen Police Detective who spends his weekends sleuthing out the habits of sea gulls. Perhaps because the science of ethology has the open-heartedness of youth; perhaps because the observation of nature is often a healthy antidote to vanity and possessiveness, amateurs appear to be welcome in this field as in few other professions.

Eibl-Eibesfeldt (1968) reports that: "Ethology has existed as a concept since 1762 when it was defined in France as the study of animal behavior." However, older editions of contemporary dictionaries define ethology differently, as it was used by John Stuart Mill in his famous "System of Logic" published in 1843. Mill proposed it as the name of a science which would study "the laws of the Formation of Character," by which he meant human character. Ethology, as Mill conceived it, would not study either humans or animals in their natural habitat, or be based primarily on observation. That he would leave to psychology. Rather it would attempt to ascertain by his Deductive Method the "simple laws of Mind in general" (p. 524), from which would be deduced "the laws of very complex phenomena" (p. 517) which would then be subjected to experimental inquiry. However, Mill defined *experimental inquiry* to include natural observation as well as artificial experiment.

Mill gave his reason for advocating the deductive formulation of general laws as opposed to experimental investigation of specific behaviors as follows:

> Are the laws of the formation of character susceptible of a satisfactory investigation by the method of experimentation? Evidently not; because even if we suppose unlimited power of varying the experiment, (which is abstractly possible, though no one but an oriental despot either has that power, or if he has would be disposed to exercise it), a still more essential condition is wanting; the power of performing any of the experiments with scientific accuracy. (p. 517.)

It appears that "universal laws" of the Formation of Character, or anything else, are no easier to obtain than universally valid empirical information, in view of the fact that Mill's version of ethology, which he hoped would be the "Exact Science of Human Nature" (p. 523), never became a working science at all. But it is instructive to note how Mill qualified his concept of "exactness":

> It is, however, (as in all cases of complex phenomena) necessary to the exactness of propositions, that they should be *hypothetical only, and affirm tendencies, not facts*. They must not assert that something will always, or certainly, happen; but only that such and such will be the effect of a given cause, so far as it operates uncounteracted. It is a scientific proposition, that cowardice tends to make men cruel; not that it always makes them so: that an interest on one side of a question tends to bias judgment; not that it invariably does so; that experience tends to give wisdom; not that such is always its effect. These propositions, being assertive only of tendencies, *are not the less universally true because the tendencies may be counteracted*. (My italics.)

Mill's concept of tendencies is useful in considering the relationship between the behavior of man and other animals, which does not predict that man must of necessity behave just like whatever animals are selected as examples. His really quite vague proposal for a new science of character seems to have had considerable appeal for the 19th century, particularly in education (Bailey, 1898, 1899) and leaves a scholarly mystery: why did it apparently die out, so suddenly and completely, that little more than a generation later a real living, breathing, working science could appear under the same name, but quite different, at least superficially, in objective and method? Whatever the explanation is, Mill's version of ethology and Lorenzian ethology may not be as far apart as they might seem at first glance. It may be that the final maturity of modern ethology will lead directly to the ends that Mill foresaw, even though by somewhat different means.

Ethology's special interest to planners and designers seems to me to be in the particular contribution of its modern version, that of gestalt observation. As noted, ethology's progenitors recognized the difficulties of subjecting human beings to experimental controls, which, in Mill's words, only an "oriental despot" would attempt. We have unfortunately had examples of oriental and occidental despots who did attempt that in our century, but even despots produce little by that method which can be called scientific knowledge of behavior, except perhaps that which can be derived from the opportunity to observe their own. In general the social sciences have had trouble in applying the quantitative as well as experimental methods that have worked reasonably well in the physical sciences, and less well, but still usefully, in the biological ones. Dubos (1968b) quotes Wordsworth: "We murder to dissect."

A number of sociologists, including Gerald Suttles (1968, 1972) whose work we will look at later, have used the "participant—observer method," which was originally developed by cultural anthropologists and is in many respects like the ethological one. Herbert Gans used it very successfully in his study of Boston's "urban villagers" (1962) and Levittown's middle class (1967). Some of the human observers who rely primarily on field observations might not like being called "ethologists" (and the ethologists may not like it either) but the basic assumptions seem to me to be the same, that understanding of behavior is most likely to emerge from watching it happen in the context in which it normally occurs. Hall (1974) calls this context a "situational frame."

The participant is able to obtain insights from the participation that may be closed to the detached observer from outside, but of course too much identification with the subject also can obscure judgment and bias events. With many animals "participation" is not possible, but some ethologists interact a great deal with their subjects. Jane Goodall (1971) became almost as involved with her chimpanzees as a cultural anthropologist might with a human tribal village, although she was careful to avoid unduly influencing their behavior, and to note human influence when it did occur. Lorenz (1952) has become quite involved with his geese and other birds.

Another group of observers of human behavior who have developed a method in some respects like the ethological one are Roger Barker and his associates (Barker, 1951, 1968; Barker and Schoggen, 1973). For more than twenty years they have been observing ongoing day-to-day behavior using a methodological unit called the *behavioral setting*. The investigations are carried on with the knowledge and consent of the subjects, and the observers participate in the life of the community to the extent that they blend into the environment and are taken for granted, but otherwise maintain detachment. They keep extensive records with a very detailed notation system. The records for a single day in one case filled a volume which was published under the title of "One Boy's Day" (Barker, 1951). The behavioral settings of Barker are generally not territories, but on the contrary are relatively discrete units of behavior which are a function of a particular space in the ongoing pattern of life within a larger territory. But the device might well lend itself to investigating human territorial impulses and relationships as they are expressed in objective activities. One of Barker's associates, Gump (1971), has applied the system to landscape design, and Bechtel (1970, 1974) has extended the conept from the relatively small towns selected by Barker to larger cities. Bechtel and his associates (1974) have elaborated in particular upon one of Barker's most interesting theories, that of "undermanning" and "overmanning," to which I will return in a later chapter.

As signs of breakdown in both the man-made and natural environment grow, some architects, designers, and planners have been turning to social science in an almost pathetically dependent mood, and social scientists have on the whole responded very generously. But there remain difficult conceptual barriers between the "two cultures" of the environmental art and science. Many designers tend to be overawed and intimidated by their own naive assumptions regarding the magic inherent in experimental methods, including the misleadingly finite quantifications made available by computer technology. The scale of urban problems leads planners more and more to look toward simulations of the real world rather than face it directly. However, notwithstanding the value of experimental methods and of quantification as important tools, designers and planners may find themselves more comfortable with the methods of ethology, where intuition can be used without apologies, if applied in a disciplined way. In its basic form, ethology does not require esoteric methodologies and obscure technical languages, but can be practiced by anyone willing to perform disciplined and orderly observation with open eyes and an open mind.

As with other forms of research, at some point the evidence generated must be interpreted, and ultimately ethologists arrive at hypotheses which have to be verified somehow to the satisfaction of those who attempt to apply them to life. Like other concepts in pluralistic societies, science itself has somewhat different meanings for different people. Kuhn (1962) for example, believes that it is not the generation of evidence, but the contest of paradigms that is most characteristic of science. Eventually paradigms fail to solve, or at least explain, the problems they were designed to cover, and a new paradigm is constructed which does the job better. The belief that unlimited growth is the measure of human progress is such a paradigm, which is now giving way in many quarters to the biologist's concept of a balanced ecosystem. I believe the theory of "environmental determinism" as the governing factor in human behavior is another paradigm which will soon give way to a re-established and greatly enriched concept of evolution.

My own preference in definitions of science, and the one I will use in presenting the arguments in the following chapters, is that of Sir Karl Popper. Popper believed that it is the ruthless testing of ideas that is the particular task of science. The testing of hypotheses is not peculiar to men, according to Popper, but is characteristic of even very simple animals. But in man it takes a very special and important form:

> ...According to my view, animals and men are born with a great store of instinctive knowledge — of ways of reacting to situations, of expectations. The new-born child expects to be fed and to be cared for. If its expectation, its informal conjectural knowledge, is disappointed, then it will die, unless it manages to solve its problems somehow. According to my view we do not learn by observation, or by association, but by trying to solve problems. A problem arises whenever our conjectures or our expectations fail. We try to solve our problems by modifying our conjectures. These new tentative con-

jectures are our trial balloons — our trial solutions. The solution, the new behavior, the new conjecture, the new theory may work; or it may fail. Thus we learn by trial and error; or more precisely, by tentative solutions and by their elimination if they prove erroneous. As H.S. Jennings showed in 1910, this method is used even by the Amoeba. . . .On the pre-scientific level we hate the very idea that we may be mistaken. So we cling dogmatically to our conjectures, as long as possible. On the scientific level, we systematically search for our mistakes, for our errors. This is the great thing, we are consciously critical in order to detect our errors. Thus on the pre-scientific level, we are often ourselves destroyed, eliminated, with our false theories; we perish with our false theories. On the scientific level, we systematically try to eliminate our false theories: we try to let our false theories die in our stead. This is the *critical method of error elimination.* (Original italics.) (Popper, 1971.)

In later chapters I will return to the idea that part of the "pre-scientific" reluctance to appear wrong is fear of alienation from the social group, so important to the human animal, and that it is precisely from those individuals whose life circumstances have in one way or another forced them into relative or partial social isolation that innovative ideas are likely to emerge, and the readiness to discard and replace obsolete ones will be greatest.

Popper's view of the meaning of knowledge is well expressed in his final paragraph of the Introduction to the 1958 edition of "The Logic of Scientific Discovery:"

For myself, I am interested in science and in philosophy only because I want to learn something about the riddle of the world in which we live, and the riddle of man's knowledge of the world. And I believe that only a revival of interest in these riddles can save the science and philosophy from narrow specialization and from an obscurantist faith in the expert's special skill and his personal knowledge and authority; a faith that so well fits our 'post-rationalist' and 'post-critical' age, proudly dedicated to the destruction of the tradition of rational philosophy, and of rational thought itself.

Clearly, the question of the role of genetically determined impulses in human behavior is one of those riddles. In my own view, if rational thought is to continue to offer assistance to *Homo sapiens* in his struggle for existence, it must be extended beyond the contemporary superstition that all human behavior can be accounted for by ontogeny, by social influences which completely obscure individual propensities acquired at conception.

Of course, the proper use of anything involves a recognition of its limitations. Popular misconceptions which interfere with the non-scientist's use of science, in my view, are of two kinds, and both are essentially mystical, not rational. The one attributes to science omnipotence and observational powers that it does not possess; the other proceeds directly from faith to conclusions without the need to observe anything. It appears to me that most of the controversy around the Nature—Nurture question comes from these two directions.

Before Popper's first book was published, Will Durant had summed up the relation of science to design as follows:

Every science begins as philosophy and ends as art; it arises as hypotheses and flows into achievement. Philosophy is the front trench in the siege of truth. Science is the captured territory; and behind it are those secure regions in which knowledge and art build our imperfect and marvelous world. (Durant, 1926, p. xxvi.)

The world seems somewhat less marvelous and considerably more imperfect now than in Durant's day. But still art can, and must, borrow information and techniques from science. While the destruction of his creations as hypotheses can hardly be the primary business of the designer and planner, he can nevertheless subject his works to testing to a far greater degree than he normally has until now. The chapters that follow are an attempt to offer, in terms the environmental decision-makers can use, some new paradigms which are not, to my knowledge, part of the standard reference systems of those who organize our habitats. But they are presented only as hypotheses to be tested and revised as need be in real world environments with due regard to the interests of all who live within the vicinity of the laboratory.

PART TWO

ANIMAL STUDIES

Chapter 3

Territory, aggression and society

Great contest follows, and much learned dust
Involves the combatants.
Cowper

In 1876, when John Stuart Mill was still the leading authority on ethology, an illustrious observer of the behavior of *Homo sapiens* prepared the following description:

The summer evenings were long. It was not dark yet. Presently Tom checked his whistle. A stranger was before him — a boy a shade larger than himself. A newcomer of any age or either sex was an impressive curiosity in the poor little shabby village of St. Petersburg. This boy was well dressed, too — well dressed on weekday. This was simply astounding. His cap was a dainty thing, this close-buttoned blue cloth round-about was new and natty, and so were his pantaloons. He had shoes on — and it was only Friday. He even wore a necktie, a bright bit of ribbon. He has a citified air about him that ate into Tom's vitals. The more Tom stared at the splendid marvel, the higher he turned up his nose at this finery and the shabbier his own outfit seemed to him to grow. Neither boy spoke. If one moved, the other moved — but only sidewise, in a circle; they kept face to face and eye to eye all the time. . .
. . .Presently they were shoulder to shoulder. Tom said:
"Get away from here!"
"Go away yourself!"
"I won't!"
"*I* won't either."
So they stood, each with a foot placed at an angle as a brace, and both shoving with might and main, and glowering at each other with hate. But neither could get an advantage. After struggling till both were hot and flushed, each relaxed his strain with watchful caution, and Tom said:
"You're a coward and a pup. I'll tell my big brother on you, and he can thrash you with his little finger, and I'll make him do it too."
"What do I care for your big brother? I've got a brother that's bigger than he is — and what's more, he can throw him over that fence, too." (Both brothers were imaginary.)
"That's a lie."
"*Your* saying so don't make it so."
Tom drew a line in the dust with his big toe, and said:
"I dare you to step over that, and I'll lick you till you can't stand up. Anybody that'll take a dare will steal sheep."
The new boy stepped over promptly, and said:
"Now you said you'd do it, now let's see you do it."
"Don't you crowd me now; you better look out."
"Well, you *said* you'd do it — why don't you do it?"
"By jingo! for two cents I *will* do it."

The new boy took two broad coppers out of his pocket and held them out with derision. Tom struck them to the ground. In an instant both boys were rolling and tumbling in the dirt, gripped together like cats; and for the space of a minute they tugged and tore at each other's hair and clothes, punched and scratched each others' noses, and covered themselves with dust and glory. Presently the confusion took form and through the fog of battle Tom appeared, seated astride the new boy, and pounding him with his fists.

"Holler 'nuff!" said he.

The boy only struggled to free himself. He was crying — mainly from rage.

"Holler 'nuff!" — and the pounding went on.

At last the stranger got out a smothered " 'Nuff!" and Tom let him up and said: "Now that'll learn you. Better look out who you're fooling with next time."

The new boy went off brushing dust from his clothes, sobbing, snuffling, and oc- casionally looking back and shaking his head and threatening what he would do to Tom the "next time he caught him out." To which Tom responded with jeers, and started off in high feather, and as soon as his back was turned the new boy snatched up a stone, threw it and hit him between the shoulders and then turned tail and ran like an antelope. Tom chased the traitor home, and thus found out where he lived. He then held a position at the gate for some time, daring the enemy to come outside, but the enemy only made faces at him through the window and declined. At last the enemy's mother appeared, and called Tom a bad, vicious, vulgar child, and ordered him away. So he went away; but he said he " 'lowed" to "lay" for that boy. (Twain, 1886.)

This and other adventures of Tom Sawyer reflect an inner reality, a primor- dial drama, so deep in the psyche of some members of our species that for generations in many of the habitats of earth they have continued to react with the delight of self-recognition. The scene changes from village street to suburban park or ghetto alley, but the play goes on. The basic dim outlines of the plot go back to the first stirrings; as we shall see, in a shadowy form this game is played even by plankton in the ocean.

The behavior described by Mark Twain would by any standard be called aggressive. In the juveniles of our species it is remarkably similar to the be- havior of adults of other species, in that it really is a game, where symbols appear much more important than the realities for which they stand, and the name of the game is bluff. Animals and small boys rarely if ever murder each other, unless conditions are pathological.

Aggressive behavior of some sort, at least potentially, accompanies the de- fense of territory, but not all aggressive behavior is territorial. Various types of dominance hierarchies exist among animal societies, ranging from the rela- tively simple "peck order" of some birds to very complex institutions, such as the baboon troop. The degree of aggressiveness of some type on the part of individuals, most often males, will determine their rank. Among other animals, as in man, status is often associated with possession of territory, but not necessarily so. Status hierarchies are usually associated with preemp- tive rights to food, and of males to breed with females. However, as in the case of baboons, rank also may be a concomitant of social leadership. Where status is associated with possession of territory, it may be a prerequisite of it, i.e., the animal first behaves in a manner that enables it to dominate others and as a consequence obtains a territory; or it may be a result: the possession and successful defense of a territory will provide status. In many cases social status and territorial possession seem to be so closely linked as to be inseparable.

Any animal which perceives another of its own kind and reacts to it in any specific way, even by avoidance, is to that extent "social." All sexual species are social to the extent that male and female must identify each other and, however briefly, join together at some time. As we will see later in considering the work of Leyhausen (1971), even so-called "solitary" animals, like the various species of cats, actually have very complex social relationships. Tinbergen (1951) considers that aggression itself is a social phenomenon; one cannot be aggressive without having another individual to be aggressive toward, and furthermore, there must be an individual who will understand the signals of aggression, whether directly physical or merely symbolic, and respond either by submission, defiance, or avoidance.

Evolutionists, confronted with persistent phenomena in life, ask "What is it good for?", i.e., what function does it perform in the survival of the species? Scotland's V.O. Wynne-Edwards (1962), finding a nearly universal tendency in a portion of the populations of animals, great and small, to organize into discrete groups, often in discrete territories, and to defend their position in either case by belligerent behavior toward one another, asked this question. He observed that more often than not this behavior does not favor the survival of all members of the species; in fact, it often assured the demise of some of them.

He reasoned that the survival value of such behavior could not accrue to individuals, but only to the *social group* in which such behavior took place. He evolved a theory of the *evolution of social groups*, a theory which is itself highly controversial, not from the same sources as the controversies we have been considering, but from the opposite direction, from orthodox Darwinians.

In 1834 Thomas Malthus proposed the idea that populations increase geometrically while food resources increase only arithmetically, and that populations would sooner or later face starvation except that other means, such as disease, limit them ahead of time. Darwin's theory of evolution proposed that individuals compete within a group, and species compete between each other, for whatever resources are required; those individuals best able to obtain resources and meet environmental conditions, including protection from elements and from predators, will be most likely to survive long enough to reproduce and thereby contribute genes to posterity. Those least able to obtain resources or meet environmental hazards will not survive to reproduce, and therefore each species will, through the generations, produce individuals best adapted for a given set of conditions. Thus, in the Darwinian view, if there is a shortage of food, there will be competition for it between individuals within a species, but the species as a whole best able to sustain itself will survive over those species which are squeezed out.

In noting that animals rarely starve to death in nature, Wynne-Edwards concluded that population control by starvation does not exist under normal conditions because such a mechanism would be too risky; an entire species would be likely to die out before the food resource could be restored, if at all. Excessively hungry animals are not likely to leave many members of food species — whether floral or faunal — around to propagate their own kind. If animals do not starve, some other mechanism adjusts population to resource, by controlling breeding.

That mechanism, according to Wynne-Edwards, is "competition among males for the right to inseminate females." Obviously this can only apply to sexual species, but he detects related processes among asexual beings. Competition of this sort would tend to insure that the genes of the most vigorous males are transmitted to offspring, but it would not by itself adjust population to resource. Wynne-Edwards believes that this is accomplished by combining competition for females with competition for territory: only those males who possess territory will be attractive to females or otherwise be able to father offspring. The effect of territory may be on the female by virtue of being a condition for receptivity to the male; or it may be on the male by being a prerequisite for his potency; or, especially in solitary animals, it may be merely a condition which brings the sexes together. Territory also may be a nesting place in which the young are reared cooperatively by a pair, or merely a place where the estrous female goes to mate before going off to rear her young by herself.

In species where attachment to territory is not a conspicuous factor, other manifestations of successful competition of one male over another will be required for breeding. In any case the key element in the control of breeding, in the Wynne-Edwards theory, is male rivalry. The attraction of female to male or vice versa insures copulation, but rivalry among males determines who does the copulating. In some cases the choice seems to be up to the male: the winner takes his pick of females. In other cases it may be up to the female; the dominant female gets the winner. In any case, there appears to be a very harsh rule; the loser goes off alone, or settles down on the fringe in the company of bachelors.

The important role that possession of territory plays as a population regulating device, in this theory, lies in the fact that the amount of territory, and the number of male proprietors, can be expanded or contracted depending on resources, without starving anybody (at least directly). In a bad year, territories will be large and proprietors relatively few, and fewer young will be borne and reared. In a good year territories will be smaller, competition less intense, and more males will have land and mates; there will be an increase in the number of offspring produced.

If the role of territory was simply to limit the number of individuals who could feed on it, rather than breed on it, those who were excluded would go hungry. Hungry animals are likely to be considerably more ferocious, or ferocious in a more deadly and less disciplined way, than sexually aroused ones, and the natural environment would be considerably more unpleasant than it usually is. It is the picture of "nature red in tooth and claw" in a nasty, snarling, contest for necessities that most people conjure up when the evolutionary concept of "survival of the fittest" is presented to them. Nature, as constituted in Wynne-Edwards' view, may in the last analysis be no less cruel, but it is more orderly and stable, and considerably more esthetic.

Wynne-Edwards agrees that food resources are the ultimate factor which limits populations; what is unique in his theory is that they do not do so directly. To explain the indirect process, he has advanced a concept which I find one of the three most interesting, the most hopeful, and the most pertinent to human affairs, of all the postulates in all of the ethological literature I have surveyed. (The other two will be explored in the next two chapters.)

Wynne-Edwards' basic concept is that animals do not compete for resources, even for mates, directly, but through the medium of *conventional tokens.*

Conventional tokens are symbols, possession of which entitles the bearer to partake of something else. The analogy that immediately springs to mind in human society is money, especially paper money which has no inherent worth whatsoever, which by convention serves as a means of exchange for goods and services. But human society is rich in conventional tokens, such as the flag, or even the word "country," which stands in the last analysis for "the place where I live and the people who share it with me." Jewelry, clothes, automobiles, all may serve as conventional breeding tokens for modern *Homo sapiens.*

Wynne-Edwards finds among animals an almost universal competition for conventional tokens, or indirect symbolic rewards, including those creatures, like ocean plankton, which have no nervous system and no brain.

Conventional tokens and the symbols by which they are fought for include the comb of a rooster and the plumage of a peacock, the iridescence of a fish, the mane of a lion, and the beard of a man. Unfortunately, in our species, conventional tokens may include that ersatz phallus, the sword, the gun, or the rocket.

The primary rivalry, Wynne-Edwards notes, is generally confined to males of the species. Females may compete in one way or another with each other, but for breeding they will pair only with the male dominant in status or territory or both. He calls the rivalry of males *epideictic* displays, in his words (1962, p. 16) "signifying literally 'means for display,' but connoting in its original Greek form the presenting of a sample." Epideictic displays perform a different function than *epigamic* displays, the word he uses for the rituals between males and females normally seen in mating. He believes, with many other observers, that many of the rituals, including bird songs and bright feathers, which have been attributed to courtship, or epigamic activities, are actually epideictic, products of male rivalry.

Every good theory should explain as much as possible in the simplest possible way. Wynne-Edwards' theory explains much that has been hitherto inexplicable. Among other things, it explains the exceeding amount of attention paid by evolution to *sexual dimorphism*, the different appearance of males and females among most higher species. This would not appear to be necessary merely for propagation. In species that pair for the purpose of raising young, a division of labor among an equal number of males and females, where the male provides food while the female cares for young, with advantages in size and strength on the part of the male, makes some sense. But pairing of that sort is not typical in nature; it is characteristic of many birds, but only a few mammals, and is not at all characteristic of fish, reptiles, or insects, all of which indulge in epideitic displays. In almost all species, one male can impregnate a large number of females, so that a numerical balance of the species is not justified on that ground; on the other hand, the amount of pomp and glitter and raw energy expended by males in fighting with each other is all out of proportion to their relatively minor role in sexual reproduction as compared with that of the female. The persistence of more conspicuously physical endowments and kinetic energy among males as compared with females of most species would be more profligate than nature would be likely to countenance, if it did not perform some major function in life. That function, Wynne-Edwards maintains, is population control.

> From a discussion of parthenogenesis and hermaphroditism, it would appear that the latter is reproductively very efficient, since it allows all adults to bear progeny and still enjoy the advantages of genetic recombinations. It is the method adopted by most plants. By contrast, one-to-one matings between male and female animals appear very extravagant, especially where the males (which contribute so little materially to posterity) are as big or bigger than the females, equally numerous, and excessively fecund. The conclusion is reached that there must be some major secondary division of labor between the sexes to justify such an apparent functional imbalance, prevailing as it does almost throughout the middle and high animals. The justification is at once seen to reside in making the male bear the immense burden of population-control, while the female is left to provide the material sources of reproduction. (Wynne-Edwards, 1962, p. 529.)

The function of regulating population to resources in this manner is possible precisely because the rewards sought are symbolic, essentially what in the human species is called "honor" or "prestige."

Wynne-Edwards (1971, p. 269) puts it this way:

> Because the rewards sought are only conventional tokens, which confer rights to the things that really matter, namely feeding and breeding, the competition itself becomes conventionalized. Stags roar, antelopes butt and wrestle, skylarks sing, and peacocks display their finery, but little or no blood is shed in the process. The bitterness of the struggle for existence has been sublimated and ritualized; the outcome is still as vital as ever, rewarding the successful with the right to a full life, and condemning the losers to barrenness and often premature death.

This process mediates between the social group and the environment before the latter is destroyed, because generally competition increases as densities increase relative to resources. This has some implication for democracy in crowded human societies, which we shall examine later. Long before the environment has been stripped of resources, the competition has effectively eliminated from the breeding community enough of the less-dominant males to produce a corresponding drop in population to the point where competition and resources are in balance. Wynne-Edwards described this as *homeostasis*, a word long used by biologists for adjustments made by parts of an organism to maintain a stable whole.

The concept of homeostasis in the transactions between social groups and their environments, in short ecology, is basic to Wynne-Edwards' concept of social evolution. Those species will survive which are able to maintain the most stable societies under changing environmental conditions. Such societies are "potentially immortal," whereas individuals are not. In fact, he defines a society as "an organization capable of providing conventional competition." The chief objection, from an evolutionary point of view, to letting competition turn into lethal violence and starvation, is that it would prevent the *homeostatic* maintenance of stable societies. Furthermore, if excess individuals were all killed off, rather than being permitted to survive but not breed, there would be no mechanism for adjusting populations upward, following disasters, or when resources expand. It is under conditions of reduced competition, corresponding to reduced densities and expanded resources, that formerly marginal animals may return to the breeding community. This is what apparently happens in the case of birds who control population by controlling recruitment of young birds to the flock (Wynne-Edwards, 1962; Watson and Moss, 1970, 1971).

This requires what Wynne-Edwards has referred to as biological "altruism" on the part of the marginal animals, who, having lost in the epideictic contests seemingly sacrifice themselves voluntarily for the good of the group. I think it is unfortunate that he has used this word, which he obviously means in a metaphorical sense, because it seems to aggravate the opposition to this theory of group selection on the part of orthodox Darwinians. They reason that if an animal is so "altruistic" that it refrains from breeding, such "altruism" cannot be passed on to the gene pool, and therefore will not appear in future generations. The first altruistic animals would breed altruism out of the picture. However, there seems to be no reason to believe that animals below the level of *Homo sapiens* have any real choice in the matter, and Wynne-Edwards does not suggest that they do, although the word he uses implies it.

An inescapable requirement for the functioning of conventional token systems is that the symbols be recognized by all parties concerned, and that the results of the competition be accepted as final. In our species, this is clearly demonstrated by games and sports, in which the rules are the game. In the case of the symbolic gestures of birds, fish, and mammals, described by Lorenz and Tinbergen, these are usually stereotyped patterns to which the opposing animal can respond in only one way. Even in the case of the relatively intelligent dog or wolf, Lorenz (1966) notes that when two are locked in nearly mortal combat, if the vanquished canine gives a certain submissive gesture, the victorious one will be frozen in restraint, even though its face and body give every evidence of a desire to carry the battle to a lethal conclusion. The loser probably has no more choice than the victor; when fear begins to overcome hostility the submissive gesture is inevitable.

In any case, the effect is that the defeated animal is then unable to perform a variety of activities, depending on the species. It may exhibit no sexual desire, or may fail to stimulate interest in the female, due to changes in such conventional symbols as coloration, scent, etc. While it will normally continue to feed, it will often do so only on the fringes, it will become prone to disease and will be more vulnerable to predators, either because it cannot find cover or because it will become careless and fail to protect itself. Not so clearly related to epideictic display, but related to behavior of males and to density in general will be the tendency of females to abort, or lose milk in the case of mammals, to fail to incubate eggs in the case of birds, and generally to desert the young. This is particularly conspicuous in the case of mice and rats, as we will see when we examine the work of Calhoun.

Ironically, Wynne-Edwards' theory of biological altruism appears to contradict the Social Darwinists. The idea of the submergence of the welfare of the individual in the good of the social group would seem to run counter to the survival-of-the-strongest individualism favored by 19th century entrepreneurial capitalism and later by fascism. On the other hand this theory could be used in reverse to justify the supremacy of the interests of the state over those of individuals in totalitarian countries (and under some circumstances in nearly all countries). Unfortunately, any theory can be evoked by someone for opportunistic purposes. To the propertyless individuals on the margins of any society, it matters little whether the rule is "l'état c'est moi" or "l'état c'est nous." As I suggested earlier, my own feeling is that decision-makers should keep the widest possible number of theories available in facing real life situations. For the moment I will turn to two other theories which pertain to what appears to be a universal problem for human and non-human animals alike, that of population control.

Chapter 4

The population paradox: more is less

My soul, be satisfied with flowers,
With fruit, with weeds even; but gather them
In the one garden you may call your own.
Rostand

The work of John B. Calhoun, of the United States National Institute of Mental Health, is mainly noted for studies of the effects of "crowding," but his insights cover many aspects of social organization as well.

Calhoun (1971) devised a number of environments for rats and mice of varying sizes, based on what architects would call a *module*. The mouse-house module might be visualized as a four-story garden apartment unit with a semi-public garden shared by all residents but not legally open to outsiders, and fully equipped with automatic vending machines providing all necessities. A varying number of these units were assembled in an "experimental universe," much as apartment units might be combined into a self-sufficient development to form a closed community. In fact, this "utopia" is not unlike some of the underground, or overhead, projects that visionary architects of human habitations have dreamed up for our welfare. The only investment the inhabitants of Calhoun's mouse development need make is in the energy expended to travel through the tunnels to get supplies. Lacking electric elevators, and not having much of a view, the mice achieved status in a reverse manner from human; the lower apartments were the most prestigious. In mice, as in men, rank is in inverse proportion to labor expended on necessities (but not on entertainment). On the other hand, mice, like men, tend to find recreation in social activity; perhaps even more than men, socially prominent mice are physically prominent in public places. And as with some humans, in Calhoun's mouse subdivisions, much socializing takes place around the rodent equivalent of the supermarket, the canteen, and the laundry room. In fact, the tower cans with nesting materials, the equivalent of a suburban lumber yard or hardware store, became a main focus of social activity. These experimental environments are probably vastly superior to most human ones, for they were designed to include everything that years of investigation showed necessary for the full development of mouse personality — except contraception.

Into each of these orderly communities of varying sizes (1, 2, 4, 8, and 16 cells), duly zoned for optimal open space, recreation, sanitation and the like,

Fig. 1. A 16-cell habitat for mice. Each cell consists of (1) a battery of 16 nesting compartments, accessible from four vertical wire tunnels, (2) 640 square inches of floor space containing a single structure, a ring stand holding a supply of nesting material, (3) a screen surfaced food hopper on the vertical wall, and (4) a shelf above the tunnels where the mice hace access to water bottles. The human intruder is Dr. Calhoun. (U.S. National Institute of Mental Health).

Calhoun and his colleagues introduced four pairs of colonists per "universe." His initial experiments were to determine optimum densities for mice, and thereafter the effects of unrestricted population increase. The mice were inbred to be "born equal" in genetic endowment, which included a tremendous capacity to reproduce. The initial colonists represented a real sort of racial segregation, and it is perhaps appropriate that they were white mice.

The normal male mouse, like the birds we have discussed, is aggressively territorial, and with territory will come preemptive rights to females. The normal female mouse is a careful nest builder and a devoted and resourceful

Fig. 2. A multi-cell habitat for men?

mother. There is an elaborate courtship procedure, and while dominant males are pretty rough on competitors of their own sex, they are very gallant toward the distaff side. They copulate only when invited, and are scrupulously protective of nursing mothers.

In the first phase of Calhoun's experiments things proceeded according to mouse tradition. The males took territories and mates, and produced healthy litters in comfortable "single-family homes." During the second phase, as litter after litter added to the population, each universe was dominated by one or two of the most aggressive original males. However, as younger males reached maturity, they began to contend with each other and with older males for territory and status. As this phase terminated each territory contained an average of 10—11 mice in the socially active age categories, approximately the normal social group size for mice in the wild. The sex ratio was quite constant at 4 : 6, averaging one dominant and three contesting males to six normally reproducing females, but the younger males were not yet mature enough to offer serious competition to the dominant one.

As the third phase began, serious social upheavals were on the horizon. The younger males reached full adulthood and, since there was no vacant space to occupy as territory, they began contesting with the dominant male in earnest. A few were successful, but most were driven out of the nest compartments into the public floor space. A new mouse personality appeared. The rejected males became social dropouts, withdrawn physically and psychologically, cowering in the center of the floor or on the platforms, moving only as necessary to obtain food and water. A minority became what the researchers called "Solitary Withdrawns," but most assembled in large aggregates and were called "Pooled Withdrawns." They were a mass of wounds from periodic attacks on each other. Meanwhile, dominant male territories grew smaller in area outside the nests, and within them females became excessively aggressive toward their young and toward outsiders of either sex near the entrance tunnels. At the end of phase three the population in each cell had climbed from an average of 38 (which had existed at the end of phase two) to 142. Out of these only 8% of the adults and young adults retained any sign of normal behavior. A third were the withdrawn mice who were no longer violent toward each other and had no capacity for productive sexual activity. Sixty percent were juveniles who were fated to develop yet another kind of personality.

Successful rearing of young ended in the fourth phase. Females who conceived either aborted or failed to care for offspring, which died. They ceased to build nests, merely scattering the paper around. Males attacked females, and females attacked young. Sexual behavior was erratic and perverted. The minority of socially active mice of the previous phase joined the withdrawn mice. Most curiously, a new group appeared: those who had been the juveniles of both sexes in the previous phase, entered adulthood, not only without any signs of aggression, but without any interest in sex or territory. Since they did not fight they had no wounds; they did nothing but eat and groom themselves, which accounts for the healthy appearance and bright coats. These were the mice Calhoun has dubbed "The Beautiful Ones." When densities were reduced in the smaller universes by removing all but a few males and females at the 4 : 6 ratio, the females of this group moved in together in the same nest box. When these females were placed with a corresponding number of normal sexually active mice, only six out of eight conceived and only three of those produced litters. Most of the young were abandoned. An attempt was made to start new "universes" with combinations of the "Beautiful Ones" and the various categories of withdrawn mice. None were successful.

At this point it is interesting to note in terms of the nature—nurture controversies, that the ontogeny of these mice as a result of environmental experience had apparently completely and irrevocably erased the capacity to develop what is normally instinctual behavior in this species.

At the time I visited Calhoun's laboratory early in 1971, one of these mice utopias was still in existence, a mass of eating machines, healthy but aging. The only individuality apparent was in the colors with which the experimenters had dyed the fur for identification. The mice were all doomed, and were not creatures to elicit much sympathy on that account, but only a strange sort of foreboding. In the words of Marsden (1970), "Utopia has become hell." That universe of "Beautiful Ones" is now extinct.

The numbers involved are instructive. This was the 16-cell universe. Its theoretical standing-room-only density is 4000 mice. In 1968 the population began with eight colonists. According to Marsden (1970), "6 mouse-months equal 25 man-years — 150 years of reproductive history are compressed into three. The eight mice had the capacity to double their population every 60 days. They could fill the universe in less than three years."

They didn't. The population stabilized at 2200 at the end of the third phase, about half the theoretical maximum and at about 15 times the optimum number of adults (150). In the spring of 1971, there were 1600 aging "juveniles." Now there are none. That "universe" is extinct.

Calhoun makes clear that what has happened in his experimental universe does not normally happen in the natural universe. When wild mice populations exceed the optimum 12 per nest unit, they either go elsewhere and establish breeding territories, or the withdrawn mice are removed by predators and disease. The "Beautiful Ones" are a product of human intervention. For the process of total social distintegration that is the consequence of this sort of extreme crowding he has used the term "behavioral sink."

There is a peculiar phenomenon observed by these researchers in their mice studies, which is important for this discussion. It will be remembered that the module, or cell, of each universe was provided with a food hopper, so that, for instance, in a 4-cell universe there would be four hoppers to feed from. Initially the colonizers would tend to distribute themselves more or less uniformly around the four sources of food supply. But as densities increased, more and more mice would congregate at one of these, competing with each other for space at one, ignoring the other stations. Calhoun's explanation for this phenomenon is that when densities are low, individuals will more often than not feed without the presence of another. As numbers build up, the chances for the presence of another at the hopper increases so that the mice begin to associate eating with company. This association becomes so strong eventually that they redefine an eating situation as one that must include the presence of others. Eventually it becomes pathological in that it increases the number of social interactions, and consequent increase in stress, at critical points in the environment far beyond that which overall densities would require. In mice, this compulsive gregariousness at eating stations is part of the behavioral sink phenomenon which becomes generalized to include large aggregations in nesting compartments, so that some mice would suffocate even when 30% of the available nesting spaces were unused!

Another important observation is that of a strange offshoot of the otherwise pathological behavior of the withdrawn animals, which have been excluded from nests by the dominant males. Calhoun's years of experiments led him to the conclusion that a certain number of relatively withdrawn, socially inactive individuals will appear in any group of animals as a result of dominance stratification, regardless of environmental conditions, and even if no crowding exists. In other words, a certain proportion of young in any litter will produce adults who are less dominant and less socially involved than others. We will recall that Wynne-Edwards postulated that this provided a reserve of adults who could be brought into the breeding pool as a result of catastrophes, or whenever circumstances warranted an increase in population. In speculating on the evolutionary significance of such phenomena as the presence of marginal individuals in a social group, Calhoun made an observation that produced a different conclusion.

In a study of wild rats in a large enclosure which included burrows in the earth, one group of socially withdrawn animals which exhibited all sorts of abnormal behavior, including homosexual propensities, accomplished what Calhoun describes as the equivalent of human beings inventing the wheel! (1971, p. 348.) In enlarging the tunnels of their burrows, normal rats will kick and push loose dirt out to a mound at the opening. Occasionally, but rarely, if the dirt is moist they will pack it into wads and carry it out in their teeth as they do small rocks. But these particular withdrawn rats would pack such wads together into a large ball just slightly smaller than the opening of the tunnel and roll the whole mass out into the open, saving themselves much labor. Calhoun admits the possibility that such behavior may have some obscure hereditary component, but he believes it to be a "truly creative act." In examining thousands of mounds of wild rats in natural conditions where such withdrawn individuals would not be expected to survive, he has not found a single example of it. On the other hand, he has found other examples of novel and useful behavior among the less-dominant rats. Calhoun explains this phenomenon on the basis that the high status, territorial animals develop orderly sequences in their normal activities; in other words, they follow an accepted way of doing things. The more marginal individuals exhibit greater randomness in their behavior, and the chances increase that some new patterns of behavior might prove advantageous.

It is hard to view these phenomena without speculating on their apparent correlation with equivalent phenomena which are readily apparent in large portions of contemporary human society. Such speculation is safer if we recall J.S. Mill's injunction that we are dealing with tendencies only, that mice are not men, that we are considering underlying patterns common to species and not specific expressions which will govern automatically, and that there is rarely a single contributing cause for complex phenomena, especially in human affairs.

The urban phenomenon is a particularly complex one, expressing human proclivities of all sorts, positive as well as negative, but especially for cultures like that of the United States, whose mythology prizes individualism, one of its more unsatisfactory aspects is an increasing dependence on others and a consequent loss of personal resourcefulness, which appears to be similar in psychological fundamentals to that demonstrated by Calhoun's mice. I shall return to this later in considering Barker's concept of "undermanning."

Calhoun declares (1971, p. 335) that in deliberately designing environments which would produce a behavioral sink, he obtained information on how not to produce such an effect. A critical element is avoidance of a static environment which restricts the kind of response situations that are possible. "On a theoretical basis," he says, "increasing uncertainty, enhancing the necessity for searching and demanding continual solutions of new problems, should prove beneficial as a basic strategy of environmental design." If this is true, and many students of both animal and human behavior (Rapoport and Hawkes, 1970; R. Kaplan, 1973; S. Kaplan, 1973) think it is, modern architecture and modern city planning, with their maddening predictability, seem calculated to accelerate the development of a human behavioral sink.

In this respect, his observations on creative performance in rats is most relevant. The fact that innovative behavior in such relatively simple animals appears among the marginal members of society, the "non-conformists" who have given up the struggle for social dominance on the one hand and the obligation to "play by the rules" on the other, helps to explain certain well-known characteristics of human innovators. It has long been observed that artists, writers, musicians, scientists, inventors, explorers, and even certain types of statesmen, tend to be "loners." What seems to be a prerequisite for creativity and innovation is a certain amount of isolation from group interaction, because this permits mental searching behavior which is prevented by rigid adherence to social norms, i.e., academic, scientific, technical, or artistic fashion. Calhoun poses a very critical qualification to his observation of the social marginality of creative animals: they are not the most withdrawn, but rather those animals which retain some relationship to the social group. In extrapolating to human creativity, which he feels is essential to mental health, Calhoun asserts that the capacity to withdraw from social pressure, with its emphasis on functioning in the status quo, in order to explore other possibilities, must be balanced by the opportunity to re-enter society so as to introduce the new patterns to it. He notes that in turn society will accept as creative only that which proves to be useful to it.

Lorenz notes (1966, p. 43) a relevant observation by Yerkes that chimpanzees copy only high-ranking members of their group. In one experiment a low-ranking chimp was taken out of his group and taught to use a machine which dispensed bananas. When he and the apparatus were put back in the group, the others gathered around and stole the bananas as he produced them, but none thought of watching how he operated the machine. However, when the top-ranking chimp was removed, taught to use the device, and returned with it, the others gathered around most respectfully and learned from him how to get bananas from it themselves. Chimpanzee establishmentarians, like most of their human counterparts, are not the inventive members of their society, but the conformist ones; not much can be learned from them but tradition, "the way things are always done." This makes for social stability as long as circumstances oblige by remaining the same. Calhoun provides no evidence that rats and mice learn from their creative cohorts; in their society the use of the wheel dies with its inventors. This may be one reason why mice remain mice, and chimps remain chimpanzees.

As Wynne-Edwards shows, marginal animals, especially males, which are excluded from territory as a result of losing dominance struggles, will perish from predators or psychosomatically-induced disease. In nature we may suppose most innovators will perish so, because as Popper notes, they are unable to construct hypotheses to die in their stead. It is inviting to speculate that because *Homo sapiens* protects — at least to some extent — the marginal members of his species, instead of letting them die, and so includes within his numbers those who are most likely to innovate, he was able to make the leap into language and technology that so distinguishes him from others. Rarely do other animals protect their misfits.

The analogy between the behavioral sink of mice and the growth of crime, alcoholism, drug addiction, suicide, fatherless households, child neglect and child abuse, as well as disease in our big cities, has been made over and over again by people who may never have read, or even heard of, John B. Calhoun and his experiments. There has been much loose and oversimplified discussion about human densities; the problem cannot be reduced to a numbers game. Calhoun himself has stressed quality of the environment as a fundamental factor in the densities that can be tolerated even among mice, as shown by the fact that in laboratories densities can be increased several times without harmful consequences by the way the environment is structured (Calhoun, 1952). For this reason the arithmetical concept of densities is not adequate, especially for human environments. A healthy social structure seems to have more to do with the number and characteristics of the individuals an animal interacts with, than the absolute number who occupy a given area, as we will see when we come to the work of Cassel in Chapter 7. But there seems to be a critical mass both for human and other animal societies, nevertheless.

Calhoun notes that among mammals the most common optimum-sized group is between nine and twelve. Ardrey (1970, p. 368) explores Calhoun's theory in a speculation which he himself calls "preposterous," but which does not seem so in the light of Calhoun's mathematics. Ardrey notes the prevalence of groups of that size in human organizations, 12 jurors, 9 supreme court justices, the army squad of 11 soldiers and an officer, ball teams of 9 to 11, the Soviet Union's Politburo of 11 members, and the 12 apostles of Jesus.

The hunter-gatherer bands of primitive man, before the invention of long range weapons like the spear and arrow, were apparently bound by social organizations of kinship groups averaging 12 adults and 18 children. Because man's ability to control mortality even in the primitive times tended to expand his population, early man also resorted to various forms of population control, including inter-group fratricide and intra-group infanticide. But Calhoun postulates that man also learned to live with larger populations. The mechanism for this was *role differentiation* which tends to restrict meaningful social contacts to an optimal level within small groups even as the population expands. This is what he calls *conceptual space*:

> With the first acquisition of a conceptual space equivalent to that of the physical space already occupied, man emerged as truly *Homo sapiens*. From that point on, man could continue to justify this appellation by making sufficient additions to conceptual area as population increased to maintain constant the total area available to each individual. This is my basic hypothesis: increases in conceptual area must keep approximately abreast with increases in total population. (Calhoun, 1971, p. 359.)

The organ which makes conceptual space possible is the human brain, equipped as is no other known brain, to manage abstract symbols. Conceptual space could not for long be restricted to the village sites of its origin. New constellations formed larger cultural groupings. As populations increase in size and conceptual space in complexity, these constellations continue to elaborate into nations, empires, and leagues, until eventually conceptual space too will fill the earth. By a mathematical reasoning which I confess I cannot follow, Calhoun believes the fullest development of conceptual space through the neo-cortex will closely coincide with demographic projections which show that, at present rates of increase, our population will reach the ultimate capacity of the earth by the year 2026, by which time there will be 9×10^9 people on earth. (With respect to ecological matters, it is important to note that we are talking about the theoretical maximum population on social grounds, and there is no inference that the earth's resources will necessarily support 9×10^9, especially with continued exploitation of non-renewable resources.)

The elaboration of conceptual space leads to an increasing diversity of roles and a corresponding diversity in value systems. There is reason to believe we are reaching a point at which the variety of value systems exceeds the capacity of the human cortex to handle it, without periodic retreat into familiar group space. At the same time human beings become increasingly dependent on the roles of others whose value systems differ. This requires not only an acceptance of persons whose values are different from our own, but also that we actually help them to assume diverse values and roles. Whereas purely territorial delineation of space requires the defense of borders, conceptual space seems to require rather an inter-penetration of space, in Calhoun's view. In later chapters I will apply this concept to my model for urban form in which psycho-geographical provision will be made for it in terms of what I will call distemic space.

Chapter 5

Time and the tides of life

I returned, and saw under the sun, that the race is not to the swift nor the battle to the strong, neither yet bread to the wise, nor yet riches to men of understanding, nor yet favor to men of skill; but time and change happeneth to them all.

Ecclesiastes IX:11

In the last chapters we have considered the work of two major ethologists who have related possession of territory on the one hand, and social ranking on the other, to the control of populations.

Paul Leyhausen, director of the Max-Planck-Institut für Verhaltens-forschung in Wuppertal, Federal Republic of Germany, has focussed on that important concomitant of society: individuality (Leyhausen, 1965, 1971; Lorenz and Leyhausen, 1973). It is appropriate that he has chosen for his primary object of investigation the behavior of the most individualist of animals, the cat. He has discovered many things about this intriguing creature, one of which is that the cat does not, as Rudyard Kipling thought, always walk by himself, and not all places are alike to him.*

Seasonal changes in food supply and breeding cycles have, of course, been an implicit part of the behavior patterns we have considered so far. But Leyhausen notes that the motivational states of an animal, which prompt it to behave in a particular way, are also governed by daily fluctuations in its inner metabolic states, called circadian rhythms, and also to changes in the environment which include the approach of other individuals. An animal which is territorial at one time will not be so at another; likewise, dominance struggles and male rivalry may occur in connection with territory, or the opposite may also be the case, in which the animal's "home is his castle," and serves as a retreat from the struggle for dominance. Most students of animal behavior have drawn attention to the psychological advantage that seems to accrue to an individual at the center of his home territory. This contrasts with the urge that most animals exhibit to explore the surrounding range. A sort of tension seems to exist between the urge to remain safe at home and the lure of the "out there," in which the urge for security yields to the need for stimulation. Among most social animals, stimulation involves not only

---

* "The cat. He walked by himself, and all places were alike to him." *just so stories.*

exploration of the environment, but interaction with conspecifics. Thus there is a polarity between the need to stay put and the need to wander, the need for privacy and the need for company, which might be likened to centrifugal and centripetal forces that hold physical bodies, from stars to molecules, in their respective orbits.

Leyhausen distinguishes between two kinds of ranking, or dominance hierarchies. That which is determined primarily by male rivalry on the range outside the home territory he calls *absolute social hierarchy*, because it will remain constant within the group once it is established, and will depend entirely on the personal authority of the winner. It will not vary with circadian rhythms or other changes in the environment.

On the other hand those rivalries and struggles which occur within the territory will be dependent on the psychological advantages which are held by the animal closest to its home base. This type of dominance will depend on the situation and the relationship of the animal to the place where the fight occurs. Hierarchies of this sort are thus not fixed, but are dynamic, shifting with time, place, situation, and the internal state of each of the individuals. This type of hierarchy Leyhausen calls *relative social hierarchy*. He believes it is a characteristic only of vertebrates, and especially of mammals.

It would appear that in combination these two kinds of status ranking would open possibilities for complex cooperative social groups to draw on the varying capacities of differing individuals to perform varying functions according to different circumstances. In other words, individuality is the mechanism by which a social group becomes adaptable to change.

From his study of cats, Leyhausen has concluded that the so-called "solitary" animal is not non-social but simply has a larger individual space. When he first started observing cats in the laboratory he noted that adults appeared to be unable to establish a firm ranking order, and he at first concluded that solitary animals were incapable of doing so. But he noticed that siblings establish a traditional ranking order within the litter. Later, when he observed free-ranging cat populations (not an easy task), males did in fact establish an absolute hierarchy among themselves by rival fighting, but this could only take place on neutral grounds, that is, not in an area defended as a territory. Male cats, he found, do not confine themselves to territory as females do. During the reproductive season they prowl around the borders of territories and it is between boundaries that they engage in rival fighting. As every owner of a domestic tom cat knows, fighting is enhanced by the season of the females, but, according to Leyhausen, is not dependent on it. Nevertheless it is dependent on male hormone supply. A castrated cat will give up rival fighting, but at the same time, interestingly enough, it becomes more territorial like the female.

In the rival fighting outside the territory it is decided among male cats who is who, in general. But as we have noted, an animal's courage and tenacity will increase the closer he is to home and vice versa. Within his home territory even the lowest ranking animal, as determined by outside fights, will generally not be attacked, even by the biggest and most dominant. Among familiar animals, within the territory itself, dominance is relative to the circumstance. He finds that among laboratory cats the rank order at the food bowl will be different from that in resting places.

Outside the territory, cat neighbors will eventually settle down to a stable hierarchy and move around in groups, forming what Leyhausen calls a "brotherhood." Affairs in such a community will normally remain more or less tranquil until a maturing male decides to challenge the establishment. Then there may be a serious "generation gap," in which the juvenile will refuse to accept authority, and will be beaten over and over again until he eventually either finds a place in the group and accepts it, or presumably goes elsewhere.

Over a wider range, when cats catch sight of each other they will recognize authority by letting the highest status individuals move through an area long before entering it. This solitary roaming is what characterizes cats in the minds of most people, but Leyhausen has discovered a strange phenomenon which may surprise many cat owners. There are nocturnal congregations when these animals leave their territories in the small hours of the night to gather round in certain places, where they sit close together and look at each other. There they will remain for two or three hours, before going home to sleep. These get-togethers will include animals of various ranks and both sexes who will at other times of the day engage in serious rival or territorial fighting. They are apparently merely social gatherings (Leyhausen, 1965).

Essential for relative hierarchy is space to move around in, where various patterns of dominance, i.e., relative capabilities of different individuals, at different times and under different circumstances, may sort themselves out as the situation requires. As crowding occurs, with reduction of territory, absolute hierarchy will tend to become the dominant social form.

It seems to me that Leyhausen's concept of absolute and relative hierarchy, like Wynne-Edwards' concept of conventional tokens, and Calhoun's idea of conceptual space by which the animal incorporates its environment into itself by mental images, suggest behavioral forms out of which human culture might have evolved from simpler, more fundamental instincts. Such processes suggest that the special characteristics of our species make us, not so much "different" from other animals, as transcendentally more complex. Underlying these are the limitations to development that govern all living organisms, that of homeostatic balance between populations and space. There is an optimum size beyond which social organization becomes diseased, the organic equivalent of the physicist's "critical mass" beyond which disintegration begins.

It does not take much imagination to find examples of relative hierarchy and absolute hierarchies in human societies. Even the most cooperative venture at some point requires absolute authority, in that someone must make final decisions. It is notorious that committees can accomplish very little in the way of action; decisions are bogged in endless debate, and the compromises necessary for consensus often lead only to neutralized generalities. On the other hand, the democratic debate of the committee is the only source of correction for the inevitability of inherent error in a single judgment. No individual can see and know and understand everything. Even more importantly, each individual will model his decisions on his own personality, and his own needs and interests, and the very best of leaders at some point will produce decisions out of phase with the interests of other individuals. The worst of leaders will do so systematically and on an increasing scale, leading to tyranny. In this sense absolute power does and must corrupt everything and everybody, by limiting the capacity of the social body to adapt to changing circumstance.

Only that society which has absolute hierarchies in the form of authoritative leadership of some sort will have the capacity for concerted action. However, my hypothesis is that only societies which simultaneously permit variation in leadership from circumstance to circumstance, and call into action as needed the varying capacities of its members, will have the capacity to adapt to changing conditions. If we combine Leyhausen's concept of relative hierarchy with Calhoun's idea of conceptual space considered as symbolic territory, we can visualize a flexible society which will satisfy the need of most human beings at one time or another to be led and at other times and circumstances to lead. This requires that citizens have on the one hand either a conceptual or physical territory of their own where they literally "know their place" in a positive sense and at the same time have maximum freedom of movement to explore their capacities and the relative capacities of others on common ground, or range. I will return to this idea later, when I will offer it as the basic relationship in designing for diversity in a hierarchy of proxemic and distemic spaces.

At this point it is sufficient to note that healthy human societies do provide both orders. In the hunger-gatherer band, the young warrior may bow unquestioningly to taboos and the rule of the chief, but within limits he will have an opportunity to "do his own thing" in the hunt or on the warpath. Barker's theory of "undermanning," to which I referred briefly in Chapter 2, and which I will introduce again in more detail in Chapter 12, suggests that in smaller village-type settings the environment makes a greater claim on each individual, who is called upon to provide a wider variety of tasks, and each will have more responsibility and a greater sense of self-identity. On the other hand there is also greater insecurity and more chance for failure as well as success. The equivalent of Leyhausen's "absolute hierarchy" of status ranking will be somewhat less important in Barker's model (1968) of the small group, where everybody is more likely to count regardless of status. But we can assume that dominance patterns based on personal assessment of individual capacities will be explicit nevertheless, and hard to escape from.

The attraction of teeming cities, demonstrated by the world-wide migrations from rural to urban areas, suggests that there is something in the smaller communities that does not satisfy especially the young and most dynamic portions of a population, and this can only partly be explained by rural poverty. While status-ranking systems are likely to be less crucial in smaller undermanned communities, there is considerably less specialization and there are fewer opportunities for individual identity on the basis of different skills and capacities. I believe that socially diverse larger cities put a greater premium on the human equivalent of Leyhausen's absolute ranking hierarchy than the village society will, but they also offer a wider range of relative ranking systems due to a greater variety of conceptual territories. This is a most complex relationship, which occupies much of the rest of this book. For the moment I want simply to suggest that while in the industrial city a person may be more likely to feel like a cog in an office or assembly line, he or she depends for identity more on home, or leadership in a club or other association, because pervasive village identity will not be available. But the reverse may also be true; the anonymity of city life also offers opportunities for escape from the continuous pressure to perform as well as to conform.

Leyhausen's theories extrapolated to humans suggest that with reduction of space, especially when it is accompanied by blurring of boundaries between private and public space and an increase in the competition for resources, absolute hierarchies will tend to predominate. More and more in our own time, small town democracy, in which certain kinds of deviance are tolerated quite comfortably, especially from established members, as long as other definite mores are followed, gives way to actual or potential dictatorships of left and right, and the crushingly bland authority of bureaucracies in the politically moderate Welfare State. The general rebellion against authority of all kinds, appropriate and inappropriate, would appear to be compensation for the loss of the opportunity for individuality. The rural or small town boy who wishes to escape the discipline of his father or schoolmaster can retreat, alone or in company of his peers, to the swimming hole, or the woods in the back yard. Clubs are organized spontaneously and activities can be fitted to moods and seasons. In the psychologically, if not physically, cramped spaces of the middle class suburb, organized recreation takes over, and with it the abstract morality of a generalized peer group, which one does not choose, but which is provided by "Society." The ghetto child is worse off; there is no space from which to escape the irascible but so-often impotent authority of overstressed adults and the even harsher tyranny of street gangs.

The development of individual personality requires space in which to test one's own capacities without invoking physical catastrophe on the one hand and overpowering social competition on the other. We may recall Popper's metaphor of science as a method of investigation in which we let our hypotheses die in our stead. Schaller (1973) notes that the full personality of which lion cubs are capable does not emerge in the struggle for survival in the wild, but only after they were protected by humans. On the other hand, the exploratory behavior of Calhoun's low-density mice which incorporate the variety of stimuli from a large environment into the consciousness of themselves contrast with the mice to which conspecifics are the world. If the environment is composed only of peers, we will be permitted only those activities which bother nobody else, which is to say, literally, the lowest — and possibly the meanest — common denominator.

Leyhausen refers to Julian Huxley's description of territory as a kind of "elastic disk" (Huxley, 1934) which surrounds the animal. I like to think of human territory as a fluid, which assumes the shape of a container, and of the container as being constructed of those space-related functions which in any particular case are natural to the individual or his group. Not only will an individual's dispositon to attend to borders vary from time to time, but their location also may change. The emergence of an exceedingly aggressive neighbor may force a territory owner to bend his boundaries inward, much as the boundaries of the nations of central Europe, for instance, have bulged in and out as a result of wars and threats of wars. One of the great difficulties of applying territorial concepts to human relations is that the individual perceives space, not fixed on a map or an aerial photo as the professional planner tends to look at it, but as a mosaic of spaces, nodes, pathways, and boundaries, and landmarks through which he moves (Lynch, 1960). To the man or woman commuting from home to office or shop, perceived territory and range may include only the terminal points and the road in between, some outstanding landmarks, and some bordering centers for shopping and recreation. Much or most of the intervening acreage may not exist at all. This may be true of whole continents for the jet-setter who moves from the hotels and airports of one city to another. It is what made it possible for businessmen to travel from Westchester and Connecticut to Manhattan year after year on a railroad running through the slums of East Harlem without really being aware of them until the residents drew attention to themselves by riots.

Summary of Part Two

The theories we have examined in the last three chapters all underscore the idea that spacial behavior among animals is a profoundly social phenomenon. Each ethologist considered here observes the difference between *territory*, that home space defended by a small group, usually a breeding unit, and a larger area used by a number of such groups, more or less in common, which in the general zoological literature is called "home range."

Wynne-Edwards has described how territory is related both to mating behavior and to aggressive competition between individuals of the same sex, primarily males. Its evolutionary purpose, according to his theory, is to regulate population in relation to food resources indirectly, through conventional tokens, or behavioral symbols, in a much more stable manner than would be possible if hunger controlled population directly. Thus spatial organization is a function of both the physcial and the psychological state of the animal, and is both a cause and a result of the creature's transactions with its fellows and its environment. The individual's capacity to hold territory is determined by its energy level, particularly its sexual energy, but on the other hand the possession of territory releases social energy and the loss of territory retards it in the same individual. In many species territorial behavior is not constant, but is related only to breeding cycles, although its indirect effects are pervasive.

Calhoun's studies also explore this very complex relationship between physical and social organization. In particular he has demonstrated what happens when, through human intervention, the population-regulating processes are artificially impeded. Complete social breakdown occurs eventually, directly disrupting the breeding system by permitting aggressive competition normally limited to adults of the same sex to become generalized indiscriminately among males, females, and young. Significantly, it is at the point where the capacity for reproduction has been totally destroyed that aggressive behavior also ceases, leaving a terminal generation which is both socially and physically sterile, although otherwise healthy.

Calhoun has also observed some related phenomena which suggest an evolutionary basis for some peculiarly human characteristics. One of these is that animals reared under conditions of relatively high density tend increasingly to react to an environment structured in terms of others of their species, whether positively or negatively, rather than to objects in physical space, and that under extreme densities this becomes pathological, so that some available resources are actually underused while others are overexploited. (In a later chapter this will be related to Barker's theory of *under-manning* and *overmanning*.) Another observation is that some socially marginal individuals will apparently appear in any population regardless of the availability of territory and resources, and that it is out of this group that innovative behavior will be likely to develop. Calhoun also believes that the greater capacity of the human brain to code the environment symbolically in "conceptual space" has enabled man to overcome some of the constraints which limit populations in other species, but that this too has limits. Both Wynne-Edwards and Calhoun relate social status to territory in some form.

Leyhausen has observed two kinds of social ranking systems, only one of which is related to territory. Social rank based on the proximity of an animal to its home base he calls *relative hierarchy*. Another type of dominance ranking system reveals itself among male rivals outside the territory, and once established it tends to remain fixed for the familiar population. The latter is apparently dependent only on the individual's native psychological/physical power, whereas the relative dominance hierarchy enables a weaker animal to drive a larger, stronger one out of its own territory even though on neutral ground it would be subservient. Leyhausen's conclusions have been derived largely from his studies of various species of cats, among which the females are the more territorial, and the males are unusually aggressive toward each other. However, he notes that such "solitary" mammals are not unsocial, but simply require a much larger personal space. The dominance of animals through absolute social ranking is not necessarily established only by fighting; in herd animals such as cows, some individuals simply seem to have a magnetic attraction for others which gives them the power to lead.

Each of these ethologists have themselves suggested parallels in the behavior of our own species, although their main attention has been focussed on other animals. In the next section, we will take a reverse view, considering the ideas of observers whose main focus has been on human beings, but at least partially in terms of pre-human behavior. All of these are medical doctors, and two of them are also psychiatrists.

PART THREE
HUMAN STUDIES

Chapter 6

Brain evolution: from feeling to thinking

To an open house in the evening
Home shall men come,
To an older place than Eden
And a taller town than Rome.
G.K. Chesterton

If students of human behavior have tended to ignore other animals, it may be because Western man, at least, has clung to the concept of two aspects of being, one physical, one not, which conflict with each other in the primordial war between good and evil. Much of Christian thought has placed the "animal instincts" in man in association with his physical body on the one hand, and with the devil on the other. It is the soul of man which is supposed to contain the higher virtues, such as love, loyalty, and kindness.

But if we carefully compare ourselves with other animals, it is immediately apparent that it is not our capacity for emotion, but for rational and abstract thought, and for technological manipulation of the environment, which is our most distinguishing characteristic. If a divine power did imbue humanity with a special quality of its own, it is most evident in man's ability to organize and manipulate the physical world. By contrast, we apparently share many emotional states with higher animals, as demonstrated by Darwin (1872). Fear, love, joy, and grief are all evident in a number of creatures with which we share space, and furthermore some emotions are quite reciprocal in our symbiotic relationships with domestic pets, such as dogs and cats.

A theory I will introduce in this chapter suggests that the perceived dualism between body and spirit may have some real basis in the way brain circuits are organized. But if the theory is correct, we may have to turn at least some versions of Christian thought upside down. It suggests that it is our capacity for essentially emotionless objective ideas, for abstract concepts of reality, permitting us to manipulate events vastly beyond our power to experience them directly, which put us on the side of the ideal but bloodless angels. On the other hand it is from our primitive mammalian origins that we have obtained our emotions for better or worse, and perhaps even our sense of good and evil, including the most noble feelings of loyalty, love, and reverence, which link us with the living cosmos in a bond of sensory experience, of pain and pleasure, in the company of spooks and demons as well as bacchanalian harbingers of joy.

Paul MacLean, Chief of the Laboratory of Brain Evolution and Behavior at the United States National Institutes of Mental Health, has postulated what he calls "the brain's generation gap" (MacLean, 1971, 1973a). According to this theory there are three imperfectly integrated layers of neural tissue which correspond to our evolution from vertebrates through mammals to man (Fig. 3). The lowest of these is an enlargement of the brain stem which he calls the *reptilian brain*, and it contains, in his words, the "raw stuff of awareness." It mediates those responses to the environment which are essential for species survival, such as attack or flight, territorial defense, aggressiveness, and mating. In mammals there appears what has become known as the "limbic system" or "old cortex" which contains the centers governing emotional experience. The apparent function of emotion in mammals is to make possible much finer distinctions regarding the environment, more complex forms of social organization, including status hierarchies, and a far greater range of memory storage and recall. MacLean calls this the *paleo-mammalian brain*. In the higher mammals, especially the primates, and fully developed only in man, is the new cortex which MacLean finds governs the intellectual process of anticipation and planning. He calls this the *neo-mammalian brain*. According to this theory, all these levels func-

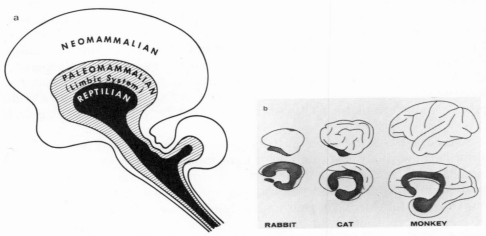

Fig. 3. (a) Diagram of hierarchical organization of three basic brain types, which in evolution of mammals become part of man's inheritance. The three types are radically different in structure and chemistry and in an evolutionary sense are countless generations apart. (b) Drawings showing medial view of brains of rabbit, cat, and monkey illustrate that the cortex of the old mammalian brain (limbic system) is found as a common denominator in the brains of all mammals. Shown in black, it occupies the limbic lobe which forms a border around the brain stem. The cortex of the new mammalian brain (shown in white) mushrooms late in evolution. (From MacLean, 1973a.)

tion together in what he has named the *triune brain* (MacLean, 1970, 1973c). But each center is partially independent. In his words "The result is the remarkable linkage of three brain types which are radically different in structure and chemistry, and which, in an evolutionary sense, are countless generations apart." (MacLean, 1973a.)

What is most significant for designers and planners in this theory is that the information processing systems are different, that the well-known conflict between thought and feeling are the results of at least partially separate physical systems with different perceptions of space.

There is also a functional dichotomy between these areas of the brain. MacLean has studied the effects of epileptic seizures involving the limbic system, and of frontal lobotomies in which portions of the neo-cortex are surgically removed to ease mental illness. Epileptic attacks in the limbic area can elicit the whole repertory of emotional feelings capable of intense memory recall, but in many cases they will not interfere with rational processes. He cites, for example, the case of a doctor who made a correct diagnosis, and that of an engineer who safely brought his train into the station, while having seizures, without remembering the events. Emotion seems to be required for some types of memory storage. In contrast, frontal lobotomies have long been known to interfere with planning functions. MacLean reasons that they reduce anxiety by reducing the ability to anticipate events connected with guilt or fear of consequences. This seems to be a neuro-surgical expression of saying "ignorance is bliss" and "what he doesn't know won't hurt him." Alcohol and certain drugs seem to have the same effect by freeing the emotions from the controls that come from the capacity to anticipate events and plan for consequences, which may undoubtedly explain their popularity (and inherent danger) in highly planned societies.

The great problem in attempting to relate the kind of animal behavior I have described in the last three chapters to human behavior is that, while in so many respects we clearly do behave more or less like other animals (to our credit or discredit, depending on the point of view), what is known of sub-human behavior quite obviously cannot adequately account for all of our own. MacLean's theory seems to explain, better than any other I have come across, how it is that we can at one and the same time be so self-evidently similar and so conspicuously different.

According to MacLean, the lowest level of our triune brain is where the atavistic impulses for ritualized aggresive displays in defense of territory, of the sort explored especially by Wynne-Edwards, originate. One of the criticisms of Wynne-Edwards, and also of the conclusions regarding humans which allegedly are drawn by Lorenz from vertebrates like birds and fish, is that such rigidly programmed responses do not characterize the higher animals which are closest to us. That behavior becomes more complex than this among the higher species is recognized by all ethologists, and certainly by Wynne-Edwards and Lorenz (a fact that will be clear to anyone who reads further than the dust jackets of the popular books on the subject). But, MacLean's theory suggests how such primitive instinctive responses can be incorporated within higher stages of development, modified but not eliminated. However, what is most significant about the social behavior of mammals studied by Calhoun and Leyhausen is not so much that it is more complex as that it is much more flexible and discriminating.

In MacLean's view, the function of emotion in the paleo-mammalian limbic system is to enable mammals to distinguish familiar conspecifics from non-familiar ones, in short, friends from enemies. To a lizard another lizard is another lizard, to mate with if it happens to be a female at the right place and time, and otherwise to attack if it happens to be on one's own territory or too close to one's personal space. The perceptual equipment with which one reptile distinguishes another seems to be very limited by mammalian standards. This enables experimenters with reptiles and lower forms to use dummies to elicit behavior which would not fool a mammal. The duck hunter's decoy is a familiar example. A decoy will not catch a fox, or even a rabbit. MacLean reports trying to attract the attention of an indifferent lizard in a zoo without success, until he sketched the animal's own silhouette on a note pad and held it up to view. Immediately the lizard charged with a full aggressive display. It is apparently the "lizard" in us which responds to the psychologists' Rorschach test and some of the more basic archetypical symbols that recur in dreams and also in primitive art, as observed by Jung (1964). The paleo-mammalian limbic system enables the mammal not only to recognize his own kind, but individual differences within it, and to make alliances accordingly, through the capacity for emotional attachments as well as aversions. This also makes possible the complex status-ranking systems described by Calhoun and Leyhausen (not to be confused with the programmed ranks of insects).

Both the reptilian and the paleo-mammalian brains lack the neural machinery for verbal communication, and for mathematical and other abstract symbolic systems. That is the province of the neo-mammalian brain, which is highly developed only in man. This difference alone can account for the great gap between us and other animals. This distinction justifies the emphasis of social sciences on culture, but if MacLean's theory is correct, it does not justify looking on culture as the only determinant of our behavior, as asserted, for example, by Montagu (1968).

A.H. Esser, who is one of the pioneers in relating ethological concepts of animal and human behavior, has elaborated MacLean's theory in applying it to his own research, especially as it pertains to communication and cooperation, for which Esser uses the term *synergy*.

He calls MacLean's three levels (1) the *biological brain* (the reptilian level), (2) the *emotional brain* (the paleo-mammalian limbic system), and (3) the *intellectual brain* (the neo-cortex as it appears in man) (Esser, 1971a, pp. 13—14). Because the limbic system, or emotional brain, is so important for social organization, which is reflected in shared feelings, Esser also calls this the *social brain*. In Esser's words (personal comment) the animal on this level can say to himself in effect, "I like that fellow, he makes me feel good," or "I'd better watch out for that one, he's stronger and he'll hurt me if I get in his way." In contrast, the kinds of mental images of the environment which are shared by human beings through the neo-cortex, or *intellectual brain*, are largely independent of direct sensory experience. Because this intellectual image system can be viewed as an artificial extension of experience, Esser also calls this the *prosthetic brain*. It is this part of our brain which makes possible speech, rational thought, and abstract concepts.

Esser believes that the emotional brain of the limbic system and the intellectual brain of the neo-cortex code experience in ways which are often incompatible, and for which the integrative functions are imperfect. The emotional brain is designed for environmental relationships which are appropriate to living in small groups, in which each individual in the social unit and each element that makes up the territory is experienced personally. Anything outside the territory and anyone outside the group is regarded as alien and will be viewed with suspicion if not hostility. He cites the example of the Australian aborigine who will simply die if ostracized from his group. On that level man literally has no existence outside his community. Furthermore, each individual is perceived in terms of his place or rank within that society. Affection for one's own and hostility or indifference to that which is not one's own is, according to this view, the very basis for social organization on the primitive mammalian level. This is the basis Tiger (1969) gives for male bonding and it would certainly seem also to imply female cooperation and also cooperation between the sexes. On the other hand, the neo-cortex provides the instrument for what Calhoun calls "conceptual space."

The conflicting functions of the emotional, paleo-mammalian brain and the intellectual, neo-mammalian brain lead to what Esser calls "social pollution" (Esser, 1971a). This results from a clash of images between one level of perception and the other. The image systems of the reptilian brain relate to demands for personal space and territory; those of the limbic system to small-group cohesion. Those of the intellectual brain pertain to the elaborate but essentially impersonal and abstract systems of technical, legal, and political cooperation in which the interests of individuals interlock with the welfare of many others with whom they have no personal identification at all.

If this is so, we may logically expect that in a human being whose neo-cortex is not operative or malfunctions through injury, birth defect, or mental illness, behavior would more closely resemble that of other animals than it does when the brain is intact. And this is what has been found to occur. Esser and his associates have been observing disturbed or brain-damaged children, and schizophrenic adults in a variety of institutional settings (Esser et al., 1965; Esser and Etter, 1966; Esser, 1968, 1970a, 1971c, 1973).

Such individuals seek to establish territorial and dominance relationships in a manner that appears to me to resemble very closely the two types of animal dominance which Leyhausen has called *absolute social hierarchy* and *relative social hierarchy*:

> The mentally most fit patient, who is capable of verbal communication, is most likely to acquire an accepted position in the social rank order existing among staff and patients in the ward. If the patient is less capable of social contact, he may only be able to satisfy his drive by occupying a certain space and literally defending this as his territory. (Esser, 1965, p. 3.)

Behavior within a rigidly controlled institution is not wholly comparable to human behavior outside, because the institution itself limits opportunities and forces codes and attitudes of its staff on the inmates who have no choice in this matter. Esser makes full allowances for this in his conclusions. On the other hand, the institution also forces its members to come to terms with each other in one way or another. He has found that they will do so in terms of territorial behavior, or social ranking, or a combination of both. Here as elsewhere the relationship between these two components of social organizations is complex.

Possession of territory among mental patients will tend to correlate with status in the ward (i.e., the ability to dominate); on the other hand, status will also correlate highly with the capacity for social interaction. The least-capable of social behavior will be most territorial! The picture which emerges, as it did from Leyhausen's studies of cats and other mammals, suggests that social cooperation frees the individual from dependence on territory, but at the same time is a function of having a territory to be free from. There is a tragic irony in that it is the least dominant who are the most dependent on a physical territory alone, but who also may find territory hardest to obtain.

Esser's studies are based on a technique which corresponds to the ethologist's *ethogram* and also to some extent to Barker's *behavioral settings* (1968) and Hall's *situational frames* (1974). Trained observers, usually watching through a one-way window, note the number and types of social contacts, and the geographical distribution within the room. Whenever possible, those observations are made where the subjects are most free to do as they wish, and not in classrooms or dining rooms where staff control will be maximum. He has found that position in a dominance hierarchy corresponds closely to the diagnosis: among hospitalized children, those with behavioral disorders (whole but poorly integrated brains) will rank higher than brain-damaged children. They will fall into three classes: (1) those who show cohesiveness as a group and who display dominance over those outside that group, (2) those who will play largely by themselves and show little social awareness, and (3) those who are merely an aggregate of individuals unable to make any form of contact (Esser, 1968).

Social contact, whether positive in terms of cooperativeness or negative in terms of fighting, generally conforms to a good prognosis for adjustment outside the institution. However, not all social contact is related to dominance or social adjustment; some children are obsessed with maintaining close proximity to others and cannot act independently, and it is difficult to observe their own relation to territory because they are inevitably involved in others' territorial fights (Esser, 1973). Depending on the situation, Esser's observations show that territory may also be correlated with high status and good prognosis, but in either case the establishment of rank or property tends to reduce fighting. As with animals, the most intense fighting and the most chaotic situations will occur when new groups are formed, or strangers are introduced to an old group, and firm relationships have yet to be sorted out.

This is particularly evident among schizophrenic adults. In one study Esser notes "recently admitted patients tend to fight more frequently than older inhabitants of the ward. . . instability in dominance position is related to aggressive behavior in 10 out of 12 cases." (Esser et al., 1965.) In this study patients fall into three categories: (1) Those who are free to move wherever they want and do not seem to need to establish ownership of a particular spot in the ward, (2) patients who show restriction of range but tend to occupy territories located so as to increase chances for contact, (i.e., near the entrance corridor) and (3) those who withdraw into secluded spots where they are least likely to be contacted. Esser and his colleagues hypothesized that among those in the middle group there would be the most frequent involvement in aggressive acts. After examining these data, he found the opposite to be true: fighting occurred primarily in the upper and lower groups. Members fought among themselves and with patients low in status.

The researchers concluded that members of these two groups maintained unstable positions in the dominance hierarchy, on the one hand fighting with equals for status, and on the other bullying those far down from whom they had nothing to fear. Of course, people are in mental institutions in the first place because they are not capable for one reason or another of more constructive kinds of social stability, so that we cannot take these as models for the larger human society. These particular studies of Esser (his work covers a very wide range of behavior) are instructive, not because they adequately describe normal human relationships, but because they reveal what happens when normal social structures are not fully operative. Esser sees it this way:

> Our tendency to accommodate aggressive attitudes will continue as long as we do not view them as part of a simple form of organization based on threat, force, and intimidation, as this exists in any animal society. . . . Behavior in human sub-cultures, just like ritualized behavior in animals, is an adaption of life in a given society. . . .
> Now that our attention has been drawn to the mental schemata of our natural evolution, the ethological approach, the study of naturally occurring behavior, should be directed to reveal other, equally basic, forms of social life, based on love, compassion, and altruism. (Esser, 1973, p. 144.)

Because in actual operation the brain appears to be drawing on neurological circuits all over itself, some researchers do not altogether agree with

MacLean's formulation. One of these is Dr. John Flynn of the Yale Medical School, who has been implanting electrodes in the brains of cats to study, among other things, aggressive behavior (1970, 1971a, 1971b). He believes that the emotional functions of the limbic system are always involved to some extent in the intellectual actitivies of the neo-cortex. In his words, "The brain uses whatever it needs for its purposes" (personal comment). Another is a University of Michigan psychologist, Stephen Kaplan, who believes that the main satisfaction in cognition is the process of linking these various brain levels. Kaplan feels that the excitement of cognition comes when the brain actually jumps the gap, resulting in a fully integrated perception (personal comment). Calhoun describes such an integrating process on the fantasy level as "an intellectual orgasm, the eureka experience of the truly creative episode" (1971. p. 359). I see nothing in MacLean's theory or his own writings about it which precludes such integration, and much that supports it. If I understand MacLean and Esser, one object of civilized behavior would be to facilitate such integration. My own conclusion is that the activity which does so most completely is design, especially when it is also art.

While the "generation gap" in our brains can be blamed for many of the ambiguities and contradictions in our behavior, neither MacLean nor Esser suggest that they are unbridgeable. Both define the closing of these gaps as *empathy* (MacLean, 1967, 1973a; Esser, 1971a, 1972), a neo-cortical function which enables us to identify our personal welfare with the welfare of others on a scale which other mammals cannot. MacLean finds this is made possible specifically by the development of what is called the "cingulate division of the limbic system" and its linkages with the neo-cortex (1973a, p. 125). However, he believes this is in part a learned sense, and that if it is not taught and learned at a critical period in the brain's development, it may never be fully awakened (1967, p. 374). He notes that although civilization is measured in thousands of years, the humanitarian movement, which is the most recent expression of this faculty of the human brain, is less than 200 years old.

While MacLean clearly postulates a dichotomy in these brain levels, he reiterates that they are part of one entity, the triune brain. He says "The emphasis given to the dichotomy in function of the limbic system and neo-cortical systems should not lead to the impression that they work independently of one another. At the subjective level, one suspects that their communication problem is a little like that of horse and rider. But just where in the brain this metaphorical interplay takes place is not clear." (1958, p. 623.) The difference of opinion between MacLean and Flynn seems to be that the latter does not think this interplay takes place at any specific point, but all over the nervous system.

The controversies of this sort reach into a range of theoretical and technical questions which are well beyond the scope of this book, and in any case beyond the competence of its author to enter into. It is sufficient for my purpose that MacLean's theory does explain some of the ambivalencies that are so readily observable in human behavior. It explains our behavior so well that I shall use the triune brain as the foundation for a conceptual model which I hope may help us to plan and design our human habitats so that the cognitive parts can find a place, each on its own terms, within a synergistically whole environment.

To avoid the implication that I have a sophisticated technical knowledge of neuro-physiology, which I do not, and to avoid confusing and irritating those who do, I have sought for words which will allow me to use these brain functions as metaphor without invoking such precise terms as "cortex". The word "mammalian" is within the province of this book, but it does not allow for the distinctions with which the model is concerned.

Esser's "biological," "social," and "intellectual" brains are appropriate to the general discussion, but they do not fit the model either. "Biological" is the basic frame of reference for my whole concept, and "social" fits both sides of its equation, as I will show when I descibe the model in more detail in Chapter 8. The word "intellectual" which accurately describes the major function of the human neo-mammalian brain, as Esser uses it, also can refer to a particular type of human social unit with strong paleo-mammalian proclivities, as I will suggest in Chapter 10. Esser's terms "emotional brain" and "prosthetic brain," expressive as they are, are too clinical for what I have in mind.

There is a further problem in that my model is a bipolar one, and there are certain structural difficulties in balancing this on a tripolar foundation. The model is concerned with the distinction between human and sub-human cognitive processes as they pertain to urban environments. For this the urge for territory, which MacLean finds to be a primitive reptilian impulse, and the emotion-loaded impulse for social differentiations and cohesion which appear to be peculiar to the paleo-mammalian phases of brain evolution, can be lumped together as "animal" characteristics which we share. But they cannot be accurately combined using the triune brain as presented by its discoverer.

I discussed this problem with MacLean, who kindly offered the term "draco-limbic" to describe for my purpose the combined functions of the reptilian and limbic systems. The term is particularly fortunate because it has mythic overtones that imply metaphor, rather than precise physical description, and it has connotations of irrational danger which I think are quite appropriate. For the human version of the cognitive processes of the neo-mammalian cortex, I shall use the term "conceptual" rather than "intellectual," since this word pertains to abstract thought. Henceforth, I shall refer to them as the *draco-limbic brain* and the *conceptual brain*, except where more specific terms are in order.

For design and planning purposes, one of the critical differences between the conceptual brain and the draco-limbic brain is that the former processes information much more rapidly. As MacLean puts it, "with its imagination that exceeds the speed of light, the neo-cortex may be able to keep up with the present accelerated tempo of life through speed-reading, help of computers, and other contrivances, but the two animal brains which are our constant companions move at their own slow pace. They have their own biological clocks and their own sequential, ritualistic ways of doing things that cannot be buried. Courtship, for example, does not lend itself to the rules of speedreading."

MacLean had likened the cortexes of the triune brain to different experimental versions of an airplane pilot's radar screen (MacLean, 1958). I should like to extend this analogy, to suggest that the draco-limbic version of the screen tells the pilot what is going on inside. The draco-limbic system can be visualized as those instruments and controls on which the pilot can actually put his hands. These are the ones that govern the internal events that directly determine the spatial orientation and state of the airplane. For these he has immediate feedback on his instrument panel and he adjusts to changes in the environment by adjusting the ship itself. The conceptual brain can tell him what the external environment is like, but can lead to adjustments in relation to it only by being reprocessed into the internal system. It is important for the present discussion to recognize that in terms of the qualitative state of the pilot and his passengers, the only significant reality is what is happening to and within the aircraft.

In the next chapter I will examine some theories of how scrambled signals in the draco-limbic part of the system may cause functional and structural breakdowns in the whole system.

Chapter 7

Space, symbols, and health

The body responds not only to the stimulus itself, but also to all the symbols associated with memories of the past, the experiences of the present, and anticipations of the future.
Rene Dubos

Fred Fischer (1965) is a Zurich psychiatrist who has explored the role of territory in human psychic wellbeing, influenced in this by a friendship with Hediger on the one hand, and the late architect Richard Neutra on the other.

Fischer observes that the first home, or "territory," is the womb: "Life on earth begins with the process of birth, with a change of living space, of habitat." According to Freudian doctrine, every person longs to return to the security of this original protected space. Whether one accepts that paradigm or not, clearly the newborn infant is helpless and for good reason seeks the protection of the temporary habitat of the mother's arms. As the child becomes increasingly social, it begins to distinguish between individuals who belong to it and those who do not, and between objects and events in the environment. As it does so it will begin to structure its image of a home, as a place which includes this and keeps out that, but as it grows it will also incorporate a larger environment into its territory, and become increasingly aware of the territory of others, and of common non-territorial places.

Fischer reduces space to four *cardinal distance values*, two pleasurable and two unpleasurable. They are *security* and *freedom of movement* on the one hand, contrasting with *confinement* and *sense of being lost* on the other. I shall re-introduce this concept in the next chapter.

Fischer finds a common denominator between man and other mammals in a four-part time/space hierarchy relating to stages of the life cycle:

1. In the mother's body.
2. Under the mother's wing.
3. Within the parent's territory.
4. Within the personally occupied territory of the adult being.

Maturing humans generally leave the parent's territory to seek their own, as do the young adults of other species. But as the studies of Calhoun and Wynne-Edwards show for mice and birds, so for human beings, overpopulation makes it increasingly difficult for marginal individuals to establish their own home base. Fischer notes that in the denser urban environments, more and more people settle in rented quarters, where some territorial prerogatives

65

exist, but where they are considerably qualified. "For the great majority, then," he notes, "the 'security of the home' is conditional, so to speak secondhand — in the eyes of the law they are perpetually on foreign territory." (1965, 1971, p. 57.)

Fischer puts an ethological slant on the relationship, often noted by architectural historians, between the emergence of the private room in houses and the development of the individualized western personality; and his observations in this respect tie in within Leyhausen's concept of relative and absolute dominance hierarchies:

> If several individuals occupy one living area and there is, therefore, no possibility for each person to select his preferred area freely, the resulting clash of interests will be settled along hierarchical principles governing the animal collective. Conflict situations arise which prove often to be insurmountable and the solutions to these are not often just. Within the community there will emerge a *balance of power* which must be reestablished with each departure and each new arrival. In the clash of drives which results in such a collective, we observe also the formation of a system of surveillance implemented by the collective, be it a clan, a people, or a state. Each individual observes his neighbor closely and seeks to check any of the latter's drives which run contrary to his own interests. The living space leads to the formation of collective cells which cannot be avoided easily. Economic development and human division of labor have resulted . . . in the loss of the individual's ability to construct his own home . . . The subject seeking protection within his home becomes its captive instead. (Fischer, 1967, p. 61.)

That various cultures have various ways of organizing space in terms of these relationships has been demonstrated by Hall (1966), whose theories will be examined later. Chinese planning students, for example, have told me that they do not understand the American concept of privacy, that for them privacy is the state of mind maintained by the individual within shared group space. For them, "home" seems to be more nearly synonymous with "family." They seem to develop ways of retaining privacy in what Calhoun calls "conceptual space," in a manner not unlike that which Hall describes (1966, p. 130) for the English upper class raised in nurseries. It is risky to generalize too far in these matters, and certainly dangerous to apply moral values to differing arrangements, but it may be reasonably safe to conclude that the strong emotional dependence on group interaction, especially of family, observed by Gans (1962) and Fried (1963), among many others, and the importance of kinship networks long noted by anthropologists, may be a function of homes in which children grow up collectively in rather high home densities. However, for the middle classes in cultures based on Northern European traditions, Fischer's observations in this respect are a frame of reference which designers of apartment buildings and town houses might do well to keep in mind.

There is a great deal of literature on the social and psychological aspects of housing design, and in recent years increasing attention has been given to territorial arrangements, usually in terms of privacy. Cultural differences in this respect have been noted (e.g., Rapoport, 1969) by anthropologists, and differences by class and income groups have been noted by sociologists, like Rainwater (1966, 1971). While diversities in this regard are still not adequately understood and provided for, the full social significance of basic territorial relationships is even less clearly recognized.

John Cassel, Professor of Epidemiology at the University of North Carolina, reveals that the close and intricate relationship between physical space, conceptual space, social organization, and social communication affects not only behavior but also physical health. The grim statistics of poverty have long showed a correlation between certain kinds of disease and low socio-economic status. In this country these statistics show up conspicuously among the black population. It is generally assumed that poor physical conditions such as sanitation and exposure, as well as poor nutrition due to limited food budgets, are the primary causes. These have often been attributed to crowding. But studies by Cassel and others in his field suggest that this is a grave oversimplification. He reports:

> Comparative recent findings would tend to suggest that we need to modify some of these existing theories to allow for the possibility that one of the more important, and hitherto unconsidered, aspects of the environment (from a disease etiology point of view) may be the presence of other members of the same species. (Cassel, 1970a.)

According to the pioneer microbiologist, Rene Dubos, microbial disease is not necessarily acquired through exposure to a new microorganism, but is a function of the balance between these organisms, which are present in the environment, and the general state of the individual harboring them (Cassel, 1971; Dubos, 1965). The question raised by Cassel is, what are the actual factors that make the individual receptive to the disease? His answer directly ties in with the theme of our study:

> Paradoxically, some of the more convincing evidence supporting this point of view comes from animal studies. To a large extent, these have been concerned with variations in the size of the group in which the animals interact and in situations which lead to confusion over territorial control. A number of investigators have shown, for example, that as the number of animals housed together increases, with all other factors such as *genetic stock, diet, temperature, and sanitation kept constant*, maternal and infant mortality rates rise, the incidence of arterio-sclerosis increases, resistance to a wide variety of *insults, including drugs, micro-organisms, and x-rays*, decreases and there is an increased susceptibility to various types of neoplasia . . . Lack of territorial control has been shown to lead to the development of marked and persistent hypertension in mice, to increased maternal and infant mortality rates and also to reduced resistance to bacterial infection and decreased longevity . . . (My italics) (Cassel, 1970a.)

It is significant that among the factors kept constant, that is, which are not allowed to influence results, are precisely those which vary most negatively with low economic status in man — diet, temperature, and sanitation. It is important to note also that genetic control in the experiment would rule out any racial assumptions about susceptibility to this or that when the theory is applied to humans.

At first glimpse the animal data suggest that there is something inherent in the situation of being crowded that may cause disease independent of the physical situation, but Cassel believes it may not be crowding per se. He provides a long bibliography of research on this question, but for our purposes it will be sufficient to refer back to the studies we have already considered. We may recall that Calhoun's mice did not all react to crowding the same way at the same time, and that there were marked differences between generations. The final result of his experiments, in fact, produced the "Beautiful Ones," which were physically sleek and healthy. Cassel's data on both animals and man lead him to the conclusion "that the relationship between crowding and health status is a far more complex phenomenon than was originally envisaged, and that while under certain circumstances crowding is clearly associated with poor health states, under other circumstances it may be neutral or even beneficial" (Cassel, 1971). It is important here to distinguish between densities as they affect social relationships and the demand of people on non-human resources, on the ecosystem.

Cassel cites Dubos' (1968a) report that despite the fact that Hong Kong and Holland are among the most crowded areas in the world, they enjoy the highest levels of physical and mental health in the world, and he provides data from Britain which also suggests that pathology does not correlate per se. In seeking the answer to this riddle he examined the history of disease patterns which accompanied the industrial revolution with its mass migrations and urban concentrations of working people, which have preoccupied social reformers ever since. Tuberculosis has been a prime example of a disease which is associated with crowding, poverty, and unhealthy living conditions. He notes that disease rose sharply for 75-100 years after the beginning of industrialization in Britain and the United States, and then started to fall spontaneously between 1850 and 1900, 50 to 100 years before effective means of treating it became available, and furthermore the rate of decline in this disease has not changed significantly following new drugs for its treatment. As TB began to decline, it was replaced by malnutrition syndromes, such as rickets and pellagra, which also peaked, and for reasons only partially understood also began to decline. These in turn were replaced by childhood diseases, which waxed and waned, "largely but not entirely" due to immunization and improved sanitary conditions. A new cycle introduced an increase in duodenal ulcers, particularly in young men, to be replaced in the present time by epidemics of heart disease, cancer, arthritis, diabetes, and mental disorders, some of which have already peaked and declined (Cassel, 1970b). Cassel believes these cycles cannot be attributed entirely to developments in medical practice. Apparently they do not correspond to equivalent fluctuations in crowding, either, which as a general phenomenon has continued to increase more or less constantly.

He has looked at data from military camps, for instance, where upper respiratory disease is common. The agent responsible is *Adenovirus IV*, and the orthodox explanation is that crowding in barracks and elsewhere facilitates the spread of the virus, but he notes that the virus is equally present in schools and colleges where it is rarely implicated in similar infections. Examination of military camps revealed that the permanent staff were not involved in the outbreaks under study, but only the recruits. When the latter were immunized against *Adenovirus IV*, they continued to experience the same amount of respiratory illness, now associated with a different virus. Even more importantly, studies at a Marine base found that there was a definite cycle of the disease during the eight week basic training period, in which the number of respiratory infections increased from the first to the fourth week, decreased during the fifth and sixth, and rose again during the last two (Cassel, 1971).

Data from epidemiology developed by Cassel show furthermore that increases in diseases do not always take place in the crowded cities, but that often the reverse is true, and that this cannot always be explained by improved health services in the city. He cites as an example the greater preponderance in rural areas of streptococcal infections, for which there is no known preventative. Looking more closely at urban data for tuberculosis, he finds that it is not more prevalent among people who are most crowded, but rather among people who are socially isolated in what must be considered relatively low densities on a person per room basis. A study in Britain found the tuberculosis rate among lodgers living alone was three to four times as high as among families living in otherwise similar conditions (Cassel, 1971).

Cassel believes that data from both humans and animal studies of crowding can best be examined in terms of four principles (1970a): The first is the hypothesis that "the social process linking high population density to enhanced susceptibility to disease is not crowding *per se* but *the disordered relationships that in animals are inevitable consequences of such crowding.*" (My italics.) The clear implication of this hypothesis is that for human beings crowding may facilitate social disorganization, but will not necessarily produce it. Cassel's second general principle is that not all members of a population will be equally susceptible to these processes, and that the most dominant individuals will show the least effects, while the subordinate ones will show the most extreme responses. His third principle is that two types of buffers will cushion the individual against the consequences of social disorganization, one biological, the other social. The biological buffer is the capacity of all living organisms to adjust over time psychologically and physiologically to new circumstances. The social cushion is the strength of group support given by familiar conspecifics. The fourth principle he advances is that the consequences of social disorganization in these terms do not directly cause a specific illness, but rather that they enhance susceptibility to disease in general, and that it will be a matter of which disease agents, independent of social factors, happen to strike at any particular place at any particular time.

Among the examples which support his first hypothesis is a great deal of information linking various indicators of social or family breakdown, such as divorce, or sudden unemployment, to various diseases, and conversely, the examples already given of very crowded societies which do not have a high incidence of disease but which are also very stable socially. The second is supported by similar data which show a high correlation of illness to low social status and job positions which occupy a subordinate role in society. The biological adaptability in his third principle is confirmed by experience with animals raised in crowded conditions as compared with those moved into them after maturing in less-crowded ones. In humans the incidence of lung cancer (when controlled for cigarette smoking) is actually higher among farm-born people who move to air-polluted cities than for lifetime urban residents, despite greater exposure of the latter to cancer-producing agents. The group-support hypothesis is reinforced by studies of rats, for instance, where peptic ulcers caused by electric shocks are much less likely in animals which are shocked in the presence of litter mates than those who are stressed that way alone. In humans, stress induced by giving unsolvable problems to solve was much greater in a group of strangers than in a group of friends. There is much evidence that diseases such as TB are more common among marginal people who for one reason of another are deprived of meaningful and stable social contacts. His final principle, that disturbances in group relationships will not lead to specific illnesses (such as job frustration causing ulcers), but rather to a susceptibility to disease in general, as supported by data which show that those regions having highest death rates, for instance from cardiovascular disease, also have higher than expected death rates from all causes.

It is apparent that all such phenomena are interrelated. It has been observed that male red grouse which failed to obtain territory were also unable to make a pair bond with females, generally were prone to various illnesses, failed to protect themselves from predators, and did not survive the winter (Watson and Moss, 1970).

If Cassel's theories are correct, we may conclude that the mechanism which enables man to remain healthy at densities higher than most animals could tolerate, also enables man to structure his environment and his social relationships conceptually, as suggested by Calhoun and Esser. In a very real sense the degree to which a person feels crowded depends very much on what he thinks being crowded is, and the effect this has on his social interactions. Not only does crowding affect the amount of interaction, but the nature of the interaction changes. At the same time an individual's concept of status and of family or other in-group relations will be very critical in determining how he adjusts both to crowding and to change. A study by Christenson and Hinkle (1961) showed a much lower incidence of disease among a group of managers who had completed college as compared with those doing the same job for the same pay who had only completed high school. The college graduates were generally sons of high-status managers and white collar workers from middle class neighborhoods; the non-college managers were children of working class immigrants. One may assume that not only did social class status play a role in this phenomenon, but also the symbols of middle class life which would normally be part of the managerial world. Cassel and an associate made a series of studies of two groups of rural mountaineers who had moved to urban areas and taken industrial jobs in factories. The groups were similar in age and other factors, but one had recently migrated from the mountains, while the others were the children of factory workers who had previously come from the same mountain coves. It was hypothesized that the second generation workers would be better prepared for the expectations and demands of industrial living than would the first group, and would, therefore, exhibit fewer signs of ill health. Health was measured according to the Cornell Medical Index and various indices of sick absenteeism. As predicted, the highest health scores and lowest absenteeism were from the group whose parents had been employed in industry before them (Cassel and Tyroler, 1961).

In view of the fact that our core cities are more and more populated not only by poor, low-status, minority people, crowded into slums, but also by people who have recently migrated from rural areas, this is pretty crucial information for planners to chew on. In other words, many of those now living in cities are ill-prepared for city life. This may be particularly crucial in terms of the dissolution of family life that so often accompanies rural-to-urban migration, aggravated by lack of housing and the inability of male heads-of-households to find work. It may help to explain why our welfare programs have failed to offer even a palliative for this kind of poverty.

Common elements we can find in Cassel's reasoning may be summed up in two words: *feedback* and *control.* We might extrapolate from this the following picture of the human condition: ultimately man's health and welfare depend, as they do for all other species, on his ability to control his relations with the physical environment, either by adjusting himself to it or it to himself. At some point an individual isolated in an extremely unfavorable environment will succumb to starvation or thirst, cold, or exhaustion, but these are not normally conditions experienced by most human beings, at least at present in the more affluent countries. While it is evident that many species can adapt quite well in a solitary manner, evolution has apparently provided physically defenseless man, as a primary means of adjusting to his environment and vice versa, with strong impulses for cooperative action with members of his own species.

Animal studies show that when an intruder approaches a conspecific's home territory, a ritualized set of behavior will be initiated on both sides. If for some reason one animal doesn't respond predictably to the other, the confused animal will tend to indulge in behavior which is quite bizarre; it will do inappropriate things like pulling up grass, attempting to copulate, or even lying down and going to sleep. Lorenz, we may recall, describes this as displacement behavior, which in his theory performs the function of diverting aggressive energy into harmless forms. Cassel notes, however, that a more common consequence of failure to get a proper response is that the animal will continue to repeat the behavior and that this is accompanied by very marked changes in very powerful neuro-endocrine processes and the disstribution of crucial hormones in the animal's body (personal comment). It is these physiological concomitants of failure to get a proper social response to conventional behavior signals which, in his theory, lead to making the body vulnerable to various insults. What these insults are, whether a disease-bearing virus or a functional breakdown like stomach ulcers, will depend on the circumstances.

Human beings communicate not only by spoken words and written symbols, but by very subtle changes in gesture and inflection, facial expression, or bodily movements, which, like all language, are learned, and are a function of a particular culture (Hall, 1959). We have our ritualized aggressive and submissive gestures, such as a handshake or a cold stare (both of which are used by chimpanzees (Goodall, 1971)). Whether one says "Hi" or "How do you do?" can make a tremendous difference in the response elicited from the greeting, depending on the culture of the greeters. Use of a first name to a stranger may be an essential submissive gesture meaning "let's be friends" in one culture, notably our own, whereas in another, such as parts of central Europe, it is an intolerably aggressive act and an unpardonable invasion of privacy.

Thus Cassel's first hypothesis, that disease correlates with the disorganization of social cues (which in other animals will normally result from crowding), rather than with densities as such, is based on his observations that among humans this social disruption may show up in both crowded and uncrowded situations. We can assume that one of these is where the culture of a migrating population conflicts with a resident one, even in low density environments, and I shall come back to this in a later chapter. Cassel notes, however, that even among animals, crowding will be tolerated much better among litter mates than among strangers. He feels there are three situations in which social dysfunction of this sort can occur. The first is where a newcomer simply does not know the proper cues. While this is most likely to coincide with migrations from lower to higher density areas, in Cassel's view it will be the changed social situation and not the density that matters most. The second is where there has been a breakdown in social structure, such as through death of a family member, unemployment, or divorce. The third is where crowding makes a retreat from an aggressive encounter impossible for the loser. The extended family with its close social relationships among relatives, which tends to be typical of American working class families, where grandparents, aunts, uncles, and cousins fill in as buffer groups, tends to protect many of them against the first situation. These are often disrupted by enforced migration. While voluntary migration usually occurs in the most enterprising sections of a population, forced relocation such as in urban renewal usually hits those most dependent on a familiar environment. More migration often follows, as a result of some of the factors in Cassel's second situation, because people move when they cannot afford to stay where they are. Migration to a higher-density environment may then lead to the third situation, so that one compounds the other.

Cassel's second hypothesis, that social disruption hits hardest on the least-dominant, also compounds his first hypothesis, that social disruption leads to disease, because, especially among the poor, migration is likely to be accompanied by a loss of status, if only because the individual becomes a newcomer and, even when potentially a leader, must establish that fact in a new group. In any case, it is the least dominant who are most likely to be forced to migrate.

The third principle, that time and group unities provide buffers, also relates to migration; the group is left behind, and the instability resulting from the first situation may force continued migrations which will not permit the healing adaptations in one situation long enough for new codes to be established. In any case these may often require more than one generation, especially in people with limited educational, and therefore limited conceptual, resources. So all three principles become negatively reinforcing, and lead inevitably to the fourth, a propensity for disease.

Summary of Part Three

MacLean has postulated that the evolution of the human brain incorporates three stages in development of the vertebrates from reptiles through mammals to the higher primates, and that these are represented within the brain itself by imperfectly integrated layers of neural tissue. In this theory, the phyletically oldest part of the brain of mammals, including humans, contains essentially the same neural circuitry as the brains of living reptiles, and that for all vertebrates it governs the more or less automatic reactions to the environment concerned with basic survival behavior, such as feeding, flight, procreation, and defense of territory. In the mammals, there appears around the primitive brain stem what is called the *paleo-mammalian brain* or *limbic system* which enables them to make much finer social distinctions and to develop more complex social organizations based on status ranking. These basic neural systems are similarly located in human beings, and MacLean finds that the limbic system is where emotional experience appears to occur. In the higher apes, and fully developed only in man, is the so-called "neo-cortex," or *neo-mammalian brain* which MacLean finds contains the areas pertaining to abstract thought and planning, and the more complex forms of motor behavior and speech. Experiments have shown that when these higher centers are disturbed, planning and abstract thought is impaired, but the emotions continue unabated, and vice versa. For the purposes of this book, MacLean's hypothesis that human social-territorial impulses derive largely from the older reptilian and mammalian centers will be presented in terms of one system, the *draco-limbic brain*, in contrast to the human *conceptual brain*.

Studies by Esser and his associates of brain-damaged and mentally-ill individuals support the conclusion that human beings do share with other animals basic territorial and status ranking impulses, and that these are centered in the phyletically older parts of the brain. They appear in a form most like that of other animals when the more highly evolved brain centers, which presumably enable human beings to construct more elaborate social and cultural systems, are impaired through injury or disease.

Fischer, using a Freudian frame of reference, has combined behavioral concepts from ethology with architectural theories, based on insights derived in his practice of psychiatry. In his view territorial impulses begin at birth with a change of habitat caused by leaving the womb, and evolve in life between the need for security and the need to explore the environment. The human institution of rented property creates a kind of partial, qualified territory which offers special problems for urbanized man. In Fischer's view, the erection of private rooms within the family territory of the home permits an elaboration of personality which can free man from the constraints of the animal collective.

Cassel's work in epidemiology is based on the postulate that disease is a consequence, among other things, of the disordered social relationships that often, but not necessarily, accompany extreme crowding. One function of territory, in this view, is to facilitate social group support systems which research has shown correlate very highly with resistance to disease. Health also correlates strongly with social status. Extreme social heterogeneity in non-territorial or overcrowded conditions which do not permit the individual to withdraw to a safe and familiar social-physical home base may facilitate either physical or social pathology, or both. Cassel's work also supports from a medical point of view the central thesis of this book that territory is a fundamental expression of social organization and not its antithesis.

The following chapters, Part Four, will attempt to relate these concepts of territory, as an essentially social phenomenon, to the planning and design of human habitats.

PART FOUR
HUMAN ENVIRONMENTS

Chapter 8

The paradox of scale

Good fences make good neighbors.
Robert Frost

Something there is that does not love a wall.
Robert Frost

In the course of pursuing the subject of this book I have frequently encountered the question, why look at animals? Why not just concentrate on human behavior? Even if man and animals have much in common, is it not the differences that matter? As the title suggests, my own belief is that the differences are indeed what matter, in studying — or being — anything. It seems to me that one of the benefits in looking to man's evolutionary ancestors and contemporary cousins is that it helps us to detect more clearly in what respects we really are unique and to realize that our uniqueness can not be taken for granted. Presumably what is entirely human may to some extent be changed by design, depending on our understanding and our goals. That which is common to life itself obviously cannot. Intelligent contemplation of our fellow beings may enable more of us to achieve, with Niebuhr, the wisdom to know the difference.

It has long been observed that one of the great differences between us and other animals is the capacity for language and the use of tools. Ethology is turning up evidence that even these, however, are not the exclusive prerogative of our species. Chimpanzees have been taught to communicate in human sign language (Gardner and Gardner, 1965) and they have also been found to use rudimentary tools (Goodall, 1971). At the Yerkes Primate Laboratory they are being taught to communicate with machines. Since the higher mammals also have a considerable neo-cortex, they must conceptualize to some extent, and these experiments suggest they do, although the chimp's brain is no bigger than that of a four-month-old child, according to MacLean. The differences, like so many others seen from an evolutionary viewpoint, are differences not as much in kind as in degree. Still, no one will deny that they are very great, nevertheless, and that with the emergence of mankind there appeared a qualitative leap in which the capacity for language and technology could transform society into culture. With the elaborations of the more elemental forms of social organization gained through culture, human beings not only extended the differences between themselves and other species, but greatly expanded differences among social constellations of their own kind. However, precisely because human cultures vary so much, and can change so much more rapidly than older evolutionary behaviors, they are extremely fragile.

Edward T. Hall has used the word *extensions* for the elaborations of biological equipment through language and technology. Hall views culture as basically a system of communication, and he observes that the languages humans use actually determine the kind of environment which they experience. In "The Silent Language" (1959) he showed how people communicate with the whole body by means of all the senses, and not merely by verbal expression. In the "Hidden Dimension" and other writings (Hall, 1966, 1968, 1974) he suggests that human use of space is also a communication system, at once a determinant of culture and an expression of it. He has coined a word for the latter process, *proxemics*, which among some research-oriented designers and design-oriented researchers has in recent years become almost a generic term. Hall defines proxemics as "the interrelated observations and theories of man's use of space as a specialized elaboration of culture" (1966, p. 1).

Hall has not only been a pioneer in considering use of space as a culturally relative communication system. He has also been among the first and most forthright students of human behavior to invoke ethological references. Hall considers proxemics to be the human extension of territorial and status-ranking systems and the impulse to display, mate, fight, or take flight. The reason cultural differences in the proxemic use of space have not been widely recognized, according to his theory, is that they are largely out of awareness, that is, that they respond to environmental cues coded in the non-verbal lower brain centers (MacLean's draco-limbic brain). Hall's name for the underlying processes is *infraculture*.

The difficulty with Hall's theory for many of his critics (see the invited responses to Hall, 1968) is that proxemics call for close attention to the culture-specific differences in the human use of space as a social phenomenon, whereas his philosophical underpinnings suggest a basic commonality which he does not explore beyond establishing that it is there. I do not myself understand the problem of these critics, since it seems to me that the paradox simply reflects the dialectical unity in diversity which seems to underlie all natural processes, so well described by Emerson:

> Nature is a mutable cloud, which is always and never the same.

But I suspect many will have the same problem with my own theory, and I will attempt to deal with it here as best I can. The practical values of recognizing these more primitive substrates of human behavior seem to me twofold. The first is that they explain, much better than a purely cultural view can do, the powerful tenacity with which the adherents of various cultures, subcultures, and social classes will cling to the particular diversities which characterize their groups vis-a-vis other groups. What seems to be a relatively trivial matter from a survival point of view when considered only in terms of diversity, becomes a life or death matter when viewed in terms of the under-lying unity of animal behavior systems. If the external expressions of prox-emic cultures are so often made out-of-awareness, the powerful motivations for them are also buried in the non-verbal, non-rational draco-limbic system.

The second practical reason for looking at the evolutionary origins of culture is that culture is very vulnerable. Ethological observations of animals in general are admittedly not likely to be useful as definers of human be-havior so long as cultures are functioning reasonably well, but they can be-come terrifyingly applicable when cultural systems are impeded or destroyed. There are unfortunately no end of examples in any day's headlines. Civilized non-combatants, and often the combatants themselves, are dismayed by the departures from cultural norms which become possible in the systematic atrocity which is war. Even the cultural norms of war itself are disintegrating as combat between individuals and groups of one sort or another increasingly takes place on the streets of the world's cities.

The danger in over-reliance on human culture is increased by all the pro-cesses of industrial life which impinge on cultural norms. The world-wide rural to urban migrations with consequent strains on village proxemics are but one example. In addition, the political climate in many industrialized and industrializing nations is committed to the principle that cultural change per se is both a necessity and a sure-fire improvement over the status quo. This view is supported quite naturally by swelling populations of partly-educated youth, so many of whom, like the youth of other species, are impelled to test their strength somewhat indiscriminately on every establishment in sight. Toffler (1970) has suggested that in industrialized societies change may be occurring much faster than the human psyche can handle it. My own interest in looking to the evolutionary similarities is to understand the substructure which may help us protect human culture in all its splendid diversity in the face of inevitable change. Toffler asserts that we are moving toward greater diversification, but all the changes I see point in the direction of the most dismal kind of sameness. Because cultural diversity is so important to human wellbeing and human evolution, and also because human culture is not a stable compound of nature but a rare artifact, it seems to me well to keep in mind at all times that culture is not all there is to life. (For a grim view of what can happen when a culture is arbitrarily destroyed (see Turnbull, 1972).)

The failure of neo-technic environments to accomodate animal unities and proxemic diversities can account for much of the current cultural breakdown world-wide. But this failure cannot account for all of it. Important aspects of economic and technological decision-making do not fit the proxemic model of behavior very well, notwithstanding the role of technic extensions in cul-ture itself. There is an important aspect of human experience and behavior which, although not wholly independent of proxemic relationships, is significantly different and must be provided for, spatially and otherwise, on its own terms. This aspect of experience is organized first of all by the conceptual brain. Proxemics provides input to only one side of the human spatial equation. In any case, vital as proxemic-type research is, it is a long-term process. Planners, designers, administrators, and statesmen are meanwhile called upon to deal with problems that cannot await the results of patient, detailed study. Somehow or other we have to find a way of structuring the environment so as to accomodate these diversities, whatever they may prove to be, without necessarily having to understand them in depth.

A possible solution may also be derived from an aspect of animal behavior which is less widely known to non-ethologists than territory but which is very significant to some ethologists, like Paul Leyhausen, whom we met earlier. It will be recalled from Chapters 3 and 5 that whereas territory is a defended space, the home range is a relatively neutral space which may be used by a number of territorial groups or individuals. A familiar example is the bird feeding station of the suburban yard or apartment windowsill.

As a basic expansion of social-territorial behavior, proxemics might be viewed as a relative social hierarchy, in Leyhausen's terms, on cultural territories vis-a-vis other cultural territories. Those members on their own turf have a sense of security which they do not have outside it. For us, urban environments contain a great deal of space which is actively used but which cannot be considered anybody's turf. Such largely non-proxemic spaces may be viewed as the human extension of the animal's home range. While the home range as defined is not defended in the sense that territory is, it is a space which is well known to the animals who frequent it, and in many cases it is used only, or primarily, by animals who are known to each other. It has definite limits which in socially cooperative species often appear to coincide with the limits of social contact. With our technic extensions, the human range has expanded to include the entire planet and now is pushing out into the solar system. This is possible, in my model, precisely because the human conceptual brain is partly free of the draco-limbic brain, because it can operate somewhat independently, as MacLean believes, and therefore is able to construct a cognitive world that is not limited by the mammalian types of social organization that bound our evolutionary ancestors to relatively small groups in more or less discrete spaces. This phylogenetically new cognitive world is, as far as the rest of the brain is concerned, very much like the artificial earth in which humans can now travel into space. Like the space capsule, we cannot reside in it for very long without returning to the original base on which we evolved.

The name I will give this cognitive world is *distemic* to maintain continuity and establish a polarity with Hall's concept of *proxemic*. Both are a function of the use of space and to talk of "proxemic space" is, strictly speaking, redundant, and so it is of "distemic space." But Hall has a forthright communication bias and continually refers to proxemics in linguistic terms. I have physical-form bias which I wish to keep clearly in evidence, and for this reason I am going to talk of proxemic and distemic *space* despite the implicit redundancy. There are forms of proxemic and distemic behavior which, while they use space in a generic sense, are not limited to particular spaces. I have major interest in the appropriate spatial morphology for each, although the model I have in mind is only a first step in defining it.

The basic theoretical difference between distemic space, in this model, and proxemic space is that the former is primarily functional or structural, whereas the latter is first of all experiencial. Hall (1974) has asserted that proxemics is concerned primarily with *context* as opposed to *information*. By context, he means the entire gestalt experience in a particular man— environment transaction, involving all appropriate senses in combination with relevant stored memories, and processed in the non-verbal limbic portions of the brain. Information, in his view, is based on abstract symbols with specific assigned meanings, consciously processed in the conceptual brain. Information, in this sense, is a function of verbal (and presumably also mathematical) language, and is linear in structure rather than gestalt. Hall notes, of course, that no situation is entirely contextual or informational, and that people draw meaning out of the relationship between the two. But he feels that the relationship is generally inverse, that is, a high-context situation is a low-information one and vice versa. The purpose of introducing the word distemics is to deal more adequately with the low-context high-information situations which he identifies but otherwise does not pursue very far.

The basic practical difference between proxemic space and distemic space, from an urban and regional planning perspective, is that whereas proxemic use of space is culturally determined, distemic space can be trans-cultural or super-cultural. This is the essential premise of my design for diversity. That is the arrangement and use of space so as to facilitate at one and the same time both the freest expression of diverse cultures on their own group territories and at the same time optimise possibilities for coexistence, communication, and active cooperation between them. This is possible, in my view, precisely because perception of, and appropriate behaviors within, distemic space can be learned abstractly, consciously, and much more rapidly than proxemic behaviors in proxemic contexts, which require a lifetime of experience to develop. One can fully learn to be a German, an Arab, or an American only by being born one: much of the learning takes place in the infant dawn of consciousness. With sufficient good will and discipline proxemic groups can learn to tolerate, to respect, to accommodate, and in some cases to actively enjoy each others diversities, but only in the most limited ways to experience them. By contrast, in a relatively short time a fully adult member of any culture with the right mental and physical equipment can learn to be a physicist at home in a laboratory, a pilot hopefully in unambiguous communication with a control tower, or a stevedore doing a first-rate job with a multi-ethnic crew in the docks. In all three cases very specific behavioral systems involving the use of space, with clear understandings as to the conventions of its use, are taking place in spaces designed for such behavior, but not culturally so. Rationally so*. Distemic behavior in distemic space ideally accommodates proxemic differences without infringing on them, by making them essentially irrelevant in that context. So, while proxemics has been defined to encompass high-context behavioral situations, distemic behavioral situations nevertheless have a context all their own.

No mammal has a range that can accommodate such diversity because no mammal — so far as I know — can structure a cognitive environment so largely (if temporarily) independent of its draco-limbic need to know conspecifics personally. Distemic space derives from the capacity of man to abstract, to depersonalize, and therefore to desensualize events so as to observe them independent of their immediate consequences for survival. The conceptual planning brain, in this view, makes possible the evolution of science in Karl Popper's sense, the construction and testing of hypotheses. The typical animal when viewing a quiescent but potentially dangerous prey may try to trick it into moving, but more often than not will eventually have to nudge it personally to see if it is alive and harmful or edible. The ape can poke it with a stick and let that get bitten instead of a nose or a paw. Man can work it out in his head, even to visualizing, without participating in, his own destruction. Hypothesis is essential to exploring unknown regions of space, whether physical or conceptual, beyond which the sensually limited animal cannot go. Columbus and his counterparts conceived a world which no human had ever "seen," a world that was round, which corresponded to no proxemic perceptions of his place and time, and on the security of that conception he risked "sailing off the edge" to return and confirm that his hypothesis was at least partially correct.

As noted, Hall believes that there is an inverse relationship between the proxemic high-context low-information situation and the low-context high-information one that I am calling distemic. I have another inverse hypothesis to suggest shortly (p. 88, paragraph V). However, as I visualize them, distemic space and proxemic space are not mutually exclusive. The same space may perform both functions, or one of the functions for one group and not the other. For instance, a traditional street market in an ethnic neighborhood of a cosmopolitan city, or a village frequented by tourists, may be largely proxemic for its proprietors and largely distemic for visitors.

---

*The word "culture" is often used to mean almost anything human beings do that alters the environment. But I am using the word as Hall uses it, to comprise the entire social ontogeny plus phylogeny that make up the perceptual world of the human being, most of which is non-verbal, non-rational, and much of which is below the level of conscious decision-making and consciously directed learning. It may include technological manifestations which have acquired proxemic meaning, as, over time, most of them do.

On the one hand, it must be partly distemic even for its proprietors, who will have to deal with alien behavior to an extent far greater than they would be likely to tolerate comfortably in their homes. But it may also have proxemic value for the visitors who vicariously enjoy the foreign culture as culture, in contrast to the more objective activity of selecting a commodity. There is no presumption in this postulate that human beings always, or even usually, perceive either activities or spaces entirely in proxemic or distemic terms. I am theorizing about the spatial behavior of an animal with a segmented but not segregated brain, a unitary but very complex creature which is rarely if ever likely to be only one thing or another. My theory, like all theories, is an intellectual construct and not a slice of life.

Since the proxemic—distemic relationship is a continuum, one set of relationships can turn into the other. Distemic relationships which exist for a long enough period of time (more than a generation) may become proxemic in their own right. This is one way in which social evolution occurs. Perhaps both the distinctions and the possibilities for convergence can be illustrated by assuming four different kinds of recreational settings prevalent in the United States: (1) a pool hall in an ethnic working class neighborhood, (2) a bowling alley in a shopping center, (3) a bridge club, and (4) a golf course in an exclusive country club. The first will be organized most entirely along ethnic lines, or a narrow mixture of proxemically similar ethnic cultures, such as perhaps second or third-generation-American Polish and Italian Catholics. The second may include a broader ethnic spectrum, but be proxemically limited by class, say lower-middle. The third may be ethnically quite mixed, but be proxemically limited by class, say suburban upper-middle class. The last may be limited in terms both of class and ethnic origin, say upper class white Anglo-Saxon Protestants. Each of the games played will have two components, one the proxemic behavioral systems identified by Hall, the other the objective rules of the game. Any of the groups can readily learn the rules of any of these games and play them. However, the proxemic behaviors that make up the entire gestalt in each of these settings are not readily transferable. A member of one who attempts to join the others on this level may at least to some extent inhibit or embarass the group or be inhibited and embarrassed in it, and may even invoke covert or overt resentment. As a San Francisco columnist once observed, for a stranger, "there is nothing less friendly than a friendly neighborhood bar." (This is not always true of course, but true enough to be meaningful.)

Now let us shift the scene to the Yankee Stadium in New York City. All of these groups may very happily enjoy the ball game, booing or cheering in harmony, and generally enjoying each other's company without much inhibition. Behavior which would be a rude breach of etiquette in any one of the other four settings, will be cheerfully tolerated or ignored. A common understanding of the rules of the game being watched (a conceptual process) combines with the primitive infra-cultural excitement of competition and aggressive, cooperative teamwork to create a heterogeneous functional social unit. This is what I mean by a distemic situation and distemic space. However, the passionate attachment of many Americans to baseball, with its special jargon, and certainly some of the behavior patterns of ball players, have through time also begun to acquire proxemic meanings which differ, for instance, from the equivalent European proxemic identification with soccer. Even so, such large-scale spectator sports will tend to remain toward the distemic end of the continuum, because with relatively little instruction in the logical rules of the game, people of any nation and social class can quite easily share the enthusiasm.

It is extremely important to recognize that while distemic situations are by definition those not primarily determined by life-long cultural consider-ations, they nevertheless do not exclude the emotions and a wide range of gestalt feeling states. Just as purely conceptual functions are not ruled out of proxemics, neither are draco-limbic ones ruled out of distemics. As creative scientists well know, there is an emotional color and excitement in the pur-suit of abstract ideas that can rival in intensity and pleasure (as well as fear and depression), more mammalian activities. As far as I am concerned this is among the greatest blessings in being human. This is true also for technicians of all sorts, whose working lives may be spent in cognitive environments pre-sumably structured largely in conceptual terms. In fact, distemic space uni-fies human beings on two levels: on the level of pre-cultural or infra-cultural experience as well as super-cultural experience. All artists (including poets, novelists, and dramatists, who use words for evocative instead of descriptive purposes) work out of the centers of gestalt, non-verbal experience on a level which in some respects transcends culture, presumably by touching those substrates of experience which are innate and species-specific. The best art of any culture will find response in the more open members of any other, even though creators and responders could not live together on close terms. Thus the Louvre and the Metropolitan Museum of Art, the Vienna National Opera and the New York Carnegie Hall are primarily distemic rather than proxemic.

In justice to the proxemic concept, I must note that Hall has provided for situations where different proxemic patterns interact, using a complemen-tary term of his own, *proxetics* (Hall, 1974). The suffixes of this word and *proxemics* have been derived from the words *emic* and *etic* coined by Pike (1966) to distinguish between describing behavior from the inside (emic), and from the outside of the system (etic). However, as presented, proxetics appears to define an approach to observing or analyzing proxemic behavior, and not the overarching behavioral situations which I am calling distemic. I was not aware of Hall's new word when I developed my own concept, and I shall stick to the formulation for the present. Among other things, the con-trast in the prefixes has a much stronger spatial connotation, relating as it does to *proximate* and *distal*. However, the contrast in scale, as I perceive it, applies not only to geographical, but also to psychological and social distance.

The differences between proxemics and distemics in my model are similar to the primary group and secondary group relationships traditionally identified by sociologists. But they are not identical for a number of reasons which I will return to in a later chapter, but especially because the sociological concepts are not predicated on the use of space. While some sociologists are of course quite interested in the role of space (Michelson, 1970) others largely ignore it or deny that physical design has significant influence on social behavior (Gans, 1968).

At this point, it might be useful to synthesize my main conclusions from the ethological work explored in the foregoing chapters, using MacLean's "triune brain" as the pivotal concept. The following ten postulates or working hypotheses are clearly not all empirically testable propositions, but some are, and I hope the others will lead in that direction:

I. In the evolution of the human brain there have developed complex but imperfect functional relationships between neural systems based on phyletically older animal brains, here called the draco-limbic brain, and the elaborate neo-mammalian cortex highly developed only in man (MacLean, Ploog, and Esser), here called the conceptual brain. Where animals are more or less prisoners of their physical environment and respond to a symbol system more closely dependent on direct stimuli, the conceptual brain with its correlates in language and technology enables man to inhabit a conceptual world in which, on this level, he reacts not only to direct environmental stimuli, but also to elaborate mental constructs which expand the cognitive environment far beyond anything he can perceive sensually (Calhoun). Except in pathological cases, these evolutionary levels are not distinct and will not act completely independently, although one or the other may tend to dominate behavior to varying degrees in different personalities under varying circumstances.

II. Man shares with other animals a propensity to organize into discrete social groups in discrete geographical territories at various times, especially for breeding purposes. On the draco-limbic level this propensity will pertain to attachment to familiar individuals and places on a relatively small scale. On the conceptual level man will extend these impulses into conceptual space (Calhoun) which often transcends physical time and space. Nevertheless, man will tend to defend and seek dominance within these conceptual territories as if they were their physical counterparts, because only by incorporating these images into the draco-limbic system can they be made emotionally meaningful, and draw on primal energies related to basic survival.

III. In primitive societies geographical territory and conceptual territory will tend to coincide, i.e., proxemic culture will be identified with a particular space and vice versa. As man extends his conceptual world through language, and the range of his physical world through technology, there may be increasing disparity between geographical and conceptual territory. He may then give priority in his behavior to one or the other, and may exhibit considerable ambiguity in the process.

IV. As with most social animals, man will seek security at the center of his territory when he is frightened and vulnerable (Hediger, Fischer, Leyhausen, Esser), he will often seek dominance within it and in relation to the territory of others (Wynne-Edwards, Calhoun, Lorenz, Leyhausen), and will exhibit exploratory or aggressive behavior when motivated by need or excess of free energy (Hediger, Leyhausen, Calhoun, Ardrey). He may do so in terms of physical territory or conceptual territory or both.

V. There will tend to be an inverse relationship between the possession of geographical territory and of conceptual territory. Where space is plentiful, man will tend to choose physical territory and construct his conceptual space within it. Where space is restricted, man may increasingly tend to organize his individual and social behavior around conceptual territories. In the former case, there may be considerable local social heterogeneity and interaction among status groups within the geographical boundaries, e.g., "village democracy," but considerable rigidity as regards alien customs and concepts. In the latter case there will be considerable flexibility as regards geographical boundaries, but considerable rigidity as regards alien conceptual territories, such as academic disciplines, and religious or political orthodoxies. These are not mutually exclusive phenomena, however, and varying proportions of both may be observed (e.g., the corporate or academic suburb).

VI. The larger the conceptual world of the individual, the less dependent he is likely to be on geographical territory, although, ironically, the more likely he will be able to obtain it. Conversely, the more limited the individual's conceptual world, the more he will rely on possession of geographical space. Thus it is the least-educated* who are most likely to need clearly-defined home boundaries, who are least likely to have them and are most likely to suffer from being dispossessed.

VII. Man will tend to seek three major types of social-spatial organization which correspond roughly to what for animals are (1) individual distance, (2) defended social territory, and (3) home range. In most animals the defended territory is occupied only by breeding groups while the home range may be used by a number of such groups with minimal conflict. In man, personal space will be expressed in the private room, chair, and so forth; the social territory in the home, neighborhood, club, or profession; and public (distemic) spaces by such areas as parks, markets, civic centers and places of employment. The emotional needs of the draco-limbic brain will be most likely satisfied in terms of the first two, which are essentially proxemic. The cultural heterogeneity required for expansion of conceptual space requires increasing

---

*See qualification, p. 90.

reliance on the conceptual brain and seeks opportunities in distemic spaces and situations.

VIII. Conventional tokens are symbolic acts and responses which substitute for direct aggression and serve as social organizers among many animals (Wynne-Edwards). Through his expanded conceptual space man has developed exceedingly complex conventional tokens, not the least of which are economic systems. By sublimating direct physical aggression through barter of objects, man was able to overcome the xenophobia of the primitive tribe, and establish a basis for abstract law (Esser, Ardrey). Emergence of mercantile trade was the result of man's extension of conventional tokens to inanimate objects and processes external to his own body. He was also able to extend his exploratory urges into conceptual space through increasing development of abstract symbolic systems, which may also serve as conceptual conventional tokens. These enable him to develop science, art, and technology. All of these may be civilized substitutes for the more primitive aggressive and mating displays of lower animals.

IX. By substituting conceptual conventional tokens for physical ones attached to his own body, mankind was able to develop not only more complex status hierarchies, but diverse social roles. By identifying with groups which share the same role, rather than the larger society in which the roles are performed, man could transfer draco-limbic small-group loyalties to the role (Calhoun). This enabled him, to some degree, to break out of the population controls that limit other animals psycho-physically while his division of labor and expanding technology enabled him, to a limited degree (as we now well know), to supply his expanding populations with resources. The ability to transfer the territorial and social loyalties to role on the draco-limbic level, freed him on the conceptual level to extend the scale of social relationships abstractly, to include all members of his species, conceptualized as humanity, or to the whole of nature and the cosmos conceptualized in a multitude of religions. In other words, his draco-limbic identification with a special role within the larger society freed him emotionally from the bondage to a small tribe, so that he could then transfer conceptual loyalty to a much larger population group than the limbic system can manage, to city, nation, or the world community of man.

X. The three phylogenetically distinct parts of the human brain have been shown to process information from the environment at very different speeds, using different coding mechanisms, with the conceptual brain much faster than the older ones. The consequence of this for designing human environments is that the cognitive worlds of the draco-limbic brain and the conceptual brain also have very different spatial parameters. Both must be provided for in designing satisfactory human environments. The need for emotional security and protection of both the individual and society from the more elemental aggressive tendencies through small-group cohesion can best be provided by small-scale physical space. On this level there is probably an optimum size and an optimum density for human societies. This kind of territory will tend to be culturally (hopefully not racially) segregated; heterogeneous social interaction from outside should occur by permission only, not by right. This kind of space, if I do not do injustice to Hall's concept, is proxemic space. On the conceptual level, the underlying impulses to adventure and combat must be kept under the primary control of the conceptual brain. All spaces designed to facilitate this must be fully integrated by right and by law. The physical correlates of conceptual space are culturally heterogeneous public space, parks, markets, civic centers, industries, and universities. These must be kept open to all and at the same time secure from any form of physical aggression. This kind of space — unlimited in scale — is what I am calling distemic.

In considering conceptual space and conceptual resources (paragraph VI), it is important to recognize that what the status quo of any society deems to be "education" does not necessarily assure those exposed to it large conceptual worlds, or those deprived of it narrow ones. Individual intelligence obviously plays a large part, just how large is the subject of some controversy at this time. Proxemic values are relevant also. Many highly "educated" people are very narrow conceptually; conversely it is possible for people without much formal education to possess very wide conceptual ranges. So-called primitive people often inhabit rich and complex conceptual spaces which put the neo-technic middle class to shame. But within any given society, it can certainly be assumed that whatever is considered education will tend to provide both encouragment and opportunity for the expansion of conceptual reference systems and group relations based on them, intelligence and culture being equal.

In this connection the role of the reptilian portion of the draco-limbic brain, as described by MacLean, is quite significant. This part of the brain cannot "think" in any terms but absolutes, good or bad. It cannot handle nuances, gradations, or any kind of ambiguity or paradox, because it does not have the large memory bank coded in terms of emotional experience which developed in the limbic system. We can conclude that whatever configurations of abstract symbols may be transmitted to it by the conceptual brain will become locked in reptilian jaws. On this mental level the most brilliant insights turn into dogma and fanatical conviction. Inputs from the conceptual brain which have reached the reptilian one after having been mixed with emotional experiences in the limbic system can result in fanatical small group loyalties. These can be maintained even by people with vast conceptual outlooks, perhaps even particularly by them. Armies have made use of this phenomenon since time immemorial. The process is not always negative, of course; if the psychic reptile has clamped onto something of value to the human race, it may drive the rest of the brain to magnificent achievements. The higher brains of artists fish much of beauty and value from these murky depths, but it is safe to say that while scientists may be usefully hounded by their cerebral lizards, science itself has no place there. A reptilian brain cannot distinguish between an hypothesis and a panacea.

Most importantly, it is coexistence of the rich variety of conceptual worlds that makes democracy possible and this the conceptual brain must organize. There is insufficient flexibility in the draco-limbic mind. The impulse — in fact the psychic necessity — for absolute status hierarchies and segregated geographical territories would offer no alternative to aristocratic and totalitarian societies were it not for the capacity of each individual to invent a wide range of conceptual territories designed for his unique needs and ambitions, and to seek security, stimulation, and status within them. But as the conceptual brain is an evolutionary extension of, not a replacement for, the draco-limbic one, our conceptual territories are either tied to our physical position in geographic space, or become proxemic mental surrogates for geographical territory. Because we are also mammals as well as human beings, we cannot find a real home in the echoing corridors of conceptual space, no matter how dazzling the view. We immediately territorialize ideas into intellectual proxemic cultures, as evidenced in the endless professional and academic civil wars that churn up our intellectual institutions, and the exceedingly cruel and often very bloody conflicts that historically have been waged over religious and political orthodoxies. What is dangerous is not that we territorialize our concepts, for we cannot help it, but that we fail to recognize it and make arrangements for doing it safely and constructively, with due regard to the proxemic needs of those who code experience in other ways.

A troublesome assumption of many educated people, especially those who, as MacLean suggests, have been educated for empathy, is that because we can conceptualize "one world" or "the brotherhood of man," we ourselves become free of the primitive bondage to small social groups and to territorial space. In the United States, both rhetoric and policies based on this assumption have facilitated an unnessary degree of polarization between enthocentric "middle Americans" (actually of all classes) and internationally-oriented "eggheads" (who constitute a class of their own) who have presumably been "educated" to look beyond such "selfishness." What we all do, whether we are educated or not, it seems to me, is to perceive abstract relationships in distemic space but ultimately to conceive them in proxemic terms. The more educated we are in the sense of having access to conceptual knowledge and the capacity to use it, the more likely we are to be inadequately aware of our own draco-limbic interests and make allowances for them in our constructs and behavior.

In everyday life, each of us, depending on the breadth of his conceptual experience, combines the possibilities revealed by distemic space with the need for small group identity in proxemic space. No matter how far-reaching in scale, or how large the number of individuals with whom our conceptual world is peopled, we will in our mammalian minds reduce these complexities to a relatively small number of personal relationships.

We have seen that Calhoun, who theorizes that human societies have emerged from basic nucleations which began as the original 10 to 12 members or a hunter-gatherer family, finds among mice the optimum number of nest mates also in this range. This "magic number" keeps reappearing in such institutions as human juries and army platoons. Kummer has found that among baboons, which in social organization appear to be closest to man of all primates (although chimpanzees are nearer phylogenetically), a primary group of ten, one male and nine females with their young, form the basic unit of bands numbering 30 to 90, which in turn organize into troops of various sizes (Kummer, 1968). Morris (1967) notes that the personal address books of a wide variety of different types of adult city dwellers will show that they know well about the same number of individuals, approximately the tribal group, less than 100 individuals. He invites the reader to check his own address book or Christmas card list and those of his friends to verify this. (This obviously does not apply to lists kept by salesmen, politicians, and others whose professions require a large number of more or less impersonal contacts.) Most of us will admit that we can relate conceptually to a much larger number of people than we can emotionally.

On the level of the small society in which citizens can recognize strangers and act in concert to protect the conventions that hold it together, self-organization and self-policing can occur. When human beings move out of the small group territory, most organized activities and law itself must be structured by superior authority, which may or may not correspond to small group interests. Thus, environments designed to facilitate proxemic, small-scale, closed group relations are an essential first step in planning habitations for neo-technic man, but they are only the prerequisite for healthy urban complexes, and not a comprehensive model for them.

Although the normal brain does not operate on one of these experiential levels alone, the draco-limbic and conceptual image systems may be more or less in or out of phase with each other like the different radio signals that keep a TV image in focus. I would suggest further that under post-primitive conditions, even for the healthiest and most "normal" persons to keep them in phase is very hard work; that is what real thinking is all about. To be a real intellectual in regard to every aspect of one's own life would be intolerably hard work, which is undoubtedly why so many people who think for a living confine this activity to a narrow area, and let their draco-limbic brains form comfortable social in-groups with others who do likewise.

The degree to which the persistence of proxemic attitudes will foil the best laid plans of town planners under a variety of economic or ideological systems, and also the degree to which intellectual interests persist as a form of proxemic subculture, are well illustrated by an account of a new community in Poland given by Atonin Mestan, Professor of Slavics at the University of Freiburg in Germany (personal communication). A modern industrial satellite town was built with the intention of attracting an agricultural population to a proletarian life style and to counteract Catholic influence from the nearby city of Cracow. But a generation later the agricultural characteristics were still retained by the people who moved there, and the Catholic influence, instead of being diminished, was strengthened to the point where the people requested that a church be constructed in the new "socialist" community. However, a new theatre which had been built for the local population was not patronized by them, but by an intellectual elite from Cracow, for whom a street car line eventually had to be built.

The difference between the proxemic outlooks of the skilled working-class in the United States, the "blue-collar aristocrats," and those of the white collar and professional middle-classes within a metropolitan situation has been eloquently revealed by LeMasters (1975).

The major problem in designing for diversity is to provide for proxemic needs of each subgroup on its own terms, while allowing for the cooperative activities on which all depend and which no subculture can structure only on its own terms. Design for diversity must recognize a basic paradox of scale. On the one hand, the sheer size of populations and the complexity of relationships among them require that people be considered in terms of abstract relationships, often in large aggregations. Human needs must be defined in terms of categories and met in terms of generalities. On the other hand, everything that makes human life ultimately satisfying is specific to personality, culture, time, place, and circumstance.

It is not only professional decision-makers who must deal with this paradox of scale; the environment must be shaped in a way that allows each individual to deal with this paradox himself, in terms of his own need and capacities. This requires, I believe, a much more complex view of personal identity than egalitarian theoreticians generally take, one which recognizes that we all move in varying ways and to different degrees between the two poles of experience, the primitive draco-limbic one and the abstract conceptual one. In considering the complexities of urban social-spatial relations, I have found Paul Leyhausen's concept of two types of status hierarchies, one relative, the other absolute, particularly interesting. The absolute hierarchies, we may recall, are established in rival fighting on the basis of individual capacity for leadership or dominance which is the result of personal qualities established on neutral ground, and which may be challenged by strangers able to demonstrate their individual superiority in open competition. The relative ranking hierarchy is a function of how close the competing animal is to his own territory and his familiar group; a relatively weak, low-status individual can drive off a more powerful one from his own home ground. If we extrapolate this theory to man, including not only the diverse home territories afforded by various forms and levels of culture, but also the vast opportunities for individual initiative in probing conceptual space, we have an extremely complex field of opportunity. If we also allow for the changes in motivation over time which Leyhausen has noted, the possibilities for each individual to move from one social/physical environment to another become very broad indeed.

For modern human beings, then, proxemic space might be considered as the area where the relative hierarchy holds sway, where status and the sense of self-worth which go with it are a matter of who you are and where you are, where a prodigal son can always come home, where, in periods of weakness or self-doubt, security can be found, where, as Robert Frost says, "when you have to go there, they have to take you in." When everybody's home is his castle, every man can be king somewhere and every woman queen. Human culture has enabled man to build many castles of this sort out of a wide variety of familiar group relationships, which often extend beyond kinship groups in possibilities, if not in size. As I have suggested, conceptual space can be territorialized also: a doctor's castle can be his office, a professor's castle his classroom, an auto mechanic's his shop, and each can retreat from one to the other if relative proxemic in-fighting gets rough. On the other hand, distemic space, in addition to being the area where cultural diversities can recombine, where the complex cooperative systems of neotechnic societies can be organized as impersonally as necessary to meet whatever circumstances must be dealt with, is also the area where absolute hierarchies develop, absolute in that they depend, not on who you are, but what you are. Where you are is important only to the extent that you are not on somebody else's home ground. Here the personal qualities of the individual ideally can be combined with whatever opportunity the environment offers, augmented by the human prostheses which enable us to probe conceptual space. As with animals, but in vastly more diverse ways, leadership may mean psychological or physical dominance, but it also may be simply the power to attract others to follow.

The entire socio-spatial relationship is illustrated, in a grim context, by Douglas North, a student in one of my classes who applied this model to his experience in a state prison. He had originally participated in a study of the prison as a member of a team of sociologists, and subsequently continued his observations while employed as a guard there. Here is his analysis:

> The majority of the prison population is housed in B and C blocks. Both areas consist of four tiers of cells in the center of the block. The cells occupy only about one third of the floor space and the rest is open for various forms of activity. The physical layout of the two blocks are similar, except for one important feature.
>
> All new prisoners are assigned to C block when they arrive . . . The cells, or "houses" as they are called, are about seven feet square with metal walls and a bed, sink and toilet. The front of the cell is entirely bars, running from floor to ceiling, with a sliding door . . . The open area of C block is generally filthy, littered with paper, food, and other even less pleasant material that is occasionally thrown from the cells. Several inmates have a work assignment as janitors, but it is a completely futile job and they are not over-enthusiastic workers anyway.
>
> If an inmate is generally well behaved and does not break any prison regulations for three months, he is permitted to move to B block. Inmates are allowed more privileges

in this block and it is a much nicer place to live. B block is identical to C block except that the walls are thick masonry and the only opening is a small door. The open area around the cells is generally immaculate and inmates spend most of their time in this area . . .

Territorial behavior in this society is obvious and important. The personal space of the cell is of overwhelming concern to the inmates. It is hard for most people to conceive of a fifty square foot space as a house, but that is what it is called, and that is what it is to its "owner." Entrance to a cell is by invitation only, and except in unusual circumstances, guards and prison officials observe this convention. The block is home range for each individual living in the block, and very few conflicts ever occur. But if an inmate from another block enters this area, he is watched with suspicion.

The public space of the yard is where the conflicts and battles usually take place. This is neutral ground and neither side is at a "home court" advantage. Although inmates can be seen in the yard, intervention takes longer and is more dangerous to the guards. (North, 1974.)

North's description of social ranking in this prison also corresponds remarkably to Leyhausen's dominance hierarchies, and underscores the major thesis of this book, that, essential as territorial spacing is, it is only part of the picture, even where social organization is most restricted:

The inmate society has a distinct hierarchy with four major levels. At the top, a few men have influence and control over most of the population. The common characteristic of these men seems to be interest in and ability to organize other men effectively. A tangible example of the efforts of these men is the inmates' "union" that tries to bargain with the prison officials for new privileges. Since these men can practically guarantee peace or disruption among the inmates, they have become a real force within the prison. Of course, their influence with prison officials is only a result of their power among the inmates. These men have a large following that will do whatever they say, and it is very dangerous for another inmate to incur their wrath.

The second level of the hierarchy is composed of men who are physically dominant on a personal level. Violence is fairly common among the inmates, and these men are the ones who have proven their fighting abilities repeatedly. Many of the physically dominant men are part of the organizers' following, but some are loners and are left alone.

The next rank is the "jail house lawyers." Long years of study have enabled these men to use the legal system to their advantage. Guards and prison administrators appear frequently in court as a result of law suits filed by these men.

The fourth level contains the majority of the population. Minor levels of status and social groups exist within this level, but they do not have the significance of the top three levels. Unless a man has a reputation that impresses the other inmates, newcomers start at the bottom of the hierarchy and must prove that they deserve any other type of status. (North, 1974.)

The very fact that the physical structure of prisons permits such a narrow range of social relationships and independent activities makes incarceration in them punishment. Despite the dominance of both guards and inmate alphas, personal home territory is respected even there. Also even there are people who reside in conceptual space, the "jail house lawyers." But the range of relative social hierarchies, which in complex societies offers so many opportunities for differing individual capacities under varying circumstances, is absent. This may be expected to be true to a lesser extent for many other types of institutional settings, including the military, and also for those external prisons, the ghettos. As always, the difference between security and confinement is the degree to which location is a matter of choice; the same holds true for the difference between opportunity and vulnerability.

Let us return to Fred Fischer's "cardinal distance values" described in Chapter 7: security contrasted with freedom of movement as positive perceptions of external space, and confinement in contrast with the sense of being lost as negative response. I have arranged these on a continuum (Fig. 4),

Fig. 4. Cardinal distance continuum (after Fischer, 1965).

with "security" and "confinement" at one pole, and "freedom of movement" and "sense of being lost" at the other, giving the upper set positive signs and the lower set negative signs. We may assume each one of us will view our position in such terms, depending on our state of being at the time, e.g., energetic or tired, healthy or sick, young or old, well-heeled or broke, etc. Any satisfactory scheme for organizing real world space must take into account not only distemic space and proxemic space, but also provide relative security and freedom within those spaces. Proxemic space, if my hypotheses are valid, will be concerned with security—freedom relationship within the small group, whereas distemic space will consist primarily of those relationships between groups through which individuals move as individuals, structured in terms of two continua, not one, corresponding to the two kinds of perceptual space.

The egalitarian philosophy, and the legal and physical structure which have been built on it in western democracies, as well as in socialist societies, have tended to set up an overly simplistic relationship between "private" and "public." In capitalist democracies the right to private property is a fundamental tenet in the culture. The psychological importance of proxemic territory on the level of the family is also recognized; it is protected, at least in principle, against search and seizure without due process. The private territory of the home is also implicitly recognized in communist countries because ignoring it would be virtually impossible. As practiced in industrial societies on both sides of what used to be called the iron curtain, private space is set at one end of a "discontinuous continuum" with public space and public good at the other (Fig. 5). In my model (Fig. 6) there are two kinds of privacy, one individual and the other proxemic, linked by distemic space which should be the real business of what planners call "the public sector." The

Fig. 5. Egalitarian "discontinuous continuum."

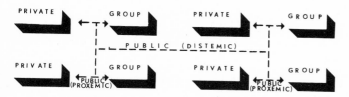

Fig. 6. Integrated democratic continuum.

personal and proxemic space should be considered relatively fixed and stable; it is related to certain innate propensities within all human beings; it has an optimum size and workable limits even though it differs vastly in form from one culture to another. The public distemic space, however, is a hierarchical arrangement of orders, capable of infinite complexity and infinite variation. What goes on in proxemic space is only the business of those who occupy it; it is "private property" in a social sense. Ideally, what goes on in distemic space is the business of anyone who cares to enter one or more of its hierarchical orders. It is the exclusive property of no one; it cannot and should not be "defended" but only protected, like air and water, from aggressive misuse or excessive monopoly by one group to the detriment of another. Of course, distemic spaces may become territorialized, as for example some city parks which may come to "belong" to certain ethnic groups, and to that extent they become proxemic. Probably few spaces in actuality are ever wholly one or the other. As a practical matter, much of distemic space is defined by regional or national associations which will have a strong cultural component, so that the degree to which an area and associated relationships can be considered proxemic or distemic is not only a matter of scale but also of the degree to which the basic functions are cultural or cross-cultural. I shall explore this idea in the next chapter.

Chapter 9

National space

What we call a nation is, in terms of my model, a fusion of conceptual with geographical space so as to give form to both proxemic and distemic relationships. The proxemic ones give to each country its distinctiveness; they provide the nucleus and the cell walls. Distemic relations are the plasma of civilization, providing life-giving exchanges among the cultural diversities, making it possible for neo-technic mankind to construct a world-wide social organism. For such an organism to exist, proxemic boundaries cannot be impenetrable walls, but must be permeable membranes. Because distemic relationships become most critical on the international level, as well as most prominent, I am going to try briefly to establish this model on that level before proceding to the regional scale which is the main focus of this book. For this purpose I will compare my own country with a highly impressionistic view of two others, without making any claim to a thorough knowledge of the latter.

In the fall of 1973 the United States and Holland were singled out by the Arab states for special treatment in the new "oil diplomacy" as a result of their support for Israel. Proxemic differences greatly outweigh some cultural similarities between the U.S., The Netherlands, and Israel, but their main links in this case are a particularly good example, on the national scale, of what I mean by distemics. Even their cultural similarities have distemic, rather than tribal, origins. Furthermore the entire context of this "energy crisis" represents not merely a conflict between nations as such, but a clash between proxemic and distemic needs on all sides.

Holland and Israel are small nations, acutely aware of boundaries. Like us, both are democratic capitalist societies in the Western tradition, with economies strongly dependent on trade in consumer goods. Both these small nations rely on technology for a continuing struggle with a difficult environment. Where Holland struggles to retrieve land from the water, Israel has the opposite problem of bringing water to an arid land. Both nations have a problem of overpopulation relative to resources, compounded by traditional hospitality to immigration. As a result both have, like us, special proxemic problems, but both are even more dependent than we are on distemic relations with the rest of the world, since they lack basic resources.

Holland is among the oldest democracies of the Western tradition in Europe, and a part of the world where Protestantism began, and where

Fig. 7.

Fig. 8.

distemic space fully started to open up for mankind. One can speculate that the self-contained Dutch trading cities and their satellite villages, linked by dikes and canals, not only enabled The Netherlands to play their historic role in the development of mercantile capitalism, but have provided to this day also much of its social stability. Everything in The Netherlands has boundaries — and everywhere there are bridges. It may not be too far-fetched to

Fig. 9.

Fig. 10.

Figs. 7—10. Contrast of scale in The Netherlands.

suggest that boundaries and bridges are symbolic of its people's outlook and a source of their sanity. But in recent years they have been (if I may be pardoned for overworking the metaphor) burning their bridges; they have been building environments which lack physical definition and as a consequence seem to have raised drawbridges over widening conceptual moats. It appears that they may be almost as uptight with each other as we Americans who have buried our boundaries in a conceptual bog.

At the end of World War II, The Netherlands faced on the one hand a catastrophic housing shortage brought about by Hitler's version of "urban renewal" in an already overcrowded under-housed land, and on the other their country's affection for its fertile, open, but very limited, space. As did most of the world in this period, the Dutch turned to the slab apartment house as a means of getting the homeless under cover as quickly and efficiently as possible. They continue to rise all over The Netherlands, and will be rising in years to come on new polders now being dredged from the sea. In small, flat, orderly, and intensely human-scale Holland, the fields of slabs reminded me, in dissonance of scale and style, of redevelopment in downtown Boston.

From my discussions with Dutch planners, it appears that the social effects are similar to the visual ones. Holland does not have our racial problems, and the country is ethnically much more homogeneous; nevertheless the passion for single family housing in small proxemic scale suburbs seems to be as intense, even though opportunities are so much more limited. Derk de Jonge, a sociologist with the Center for Architectural Research at the University of Delft outlined a pattern which seems to me very meaningful for us here in the United States. (I will quote from a paper published here, but my attention was first drawn to this and to de Jonge by a reference in Sommer's "Personal Space" (1969, p. 23)):

> Each (sub)culture has its own norms and expectations with regard to the activities and situations for which isolation from other people is desired.
>
> Modern urban society is characterized by its division of activities and spaces into *public and private*. It is only possible to live with great multitudes of people if there is relative indifference toward a majority of them. Only by restricting personal contacts to a limited number of people is normal life possible. Here we speak of *the closed family in an open society*. On the other hand, in sparsely populated agrarian areas the number of people that one meets is limited and the inclination to greet them and to know them is greater. In many parts of the Dutch countryside there are no such fixed barriers (such as closed front doors with bells) as in the cities; *society is more closed and the family is relatively open* . . . (my italics).
>
> This relatively open family type is also found in a number of urban slum areas inhabited by people of relatively low status. These, too, are to a certain extent socially as well as physically isolated from the rest of the population . . . (De Jonge, 1967).

The anonymity of big city life is, of course, well known all over the world and often deplored. But, anonymity is exactly what makes cities attractive to many people. Coexistence is possible among a wide variety of life styles in the city because of the conventions of big city life which make excessive friendliness to strangers almost the only unacceptable form of behavior, short of murder, robbery, and rape. Groups of mobile young people may readily accept strangers, but only because the youth cult itself forms a kind of open family in a closed society bounded by age. Among the rest of us, one may ask for a light or directions, one may smile at a baby or at a dog (under some conditions!), but one may not ask where another person lives or what he does for a living. These are usually the first questions which will be asked in the "closed community" of the small town, suburb, or ethnic urban neighborhood, where people will consider personal behavior part of everyone's business. That is, of course, precisely what makes such societies safe, as demonstrated by Jane Jacobs (1961) and Oscar Newman (1972).

De Jonge notes that residents of one-family houses will tend to know five or ten families in the immediate area where they have visiting contacts, whereas apartment dwellers will be more withdrawn. He finds an inverse relationship between the size of the building and the number of occupants on the one hand, and the number of contacts on the other. The way the building is designed will affect the number of contacts. Contrary to design theory that common spaces foster community feeling, there is much evidence that in general communal staircases, elevators, and even communal gardens tend to reduce contact in the absence of clear private territories.

De Jonge observed: "Here in The Netherlands, people tend to become withdrawn by the very fact that they have communal facilities. While you have your front door and a garden of your own, you have a sort of territorial security and then you are more willing to meet people and talk over the back fence and to exchange information on your garden and things like that." (Personal comment.) What apparently tends to happen when families are congregated into high-rise, high-density apartment towers with communal corridors and elevators, is that they withdraw from direct contact with neighbors, who are too many and too close, and substitute for the closed village society a closed personal society based on similar professional, trade, or recreation interests. De Jonge also confirms for Holland what has been observed in the United States and elsewhere, that among working class people the personal social activities will tend to be confined to relatives, whereas among the middle classes they will be more likely to be formed on the basis of professional or intellectual interests. In other words the middle class relates more in distemic space, but as I have suggested in the last chapter, will tend to territorialize conceptual space as compensation for lost geographical territory.

De Jonge identified a phenomenon, which is especially meaningful for Americans, which he calls a "pioneer phase" of a new settlement. He has found that it lasts about five years. During this period there will be very intensive neighboring, which will tend to continue until the community has become stabilized and presumably some sort of social hierarchy has been established. Neighboring of this sort was observed by Gans in Levittown (1967) where he saw it last two years. The modern United States, of course, emerged from a continuous process of new settlement, and ready acceptance of neighbors has become part of our cultural image of ourselves. In each successive stage of the westward migration new communities were organized on a "howdy stranger" basis. As establishment hierarchies formed, the shiftless, the rebellious, and the restless, who in tribal societies will be forced one way or another to conform, moved on.

In contrast to the frontier settlement, established village democracy depends on implicit adherence on the part of all residents within the territory to community norms, and it will be maintained by an often implicit dominance hierarchy. The fact that such a hierarchy is elected or otherwise freely chosen makes it all the more powerful. In the pioneer phase of a settlement, which will be populated by a collection of strangers, common needs and uncertainty regarding both the social and physical environment will be the unifying force. Stable leadership hierarchies, whether structured by force or by vote, or a little of both, require that individuals have a chance to size up each other's qualities and characteristics. Since in the frontier phase there is minimal authority to enforce rules, there will be few rules, and being a good citizen will mainly consist of not treading on someone else's toes, as in the fabled lawlessness of our "Wild West." As the law comes in, so do power structures. Power requires both social and physical organization. Those who view "freedom" as the absence of all restraint usually have only one freedom in any organized society, the freedom to move out of it — if they can find a place to move to and the establishment does not want them for labor. What was unusual about 19th century America was that there always was a place to move to.

On the other hand, the freedom of a stable, organized village democracy is mainly the freedom voluntarily to submit to a code of conduct which is often unconscious and a matter of course; as long as certain conventions are followed considerable diversity can be tolerated. People will be equal only in adhering to the code; in almost all other respects, in age, health, wealth, rank, skill, education, power, and possession of property they will vary widely. This is the model for heterogeneity which so many liberal Americans hold as the ideal for our time. But for voluntary compliance with village mores, the community must be small enough to know who everyone is, to recognize personal deviance and evaluate it in terms of its significance for group stability and common interest. On the other hand, the model for the egalitarian society is drawn mainly from the pioneer phase of settlement in which everybody has equal claim to health, wealth, property, and power, an equal voice because nobody has yet developed specialized interests in the affairs of the community.

To maintain equality of this sort for very long requires the deliberate repression of all differences: the freedom to be "as good as everyone else" becomes the obligation to be the same as everyone else. And this is what tends to happen in the suburbs of our socially-mobile middle classes. Rules for conduct become externalized so as to be easily recognized. Any deviation is a serious threat to the community precisely because there are no mechanisms, no enforceable codes of behavior as well as spatial divisions, for coping with differences. To this day, American societies show more interest in "equality" as you move across the Appalachian range into the mid-west, but also remain less tolerant of differences than the older communities of the Atlantic seaboard, which tend to maintain a traditional affection for fences.

As suggested in Chapter 1, the modern one-class suburb is the result of an attempt to combine two incompatible views of social organization, the structured tribal village where people unite in a common space for common interests and are more or less bound by both, and the euphoric anarchy of the frontier, where anybody can do anything he pleases as long as he doesn't hurt anybody else. Since overt social restraints are considered an infringement of liberty, society is structured spatially, and we have the emergence of zoning. Each individual has his own plot of more or less equal dimensions, all visible activities must conform to a physical code. In such a "democracy" a man may easily carry on an affair with his neighbor's wife even though it is formally taboo, but a botanist who lets wild flowers grow on his lawn will be likely to invoke hostile action against himself for "running down the neighborhood." Not all suburbs will react to the same symbols in the same way, of course. The liberal stereotype of "suburbia" is a gross caricature of actuality, as shown by Gans in his study of Levittown (1967), by Wood (1959), by Donaldson (1969), by Berger (1960), and others. Many suburbs are stable and reasonably happy communities, perhaps most of them are. More than a third of Americans now live in suburbs and they will vary from poor to middle class black suburbs, poor to middle class white ethnic suburbs, blue-collar suburbs, white-collar suburbs, and will represent every culture and class in our society from shanty towns to the automobile aristocracy of Grosse Point, Michigan. Even the term "dormitory" is not a necessary adjective for "suburb." As the Davidoffs (1971) and Downs (1973) have pointed out, suburbs often contain industry even if they don't as often contain industrial workers. In my view the chief characteristic of a suburb in our society is homogeneity of social organization expressed by homogeneous spatial division.

The old heterogeneous village, the "closed society with open family" described by De Jonge, achieves social diversity at the price of cultural conformity. This form of democracy has two prerequisites, relatively small, more or less stable, populations, and sufficient space. Under such conditions, political power, economic wealth, social status, and personal life-style do not become standards that separate people from each other, because each citizen can form a self-image based on his own physical space. These things may certainly matter, but they are not crucial for individuality. The common value system enables the "family," (whether defined by kinship or otherwise) to be open without its being interpreted as intrusion because privacy is maintained by spatial boundaries.

Such societies exist in all industrial nations, not only in rural areas, but in the ethnic enclaves of large cities. If they are not invaded in one way or another, by a horde of tourists or a "renewal" bulldozer, they may remain quite stable. But in most cases the ablest and most energetic members of each new generation will tend to leave. Small towns may often be safe, but as Jane Jacobs observed, they tend to be dull. No matter how picturesque and appealing they may be to overstressed visitors from more dynamic centers, the kinetic processes that make up most of life in technological societies cannot take place in them. When these processes move in, they are no longer villages. Although some find a way to exist as vacation resorts, if all those who find them appealing moved into them, they would — and do — rapidly lose their charm. There is no reason to believe that such a way of life can be reclaimed in its original form for any significant portion of the world's population in the future. The world-wide rural-to-urban migrations, of which the city-to-suburb migration is only a phase, points in the other direction. It is for this reason that I believe a largely proxemic approach to urban structure, while addressing exceedingly vital realities, is inadequate, and that inclusion of a distemic reference in the equation is essential.

As I have suggested, I think healthy adjustments can be facilitated by making more careful distinctions between distemic and proxemic space. The Dutch, a culturally homogeneous nation, appear to have taken proxemic needs for granted. They have become masters at managing distemic ones, which require rational planning and a willingness to submit to objective law. But they seem to be in trouble on the proxemic level, because some problems cannot be met rationally. We are in trouble on both counts.

The basic problem is world-wide, of course, a function not of ideologies, cultures, or economic systems, but of population pressures combined with abstract technological systems which are incompatible with underlying psychological needs. In Communist Yugoslavia, the confrontation between the proxemic past and the distemic present is told larger than life in a Tale of Two Belgrades. The accompanying photos (Figs. 11—18) suggest, but cannot convey, the regional cacophony of scale.

That the citizens of a supposedly classless society have as much trouble making social adaptations to unfamiliar physical scale as anyone else was apparent to me on a guided tour of one of the new housing towers on the old Belgrade side. The architects of this complex had made some effort to reduce the apparent bulk of the building by a varied play of forms, but this high-rise apartment building stood alone among acres of small owner-built single- and two-family houses on the outskirts of the city, and it provided a dramatic contrast on the skyline. It had won an architectural prize, and, compared with New Belgrade, deserved one. Standing on a windy paparet at the top, the guide explained how the building was occupied and maintained.

Fig. 11.

Fig. 12.

Figs. 11 and 12. Old Belgrade.

Fig. 13.

Fig. 14.

Figs. 13 and 14. New Belgrade.

Fig. 15. "Western ideas" reach up here . . .

Fig. 16. . . . but not down there.

I asked if there was any sort of community feeling among tenants. She said glumly, "No, they all go their own ways individualistically. They have no sense of responsibility or cooperation. Unfortunately we are getting exposed to ideas from the West." I pointed over the parapet to the mosaic of small homes below, "Do they have a sense of community down there?" "Oh, yes" she said brightly, "That is a real community." Apparently "western" ideas can only penetrate tall glass houses.

Fig. 17. Village of Zemun: private proxemic space.

Fig. 18. Village of Zemun: public proxemic space.

Hall has given the title "The Hidden Dimension" to his book defining proxemics. Probably nowhere is this hidden dimension so apparent and so troublesome as in that part of the Middle East centering on Israel. Here, also, the conflict between proxemic needs and distemic necessities transcends local perceptions and interests and affects the welfare of whole nations, regions, and the world. A great deal has been written on Israel, and I can add little except to draw attention to it as an example of this particular relationship. In doing so I will undoubtedly oversimplify a complex situation.

Holland has had to reconstruct its physical environment with each generation, and America has constantly reconstructed its social one. Israel, in its brief lifetime as a nation, has had to do both. Israel is surrounded by both a hostile physical environment and a hostile human one. Disputes over the national boundaries occupy the attention of the world. But boundaries also delineate a most complex array of subcultures within the nation. The ecological line between irrigated fields and the stony desert along the Jordanian frontier expresses not only a military—political border, but also demarcates contrasting technical and conceptual systems.

Ardrey declared (1966, pp. 305—312), in accordance with what he calls the "amity-enmity complex," that the Arabs have made Israel by uniting its polyglot people in a constant need to attend to its borders. Undoubtedly this principle works for the Arabs too. But Israel seems to offer an unusually clear illustration of my hypothesis that human beings are territorial, in both physical terms and in conceptual ones. The Jews appear to be unique in human history in that for so many hundreds of years they were able to maintain a cultural identity without the physical concomitants. To the extent that they are a distinct culture they have dwelt for centuries almost entirely in conceptual space. The "Promised Land" has been just that, a promise, and promises are artifacts of the human mind. Nature promises nothing for keeps. Maier (1975) has combined concepts from Jungian psychology and Lorenzian ethology in a most interesting analysis of Jewish history in terms of territorial symbolism. He suggests that the Torah became the conceptual substitute for Palestine as a sort of movable territory.

Where most human societies integrate physical and conceptual space over generations of intimate association in specific places, the Jews of the Diaspora built a culture on images alone. No wonder they have so often excelled in the abstract arts and sciences, and in trade with the conventional tokens called money. (No wonder also that anti-intellectualism has so often been associated with anti-semitism.) Their capacity to organize concepts has equipped the Israeli Jews particularly well to construct a nation in distemic terms. The clash of interests within and around Israel is not merely one of a conflict over the usual territorial boundaries, but also a clash between proxemic and distemic ways of giving form to human activities in space. Ardrey's amity-enmity complex can account for much of the vitality of the Israelis (and now the Arabs), and possession of an actual physical territory may well have been what transformed utopian visionaries into a tough pragmatic people. But it cannot account for most of what is going on the Middle East as far as the rest of the world is concerned. Israel is a transplant of European culture totally dependent on elaborate and complex distemic systems;

neither culturally nor ecologically can it leave alone the proxemic environment, not only of Arabs, but of native Palestinian Jews as well.

Hall, who shows much sympathy for the Arabs, has suggested profound differences between them and Americans or Europeans in the perception of self and others in space. According to him the Arabs seek both more and less personal space than we do, because space is delineated in different terms. Their idea of boundaries consequently is very different. For example, they cannot understand our concept of trespass; for them it is much more a matter of who you are than where you are (Hall, 1966, pp. 143—153). When the Israelis discuss security it is much easier for most Americans or Europeans to understand what they are talking about. By contrast, the Jews possess land by putting it to use. They point out that the Arabs in the territory occupied have a higher standard of living than they had before. The Israeli Arabs apparently don't argue that point, but conceptually the Arab world in general appears to view energetic industrial Israel and its blooming deserts as an alien body on the landscape — their landscape. Those viewing it in their mind's eye from Palestinian refugee camps beyond seem to be already doing what the Jews themselves did, organizing a social structure around a territorial image which more and more takes on a reality of its own, independent of physical space and time. On a purely local proxemic level the Arabs and the Jews seem to get along well with each other, at least so the Israelis claim. Hall notes that the Middle Eastern urban pattern is a territorial system which is marvelously well adapted to cultural coexistence (personal comment). In this system each culture maintains its social individuality within clear-cut territorial boundaries, mixing freely with others only in the heterogeneous market place and traffic ways.

This can be seen quite clearly in the old walled city of Jerusalem, which is divided into four distinct homogeneous quarters. There is a Christian quarter, an Armenian quarter, a Moslem quarter, and a former Jewish quarter, now in ruins. The Armenians are also Christians, but maintain a distinct culture. According to Professor David Amiran of the Hebrew University, these quarters have shifted around through the centuries, but each culture has always maintained its spatial integrity (personal comment). The quarters are divided from one another not only by arterial streets, but even more so by their own wall systems within the larger walls of the old city and its seven gates. The Armenians and Jewish quarters are separate from the Christian and Moslem quarters by the commercial Street of the Chain. This has been the same kind of market street in the exact same place since before the birth of Christ. There is the intense stimulation of interpersonal, inter-cultural contact. By contrast, to step off the street into any one of the Quarters, there is a strange sense of peace, security, and stability.

Old cities such as Jerusalem are not only divided horizontally by walls, but vertically by stairs and terraced courtyards. The corridors and stairs are deliberately crooked, as in the medieval European cities; that is part of the

Fig. 19. Ecological border: Israeli groves/Jordanian desert.

Fig. 20. Distemic public space: Jaffe Gate, Jerusalem.

security. Through the ages, these cities have grown from the ground upward, layer on layer. For the tourist, these spatial/cultural divisions provide for endless surprises. For the residents, they must be important aids in maintaining a sense of individuality under conditions of high density.

The internal structuring of old Jerusalem complements vividly the changes and contrasts outside its walls. The Arab villages face outward, as we have noted. The contemporary Jewish urbanization has developed a form all its own, a small-scale Mediterranean-style version of the Corbusier slab on

Fig. 21. Proxemic social space: Armenian Quarter, Jerusalem.

Fig. 22. Proxemic public space: a street in Jaffe.

pilotis, providing an entrance plaza off the street. This is quite useful and pleasant as a cool planted area shaded from the desert sun, but also serves as a transitional zone between the public street and private residence. The internalized urbanity of the Israeli new development is in marked contrast with the essentially agrarian Arab extensions of the city into the surrounding desert.

Israeli policy has been to atomise these socio-spatial relationships. This

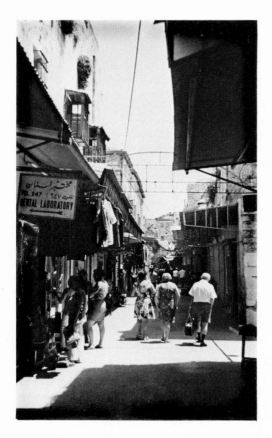

Fig. 23. Proxemic/distemic street of shops (Christian Quarter beyond).

policy can be attributed partly to military strategy and partly to the needs of industrialization. It can also partly be attributed to the egalitarian mythology which contemporary Israelis have inherited from the utopian socialism of earlier generations, as Americans have the myths of Jeffersonian democracy. As in the United States, this mythology does not find its way into general practice in a highly stratified and often effectively segregated society. As in the U.S., it has not resulted in real social integration. Israelis have claimed that if their boundaries become stabilized they will eventually get along very well enough with their Arab citizens. Whether or not the Arabs agree with this, the worst stresses, at least prior to the 1973 Yom Kippur War, internally seemed to be, not between indigenous Arabs and Jews, but between the European Jews who constitute the Israeli establishment, and the poor semi-literate Oriental Jews who have been immigrating in increasing numbers. Here as in America and Western Europe, the problems of poverty are distemically interlocked with problems of education for technical skills and the

Fig. 24. **The Christian Quarter**: proxemic public space (Moslem Quarter beyond).

clash of rural with urban proxemic systems. Amiran told me that he feels this sort of problem can never be solved in one generation, that it takes two and maybe three. As the cultural identity associated with distinct physical spaces becomes blurred, unstructured and generalized, social aspirations increase, and restless confrontations with it.

In sharp contrast to the social mood of the rest of Israel are the utopian socialist kibbutzim, where a genuinely egalitarian system developed, but one that is both spatially defined and socially homegeneous.

The kibbutzim represent to the Israelis something of the same sort of ideal that the "small town" represents to citizens of the United States. Many Israelis return to them as to a home town. In important respects they are an up-to-date version of what De Jonge calls the open family in a closed society. They are not peasant villages, however; the members are highly educated and participate actively in many of the distemic aspects of national life.

Of course, for their part, the Arabs too are interested in the distemic

116

Fig. 25. A proxemic public street in Jaffe.

Fig. 26. A proxemic private courtyard in Jaffe.

relationships of the neo-technic world, and like so many other so-called "developing nations" part of their problem is that they want to be more in it than they have been. (Part of our problem is that they have more control, and we have less control, of it than had been assumed.) The schizophrenic aspects of the problem are similar to those which underlie conflicts between other developing nations and the large industrial powers, where the proxemic needs of national identity sometimes underscore and sometimes contradict the distemic as well as territorial aspirations of their own establishments.

In my theory, economic imperialism, as well as much that passes for anti-imperialism, can be considered an attempt to territorialize conceptual space. Somehow or other a means must be found to render unto all proxemic Caesars that which is Caesar's so as to unfetter the distemic relationships which must evolve in a rational manner that will enable our species and our

Fig. 27.

Fig. 28.

Figs. 27 and 28. Jewish houses, Tel Aviv.

Fig. 29.

Fig. 30.

Figs. 29 and 30. Arab houses, Jerusalem.

planetary habitat to survive. This need transcends all proxemic interests; yet it seems unlikely to be met without also providing in some way for them, precisely because the latter are based in mental regions not fully accessible to rational thought. My hope is that by recognizing and accepting that most of us exist on both levels of experience, and more clearly structuring both kinds of space and behaviors appropriate to each, we can minimize the difficulties that continually arise when we confuse one set of needs with the other, allowing the more primitive urges a territory of their own where they can do most good and least harm.

Chapter 10

Opening up the suburbs: closing up the city?

There was an old man of Thermopylae,
Who never did anything properly;
But they said, 'If you choose
To boil eggs in your shoes,
You shall never remain in Thermopylae.'
Edward Lear

Lewis Mumford observes in the "City in History" (1961) that "Human life swings between two poles: movement and settlement."

Primitive human societies often moved over a wide range, interacting in various ways with other social groups. But the basic units were small kinship groups more or less isolated in large space. Under these circumstances physical territory and cultural territory would coincide in the spot which the tribe occupied at any given time. Social and physical space were one. As I have suggested, on this level, a culture could be defined in terms of the place where this or that set of social conventions held sway, and the place could be identified by the behavior which occurred within its boundaries. Extremely elaborate, but conceptually monolithic, cultures could emerge on this basis as in pre-Columbian America.

Adams (1960) observes "The rise of cities . . . was preeminently a social process, an expression more of changes in man's interaction with his fellows than in his interaction with his environment." Perhaps the impetus for change was social, but there were profound changes in the physical environment nonetheless. The city came into being to permit increasingly specialized subgroups to interact productively, safely, and more or less continuously with each other and with emissaries from other places. With the city we have distemic relationships taking precedence over proxemic ones. The essential function was to elaborate social diversity.

Social diversity within a common geographical space appears within other animal species generally only when they have begun to diverge genetically into subspecies and therefore cease to interbreed. This is because so much of non-human behavior is genetically programmed and the behavior itself controls breeding. As we know, human beings have a much greater repertory of learned behaviors and somewhat more independence regarding procreation. According to Calhoun, one of the behavioral mechanisms which enables man to overcome the density limitations of other animals is role differentiation, to which I referred in Chapter 4, since there is a limited number of individuals with whom we, like many other species, can identify meaningfully (i.e. emotionally). Nature had already devised a basic form of role differentiation for animals and plants, sexual reproduction, which made the higher stages of evolution possible. Asexual self-dividing creatures can only change their genotype through mutation, whereas sexually reproducing ones can produce a wide variety of individuals, or phenotypes, which eventually lead to new species through recombination of characteristics carried by genes. Role differentiation between males and females made possible also a wide variety of behavioral adaptations to diverse environments, especially as regards the care of young, from cooperative monogamous pair bonds to all sorts of other associations, and the great variety of territorial behaviors which we have examined here only in their most basic form. Despite man's great brain, for much of human history diversity within a particular society probably has been limited pretty much to this form: role differentiation by sex. So long as human beings were relatively similar to each other, the size of a cooperative group, whether of a clan or tribe, would be limited within a geographical space. What I am calling distemic space could exist only outside what were primitive proxemic physical boundaries.

The rise of cities coincided with the specialization of activities within a cooperative group. This had become possible because the increasingly productive domestication of plants and animals had made it unnecessary for all members to be continually engaged in obtaining food and other necessities for mere survival. As soon as a portion of the population could produce enough to feed all of it, specialized tasks led to the formation within the larger community of various subcultures in the form of classes and professions, with increasingly elaborate and exclusive ranking hierarchies. Using Leyhausen's model, we can assume that these were both relative and absolute. As individuals identified their familiar social group in terms of roles, which the psychoanalyst Erikson (1966, 1974) calls *pseudo species*, they could conceptually isolate themselves within a larger population of an otherwise similar larger community in a common area. Distemic space, which in tribal society must be outside the village, entered a geographically bound ecological area, tying together social sub-segments within a greatly complexified culture. It had territorial dimensions in that it enclosed specific forms of social relationship and kept others out, but it also included within it characteristics of the animal's home range.

The function of cities was to organize essentially proxemic tribes by transposing some ethnocentric aspects of them to classes, into a much more complex hierarchy which became a new kind of social entity, much as the cell clusters of simpler organisms have evolved into subsets of cells which form organs of an individual within the whole being. The proxemic qualities of cities could become synergistic as they interacted distemically, so that the cultures which emerged expressed considerably more than the sum of their social parts. Egalitarians will be quick to note that this did not guarantee

122

equal benefits of the synergy to all, or often even to most, of its contributors. Thus, from the individual's point of view, life could actually become worse for many than in the proxemic tribal village. But from the point of view of cultural evolution, this opened up tremendous possibilities for the development of human potential, which have led to modern technic civilizations, with all their faults and virtues.

However, to facilitate uniformity for its own distemic objectives, the industrial revolution began to aggregate in crude lumps the intricate proxemic—distemic web of relationships of earlier cities. Instead of rather delicate hierarchies (both relative and absolute in Leyhausen's terms), there emerged gross divisions into upper, middle and lower classes, which conformed more or less to the needs of those twin behavioral systems, mass production and mass consumption, and the city morphology followed with equally crude spatial divisions. The city also became increasingly distemic and less proxemic. Those proxemic spaces which survived were beleaguered ethnic enclaves in what had originally been whole, if highly differentiated, cultures.

Until the coming of the railroad, and then the automobile, it was relatively easy to distinguish proxemic—distemic boundaries at the edges of cities. But with improved mechanical transportation, the more dominant proxemic subcultures moved their territories to the suburbs. In the past century the formerly clear boundaries between city and country, and the diverse proxemic—distemic relationships they reflected, have become blurred, and we have had what has come to be known as urban sprawl. Even the distemic relationships of the former city are now moving to the suburbs, leaving only proxemic ones of diminishing quality in the urban core. Some of our cities seem literally to be dying. They are dying of boundary obliteration. The disease of boundary obliteration is cancer.

It has been argued that electronic communication systems have made the older forms of urban social-physical organization obsolete, since it is no longer necessary for human beings to meet face to face to communicate and cooperate. Certainly these extensions call for some changes, not all of which can be clearly perceived at this time. My own guess is that they will not make the older forms of city structure obsolete at all, precisely because proxemic communication does involve all the senses, as noted by Hall. It is the distemic communication systems, which lend themselves to abstract codification, that are best developed with the media. But these are not substitutes for more basic human relationships; they are extensions of them. Adequate and satisfactory distemic environments are dependent on clearly structured and mutually perceived proxemic ones, and vice versa. As of now the media seems to have contributed more to incoherence in the social/spatial environment than to the unifying of it, but there may be some new order emerging which is not yet clear.

One function of distemic space is to provide an arena for social behavior which not only transcends culture but underlies it. In that sense, distemic space facilitates communication on the basis of human similarities, where proxemic space offers greatest latitude for diversities. Human beings are able to communicate increasingly readily across cultural boundaries as they objectify, that is desensualize, experience through use of the intellectual forebrain. However, as Clynes (1970, 1971), Lorenz (1966, 1973) and Eibl-Ebesfeldt (1971), among others, have shown, we respond to fundamental emotional cues which are common to our species. These certainly are the basis of art, especially that art which can appeal to members of any culture. All forms of art, but especially the arts of defining space through architecture, and the art of defining behavior through drama, are important aspects of distemic space. This includes sports which may be considered a form of theatre. These may be distemic in two ways, when they draw with sufficient clarity on underlying human impulses to be understood regardless of cultural conventions, or where they are the expression of conventions which can be understood by more than one proxemic subculture. The conventional tokens defined by Wynne-Edwards, which instinctively govern the behavior of lower animals, are here rationalized and made explicit by the human intellectual brain. This is not to say they have lost their evocative relation to the more primitive and sensual impulses, but rather that they express these humanely. The city is the place where prosthetic conventional tokens can be most effective.

Distemic perception and behavior relate also to the non-human natural environment, which has distemic expression in public parks, especially those which are used cross-culturally or by a variety of classes and subcultures. Indeed, of all distemic urban spaces, perhaps parks best combine underlying emotional communication through art, over-arching intellectual communication through science, law, economics, and technology, and our dependence with all other organisms on an ecosystem. The fate of our cities is measured by the fate of their parks: despite an increasingly gloomy prognosis, I am reassured that New York is still alive when I can get a look at Central Park; although it is only half alive perhaps, because one dare not go through much of it at night.

The basic distemic role of a park within what is also so often a proxemic framework was illustrated for me by the comments of a young colleague of Greek descent who reported on a park planning project he performed in his ancestral land to a class in open space planning. He observed that park designers in the United States tend to look at their task in terms of organizing physical space so as to achieve presumably desirable behavioral objectives. In Greece he says the behavior is there; it would not occur to anybody to influence it. All the park designer needs to do is provide an open space, and immediately from somewhere, someone provides tables and chairs and a discussion is going on. That is, according to him, by Greek definition, a park, and it fits the proxemic perceptions of all Greeks. But the public parks are used intensively and jointly by Greeks of all social classes with equal enthusiasm, in the Greek custom of "walking and talking." Here we have space which is distemic in uniting proxemic groups which differ according to social class within a geographical context which is quite homogeneous in ethnic terms. Ironically, the expression of the impulse for public association seems to be most clearly manifest where private territorial relationships are sharpest. As suggested by Heckscher (1962), in America we have tended to blur the public with the private. These lead to social-spatial relationships which are not clearly one or the other and which unfortunately often have the disadvantages of both without the advantages of either.

Proxemic—distemic polarity is not the same as public—private, as I have stated, but rather represents qualitatively as well as quantitatively different levels of social interaction. While sociologists have attempted to deal with such complexities by defining "primary" and "secondary" relationships, at least the rhetoric of egalitarian politics tends toward one or the other of two equally simplistic models. One is that the "sense of community" is a basic human need, which can be defined in some universal way like needs for food, clothing, and sex. From this is derived the non sequitur, especially favored by contemporary young people, that since community is characterized by a group of humans living or working together, telling them to love each other will produce a community. The opposite simplistic view is that modern society, with its functional extensions and communication systems, makes small communities not merely unnecessary but reactionary and destructive. Both look at contemporary mankind as if it were merely a streamlined and transistorized model of tribal mankind. The one position proceeds from the accurate but incomplete observation that industrial society corrodes and breaks up natural community patterns. The other presumes that the larger cooperative order required by technology can simply replace the smaller, more primitive, cooperative group. In neither case is there any allowance for critical mass, for qualitative changes that occur at certain points with quantitative changes in scale or form.

Erikson (1966, 1974) believes that the propensity for *pseudo speciation*, the identification of self with a particular cultural group, is a human evolutionary adaptation, and that the development of such an identity is one of the functions of the long period from infancy to adulthood of humans as compared with other animals. Its successful accomplishment is, in his view, essential to the growth of healthy personality. Precisely because phylogenetically the newborn human being is a "generalist creature" who has the capacity to fit any number of pseudo species, ontogeny is required to develop a particular one: "Thus each develops not only a *distinct sense of identity*, but also a conviction of harboring *the* human identity, fortified against other pseudo species by predjudices which mark them as extraspecific and inimical to 'genuine' human endeavor." (Original emphasis) (Erikson, 1966, p. 606.) While he finds this essential to the growth of the human personality, he notes its dangers for species survival in the nuclear age, as do so many others who consider such phenomena. Erikson, like Esser (1972), hopes that further human development will lead to "a new spirit embodying an identification of the whole human species with itself and a universal sense of responsibility for each child planned and born." (1966, p. 620.) But contemporary planners must face the reality that, if such a development can eventually come about, it is not likely to do so within a time frame which permits the species in its present circumstances to make the decisions that can assure survival for such a benign destiny. My own view is that in the short range, which is increasingly a critical one, we have no choice but to attempt to accomodate safely, if we can, a behavioral characteristic which has been so persistent throughout the millenia of recorded history, and at the same time keep free and reasonably secure the avenues of less personal association so essential for the actual common identity of our species on this small planet.

Ethnocentrism is a better known term, generally credited to Sumner (1906), used to describe tendency of human cultures to define themselves in terms of in-groups and out-groups, and to identify as enemies and less-than-human those cultures which do not conform to the in-group norm in behavior and values. Recently an anthropologist and a psychologist (LeVine and Campbell, 1972) have teamed up to synthesize a variety of theories from diverse disciplines which have examined this phenomenon. Their objective was to reduce a number of diverse paradigms to a series of empirically testable propositions. One of their conclusions is that it is essential to make a distinction as regards variations between groups and within groups (p. 212). They found among the various theories they examined four areas of agreement: (1) that conflicts of interest tend to accentuate ethnocentrism, (2) that it is reciprocal, i.e. hostility of one group will tend to generate equivalent hostility in another, (3) that ethnocentric differences lead to stereotyping and depersonalizing of the out-group, and (4) that ethnocentrism will rise with increasing social and political complexity (pp. 222—223). The first three of these can be accepted by most of us on the basis of common-sense observation. The fourth is not so obvious. On the one hand social isolation might appear to foster intolerance and fear toward out-groups and at the same time to release internal conflicts. On the other hand we do have much evidence, some of it discussed in earlier chapters, that too much cross-cultural interaction can result in withdrawal under some circumstances. My own view is that LeVine's and Campbell's last point cannot be tested empirically as stated, because it is inherently both true and untrue. My hypothesis is that because ethnocentrism is a primitive phenomenon rooted in the draco-limbic system, it will increase with social complexity on the proxemic level, but it will decrease with diversities on the distemic level. The ghettoization of the urban environment may be expected to continue both for in-groups and out-groups who define the environment entirely in proxemic terms, but a broader view of the human community may also be expected to emerge from the appropriate distemic institutions.

For example, the concept of a "one world" community has been undoubtedly encouraged in the nineteen sixties college generation by such institutions as the Peace Corps, and yet it tended to polarize youth within American society into stereotypes of "long-hair students" concerned with world welfare and "hard-hat" blue-collar or ethnic "middle Americans" preoccupied with home. A surprising lack of sympathy for near neighbors seems to accompany an increased identification with far ones, a phenomenon examined by LeVine and Campbell (1972, pp. 182—186).

Cultural anthropologists in general have built their disciplines largely on the study of discrete, cohesive, clearly definable and easily observable ethnic groups. But Morris has observed (1967) that the preoccupation of anthropologists with primitive tribes has focussed attention on the very characteristics that have prevented such backwater subcultures from following the main course of human history. The Norwegian anthropologist Frederik Barth (1969) has taken strong theoretical issue with the idea that ethnic groups can best be considered in isolation. He offers a view of ethnicity which to my mind is much more useful for understanding neo-technic urban relationships. He points out that actual cultural boundaries persist despite considerable movement of the members across them:

> ... one finds that stable, persisting, and often vitally important social relations are maintained across such boundaries, and are frequently based precisely on the dichotomized ethnic statuses. In other words, ethnic distinctions do not depend on an absence of social interaction and acceptance, but are quite to the contrary often the very foundations on which embracing social systems are built. Interaction in such a social system does not lead to liquidation through change and aculturation; cultural differences can persist despite inter-ethnic contact and interdependence. (Barth, 1969, p. 10.)

Ethnic identity, like personal identity, is maintained precisely for the purpose of distinguishing it in some kind of cooperative interchange with those who have a different identity. Neither a culture nor an individual lacking all contact with others would have any reason to be concerned with identity in the first place. Thus Barth argues that the function of ethnic boundaries is to facilitate, rather than prevent intercourse across them. He developed this paradigm from the evolutionary-ecological viewpoint of environmental adaptation, suggesting that ethnic boundaries define behavioral traits which have varying degrees of usefulness under various conditions. The same group of people, with unchanged values and ideas, will institutionalize different forms of behavior under different circumstances.

This is what Gans (1962) found, for example, in his study of Boston's Italian "urban villagers." He observed that while they identified themselves with the culture of the new country, they pursued a way of life that retained many basic relationships derived from the place of origin. Barth notes, "Not only do ecological variations mark and exaggerate differences; some cultural features are used by the actors as signals and emblems of differences, others are ignored, and in some relationships radical differences are played down and denied."

Ethnicity, like other propensities to which we are heir, is used by human beings selectively. One of the most important functions of ethnic identity and the status derived from it, in Barth's view, is to enable the individual to perform adequately in some role. Ethnic boundaries will persist where such adaptive performance is facilitated, and will tend to dissolve when they do not. The best situation, obviously, is a symbiotic one, where various roles of interacting ethnic groups complement each other to their mutual satisfaction. The worst situation, clearly, is where ethnic status enables one group to maintain a disproportionate control over resources needed by others, and this, needless to say, is often the case. But Barth notes that ethnic symbiotic relationships are often destroyed by industrial systems where ethnic identity cannot contribute to performance in the larger society. He gives an example of Lapp fishermen, whose ethnic identity was not taken into account, and who could participate as Norwegian citizens but not as Lapps.

Melting pot America can offer no end of such problems, but one of the most difficult today is the problem of the ethnic blue-collar subculture whose identity is based on manual skills in a society more and more supported by industrial automation with less and less need for those skills. The problem for the unskilled rural immigrant in the core city is even worse; the rural villager, however impoverished, can maintain a kind of ethnic identity based on certain kinds of performance associated with long acquaintance with his environment, but the same villager finding himself in a city ghetto may have no basis at all for performance, and consequently no basis for maintaining an ethnic identity in this context.

Barth lists three choices open to members of ethnic cultures faced with a changing environmental situation in developed and developing industrial societies. They may attempt to assimilate into the dominant industrial society, they may accept minority status and encapsulate their ethnic culture into areas where it least interferes with participation in the larger society, or they may choose to emphasize their ethnic identity, using it to develop new activities within their own society which are more adaptive in the larger one. Ironically, the result of the first choice, according to Barth, is that the ethnic group will be denuded of those resources which are based on ethnic diversification, and will tend to be culturally conservative and relatively low-ranking in the larger system. Yet this is the route most emphasized in traditional middle class egalitarianism. The second route, acceptance of minority status, Barth believes parodoxically leads to eventual assimilation because it prevents the functioning poly-ethnic relationship which would make maintenance of ethnic boundaries worthwhile. (Skin color, being so visible, has kept blacks in the United States in a socially isolated subgroup involuntarily.)

The third, in his words, "generates many of the interesting movements that can be observed today, from nativism to new states." In the United States we have an emergence of a wide variety of minority group movements, which not only demand an end to the discrimination that blocks the traditional American route of assimilation, but also demand a role in society on the terms of their own ethnic identity. Black separatism is a case in point. However, it is important to note that generally these groups have not maintained the original form of their ethnic culture intact, but on the contrary have transformed it to new purposes which their ancestors would not have recognized. Some modern American blacks may elect to identify with African culture but they remain Americans, not Africans.

As I noted in Chapter 1, Gordon (1964) makes an important distinction between full *assimilation* and one stage of assimilation which he calls *acculturation*. The latter occurs when the ethnic sub-society adopts the language, basic values and standards of the larger culture as its own. At the same time, ethnic identity revolving around a "sense of peoplehood" or "historical identification" may remain, as well as the confinement of intimate primary relationships to one's own ethnic group. Total assimilation, in his view, involves a number of subprocesses or conditions involving changes in structural relationships, kinship, life styles, and values. It results in the relinquishment of ethnic identification and the merging of the individual in the larger culture, or perhaps in a new hybrid culture which is the ideal of those who espouse the "melting pot." Assimilation most often occurs through intermarriage. Gordon does not directly address the negative possibility raised by Barth, that denuding the group of psychological and other resources of ethnicity leaves it very vulnerable in the larger society, but rather he takes the more positive approach that the value of such resources causes so many to retain them, especially during the early stages of immigration. In Gordon's view, assimilation occurs most readily in the upwardly mobile middle classes, but he finds that it does not occur as much as might be expected and that it is rarely complete. What he finds in American society is a tendency for assimilation to occur within a "triple-melting pot" of the three basic religious groups, Protestants, Catholics, and Jews. Within the divisions the unassimilated, but increasingly acculturated, subcultures retain their identity, usually on the basis of national origin, but in the case of blacks, on the basis of race.

This subculture structure, however, is only half of Gordon's model; his ethnic (and the larger religious) divisions are vertical, but they are also divided horizontally by class, each of which has its own cultural norms. In fact, he finds the class norms confine groups much more strongly than the ethnic or religious ones, especially in primary relationships. Nevertheless there is a great deal of communication across both ethnic and class lines on the secondary level, facilitating and facilitated by acculturation, except where it is heavily restricted by prejudice.

Gordon finds only one neutral ground in the United States where ethnic identity is of little consequence in primary relationships, and that is among intellectuals. But he finds that intellectuals form a sub-society of their own, with many of the structural characteristics of other subcultures. This group includes university professors, media people, and the professions which have such a large impact on public values. As I have suggested, such people are likely to be freest from dependency, not only on ethnic tradition, which they often find unduly restrictive, but also on geographical territory, because they can substitute conceptual territories which offer both in-group security and an abundance of opportunity. They are most likely to be at home in and to be satisfied with what I am calling distemic space. However, they have the same ethnocentric tendency as other subcultures to project their own interests onto others, and to have little patience with those whose identity needs are of a different order.

I shall return to this in a moment. But first I would like to compare the ethnic basis for urban territoriality with another, somewhat different, but not incompatible, theory advanced by Gerald Suttles (1968, 1972), who has spent many years studying neighborhood structure in Chicago. Like E.T. Hall, Suttles accepts ethological theories of behavior as a sort of substrate for human activity. Territorial boundaries in the modern city, he believes, are essentially cognitive maps which "are part of the social control apparatus of the urban areas and are of special importance in regulating spatial movements to avoid conflict between antagonistic groups." But these, in his view, are a reflection of the changing objectives and needs of the various groups, and they are not rigidly fixed, either in physical space or in the mind: "The actual structure of most cities is best described as a series of gradients, and there are very few clear boundaries or sharp junctures which cannot be crossed by a simple decision to do so." (1972, p. 22.)

Suttles takes issue with what he believes is a sentimental view of community which puts primary emphasis on loyalty. Urban people rarely inhabit a single community: "Indeed, it is because of such a narrow focus on positive and exclusive sentimental attachments to the neighborhood that some researchers may have simply discounted the very existence of neighborhoods." The prominent characteristics for him are structural rather than sentimental or associational, and urban neighborhoods are not synonymous with ethnicity or social class. He has found strong boundaries around communities which are not ethnic and notes the persistence of certain boundaries during periods of ethnic transitions. He develops Janowitz' (1967) concept of the "community of limited liability," membership in which is partial, voluntary, and differential. Such communities are not defined by common traditions and inherited loyalties, but rather by a selected group of members who are willing to accept responsibility for it, to give leadership in defending its special interests, to keep its boundaries intact despite changes within and around it, and to keep alive those myths which give it unity and cohesion. A large number of its residents may thus join in accepting the benefits offered by the coherence and identity offered by the neighborhood, without otherwise participating in its affairs. Such communities not only can be, but in Suttles' view should be, created by conscious planning and design which provide for the structural realities of city life without pretending to duplicate rural or tribal existence. Such communities may in many cases be far more segregated than the old defended neighborhood, though not necessarily racially so. In some of the private developments, he notes ethnic and racial considerations have been subordinated to more subtle indices of cultural uniformity.

An example of one kind of defended space of the sort identified by Suttles is the proliferation of communities planned for retired persons. Johnson (1973), has described a number of such communities for a variety of groups and life styles. Each of them is highly homogeneous, in some cases economically so, in some cases culturally, in many cases both. The community of limited liability is clearly evident in her examples, where some people participate actively and/or exclusively within the community, while others live relatively private lives with most of their ties outside. Johnson cites one example where the residents, who had been content to let the management run things for them, organized a successful protest movement when the developer, advised by a sociologist of the supposed evils of running a "geriatric ghetto," proposed to build residences for younger families with children. They wanted to be segregated.

The new defended neighborhood, as Suttles defines it, may eliminate some of the very characteristics of the older defined neighborhood without implying its decline, but rather bringing into sharper relief its basic functions which were to minimize social conflict by reducing large urban populations to manageable size. However, precisely because participation in such communities is limited and permits association with other kinds of community as well, the city itself cannot be defined in terms of such neighborhoods, but rather "is instead a pyramid of residential collectivities which receive their recognition by common consent and whose expansion depends on the expansion of a hierarchy external to the community itself" (Suttles, 1972, p. 46). Even though Suttles minimizes the role of ethnic culture, there must be some sort of proxemic communication present in these collectivities to lead their members to seek security in each other's presence.

Relating this view of the urban fabric to the model I am proposing, we can broadly consider each "residential collectivity" to constitute proxemic space, whether ethnic or not, defined primarily in terms of security, and the hierarchy itself to constitute distemic space concerned primarily with opportunity. The security of the former is both positive and negative; negative in the sence of avoiding conflict with other groups, and positive in the sense of providing a physical context for identity. The opportunities of distemic urban space also have both positive and negative implications. The positive value lies in the possibilities for social evolution and elaboration of cooperative cultural and technical systems; the negative aspect, of course, lies in the increasing opportunities for inter-group conflict and the difficulties of policing it, precisely because the self-policing activities of groups that know who is who and are therefore able to mind each other's business (or hire someone to know each other's business) are lacking. But crucial to the application of this idea to real urban environments is the recognition that different human beings will have very different needs in these respects, and the same human beings will have differing needs at different times and under varying circumstances. It requires that the traditional humanist concept of the larger community of mankind, while certainly not invalid, be severely qualified.

Paradoxically, egalitarians (who are most likely to be found in Gordon's intellectual subculture) can be the most ethnocentric of human beings. As I have noted, they are usually people who, for one reason or another, have relatively large conceptual spaces to rove in, with the intellectual equipment to feel secure in them, and are thus able to incorporate the cultural symbols and social communication systems associated with technical skills, arts, sciences, and history in their own ideational territories. They often assume that everyone else will feel equally at home if only society would provide "equal" opportunity for us all to be the same. Behind this often lies the disguised and insidious aggrandisement of self through implicit annihilation of other people's self-identity which the blue-collar philosopher, Eric Hoffer, has aptly called "soul-raping." Because egalitarians have draco-limbic systems too, they must set up a territorial environment in which they feel secure. But where the ethnic chauvinist frankly admits that his neighbors are inferior, the egalitarian is precluded by his own mythology from indulging in this form of ego building. Instead he perpetrates the one form of human aggression which is ultimately unforgivable. He conceptually obliterates his neighbor's culture by pretending it is really identical to his own. This is unforgivable precisely because it makes distemic relationships impossible. It is what Hall calls "cultural imperialism." My own name for it is "conceptual aggression." Since the ability to move in conceptual space is our most human characteristic, conceptual aggression which circumscribes this activity in others becomes the most "inhuman" act of all.

That this is often largely or entirely unconscious, makes it more, rather than less, dangerous, as psychoanalysts know. Since our consciousness is always limited, we must all be guilty of it to some extent. The purpose of the true city, in my view, is to structure the distemic environment with such a balance of clearly defined diversities that conceptual aggression becomes functionally unworkable and therefore unrewarding. At the same time the proxemic environment should be adequately provided for, with safely contained personal and cultural territories which make conceptual aggression unnecessary for self-identity. Indeed, it is important to provide proxemic territories for egalitarians too. There may be thriving communities, including some communes, which are based on various kinds of heterogeneity; they may be inter-racial, international, or economically and professionally diverse. Such communities find in diversity itself a kind of common culture. But such heterogeneity must have limits, or it cannot constitute a community; at the least it must exclude the many who do not want heterogeneity on the primary level at all.

If in order to deal adequately with the structure of the neo-technic city we must reject a sentimental view of the community of man, we should also reject the sentimental view of small group ethnicity. Ethnicity is only one context in which neighborhood territory may be defined. Suttles observes that "On the West Side of Chicago, for example, ethnicity is a primordial distinction of great importance because there is not much else by which to distinguish people." (1972, p. 251.) But even in strongly ethnic neighborhoods, not all residents will belong to the primary group and not all who do will have equal allegiance to it. Certainly historic social environments should be preserved wherever possible along with historic physical ones. But such communities are growing fewer and growing older; how many generations they can survive under modern conditions is a moot question. A most important task for urban designers and planners is to understand their structural characteristics and their on-going cultural ones, so as to preserve what is vital and valuable in our changing times, and so that new cultures and new proxemic forms may emerge.

In the post-war United States, urban renewal proposed to cure social illness with architectural surgery, not only by operating on live tissue with little regard for social anatomy, but by making massive organ transplants without any consideration of how the urban corpus would accept them. In the 1970's the new prescription for chronic urban disease is "opening up the suburbs." One of the earliest, if not the first, to advance this concept was planner Paul Davidoff (Davidoff et al., 1970) who also has the distinction of being an originator of the concept of "advocacy planning," of which suburb-opening is one form. The basic argument advanced by Davidoff for shifting the poor from the central city to the suburbs is that the latter is where more and more of the jobs are. The functional logic of this argument is almost unassailable. Nothing can be done for or about the plight of the urban poor, if they are sealed off from the economic life of the larger society. Neither can anything be done about the viability of the city as a distemic entity, if its major populations are so cut off. On the level of elemental social justice, the arguments are also about as sound as any arguments for justice can be. A community which derives economic strength from industry can neither morally not functionally justify excluding from residence those who work in the industries.

Anthony Downs (1973) has prepared a more elaborate and comprehensive strategy for opening up the suburbs. He shows somewhat more sympathy with the suburbanite's side of this question than does Davidoff; in fact Downs expresses a strong bias in favor of the middle class way of life as a socially stabilizing force, which, as he himself recognizes, may not sit well with some other advocates of the urban poor. He also offers a detailed analysis of the economic processes by which even larger concentrations of poor are building up in the central cities of the United States and argues that there is no possibility of making the cities viable except by dispersing the poor populations among more prosperous communities, most of which are now in the suburbs. Both Davidoff and Downs have selected as a primary strategy a legal assault on "exclusionary zoning."

This new prognosis and proposed cure for our urban maladies is somewhat less mechanistic than the earlier urban renewal and high-rise mass housing projects. It starts with social functions instead of physical forms, but goes to the other extreme, ignoring the effect of form on function. In the Downs version, there is some attempt to view the urban organism as a system, but largely as a very generalized economic system. The cure is still major surgery, as the term "opening up" vividly suggests. The courts rather than the bulldozer and the concrete mixer are the instruments now selected for transplanting of urban tissue. But the impact on the social organism may be no less severe, and if it turns out that the diagnosis is faulty, the consequences may be even more devastating. Legal mechanisms are slower to start up than bulldozers, but they also take longer to put into reverse.

American suburbs are probably the most effective kind of community of limited liability (to borrow Suttles' and Janowitz' concept) that we have in the United States at this time, and the basic trend seems to be followed not only in other industrial countries, but in the so-called developing ones as well, wherever a middle class has access to automobiles.

The land-use controls by which many are defined provide merely a formal, and very arbitrary, legal-physical framework in which proxemic relationships can exist in a world increasingly dominated by the abstract decisions of government and coorporate bureaucracies. To recognize the function of suburban organization of people and resources is not necessarily to predict that this solution will remain viable forever, or that it is the best answer to current urban problems even now. But if, as I suspect, it pertains to certain basic characteristics of the social organization, not only of mankind, but of other animals as well, it is well to consider the function carefully before battering down the form.

Even though American suburbs are not confined to any one class or life style, they are the basis for culture of a sort, whether or not they provide for other underlying needs. (The restlessness of affluent societies today, especially among their young, suggests that they are increasingly failing to meet such needs.) If suburban land-use and building laws are an expression of a conventional culture and are relied on to preserve a predictable and intelligible environment, and if in the name of social justice these are to be radically altered, what is to take their place? What sort of cultural institutions will immigrate with those for whom geographical doors have been opened? Is the middle class, in being forced to yield many of its own conventions, expected to welcome alien ones? Is that, with the best of intentions, possible? If so, what sort of cultural trade-offs or compromises can be negotiated, and how? To what extent when social systems mix are they mutually reinforcing or mutually destructive? These are questions about which very little is known and that which is known is not being considered adequately. Such questions are not even being asked in setting up court attacks on one of the few urban structures that seems to be working for anybody in our time.

In the general pattern of United States history, whatever equality of opportunity there has been for succeeding generations of immigrants from various places has resulted in acceptance of middle class conventions, including housing patterns, by those who moved up the socio-economic ladder. Now the immigration of city poor to the middle class country-side is being proposed as a deliberate assault on the status quo, as a matter of right for the poor as poor, and sometimes on the ideological grounds that the status quo is immoral. This is predictably perceived by the middle class territory-holders exactly as what it is claimed to be, an invasion. Under such circumstances laws and institutions to resolve these contests must be imposed. There is a very real question as to whether the abrupt and forceful dislocation of community norms in the case of the middle class will prove to be any more salutary than such dislocations have proved to be in the case of the urban poor. But can the imposition of new norms, via changed laws and institutions, be limited to the middle classes on the site? Will not something have to be imposed on the new immigrants? And if so, will what is imposed on them be any more likely to provide satisfactory environments than the impositions of public housing authorities and relocation agencies back in the city core? Who is to determine the nature of the imposed institutions, and how will the determination be made, if the collective opinion of the existing community is made invalid?

Let us suppose the culture of the new residents is one which involves a lively street life, and some care has been taken in the physical design of the new residences to provide opportunity for it. How will the attendant noise and general commotion fit in with the internalized life-style of many middle class nuclear families? What of differences in manners and general deportment, especially as regards the behavior of children (which can cause a problem even in socially homogeneous communities)? To what extent will the inevitable conflicts result in voluntary withdrawal on all sides into culturally segregated enclaves, replacing big city ghettos with small city ghettos? To what extent will this raise the question Newman addresses regarding abdication of responsibility for the affairs of the community and consequent opportunity for irresponsible and criminal behavior? In short, what sorts of social organizing principles can or cannot be written into the new laws and institutions which will preserve the stabilizing functions of the older, indigenous ones?

It seems to me that identification of such principles in the context of relocating urban poor is hindered, rather than facilitated, by framing the attack on zoning as "exclusionary." As suggested in my opening chapter, it is not the exclusionary nature of zoning that is causing the trouble, but the unworkable and unbalanced distribution of populations in relation to resources, both economic and natural, that has resulted from exclusion in the wrong context. The concept of "snob zoning" in this connection is a self-righteous trouble-maker. Eliminating snobbery is not a realistic part of the objective problem. If my theory is correct, snobbery in one form or another, in the sense that one finds one's own culture superior to all others, is a characteristic of all members of our species, rich and poor, educated or otherwise, and that includes egalitarians. It cannot be eliminated, but only constructively directed.

Of course, the more sophisticated advocates of suburb opening are not attacking exclusion per se, but the consequences of its present expression. But underlying the approach to this problem is the persistent assumption that human needs are more or less identical, which is characteristic of a generalized economic model of human life. Space is the universal desirable in this case, and the suburbs are where, theoretically, the space is. But, while there is clearly more of some kinds of space in most suburbs than in most parts of the central areas of most American cities, that is not, in and of itself, what makes the suburbs attractive to planners who want to help the urban poor. The "fresh air and green grass" view of the suburbs is unfortunately highly idealized. Some suburbs have an adequate amount of attractive open space, but many, probably most, do not. A low-rise apartment building or town house facing a well preserved urban park may have much more access to a high quality natural and recreational environment than many of even the more affluent suburbs. In some cases there can be more privacy, less noise, and less traffic. Yet such urban areas are often the ones that are being invaded by the poor as they are abandoned by the middle class to structural delapidation, crime, and general social misery. Parts of the west side of Manhattan (and once upon a time even Harlem itself) are a case in point.

We should be clear about what it is that the suburbs really do offer at this time: relative social stability. Exclusion must be considered, then, not as an evil per se, but rather in terms of who is excluding whom, where, and from what, and above all, why? Like the apartment complexes Suttles and Newman describe, many suburbs may provide for social stability precisely because they are exclusionary. Thus in the name of providing the poor with a socially more satisfactory environment, an attack is being launched on the very devices that provide the basic securities that the poor most need and lack where they are.

I do not want to appear to idealize the typical suburban land-use laws. Urban designers have long been bitterly frustrated with the imbecility of their generalized geometry, which makes it difficult to relate human beings to both the social and physical environment in a more esthetic and functional manner. Among other things they are extremely wasteful of land. But their very success in providing certain kinds of physical securities across the board for large classes of people may be attributed to their crudities. The advantage of simple-minded laws is that they can be administered and complied with by simple-minded people.

A rational understanding of the structural role of suburbs requires that they be neither idealized, as Downs for instance tends to do, or disparaged, as so much pro-urban literature does. Some very affluent suburban cultures demonstrate a degree of social irresponsibility that make many low-income communities look like paragons, even if they are considerably less likely to have trouble with the law (and much better able to rely on it for security). By contrast, Jacobs, Newman, Gans, Suttles, and many others, have shown that low income communities, on their own terms, are often stable, reasonably law-abiding and relatively secure.

On the other hand Suttles, Newman, and also Downs, note that the idea of a separate life style or subculture or poverty, has been greatly overplayed and that the poor seek the same basic securities and opportunities desired by the middle classes, and that in most cases they will attempt to obtain these as best they can under the very restrictive conditions they face. Rainwater (1971) shows, however, that the residents of the most marginal ghettos do not have a culture of their own so much as a lack of any community structure at all, noting that "the lower-class community which grows up in this situation is one in which a premium is placed on the exploitation and manipulation of one's peers."

While it is quite possible that people who are induced one way or another to migrate from such environments to ones based on a more cooperative and optimistic structure might benefit from the change, quite obviously there may be problems of incompatibility in outlook which would have to be dealt with somehow (no one seems to be willing to suggest how as yet), and in any case these are problems which even the most conscientious residents of more satisfactory neighborhoods are understandably nervous about facing. Perhaps more importantly for those who are able to move from an unstructured to a more structured environment, the structure should be one new arrivals can comprehend and respond to. It would be purely fortuitous if this resulted from a generalized mixing of low or lower-middle class people with those of the middle and upper-middle class. This is not to say that it cannot in some cases produce benefits for some but to suggest that it is not a reliable basis for social planning.

For any program for the mixing of populations to be successful, in my view it must take into account the security—freedom relationship which I presented earlier on p. 96. It must recognize that the capacity of any organism to adapt to a new environment (whether social or physical) is a function of its being able to cope with the changed situation. This in turn must rest on some base of experience which involves that which has not changed. This applies to all of us, as Alvin Toffler (1971) has so forcefully demonstrated, if we are not to succumb to future shock. If the new set of relationships which is established by the mix is to be satisfactory for all participants, and particularly if it is to provide security for all concerned, the principle must apply to all parties to it, those who move into and those who live in the destination area. This is at least as important to the new migrants as to those in situ. If the more affluent proprietors of the original territory feel threatened they may be expected to have resources, overt or covert, to maintain their sense of security, with which the newcomers may not be equipped to deal, especially if the latter are both a cultural and numerical minority.

The factors which might in any given instance enable a mixing of socioeconomic populations to work are extremely complex, and they involve an array of subjective variables which cannot be encompassed in the economic and demographic abstractions of urban planners, aggregated under categories such as "deprived," "poor," "middle class," and the like. In addition to income, there are the social codes and group support mechanisms identified by Cassel; there is also the level not only of affluence but aspiration, the level of energy needed to back up aspirations, and even the aptitude for social and technical skills needed for achieving them; the very things which Rainwater shows so many of the urban poor do not have. To mix a majority that has a large stockpile of such assets with a minority which lacks them without some very clear commonly agreed upon objectives, would appear to be something far removed from justice in the long run. For instance, it would make some difference if the immigrating household or households is one with a strong family structure, no matter how poor, and a sense of personal pride based on that, or one in which an overworked female head of household may be expected to have even less control over her children in a new environment than in the old simply because it is new. It would make some difference whether an ADC mother is socially isolated with problems peculiar to her own situation or whether her family has been part of an extended kinship network such as has sustained generations of immigrants to the U.S. melting pot, and all over the world.

Leaving aside the complicated question of identifying the range and character of personal and group aspirations, it makes some difference in assimilating diverse populations with each other whether not only the desirability but the attainability of common goals is recognized by the aspirants. For some, no matter how desirable middle class goals may appear, the need to protect group identity may contradict them. It is well known that among many migrating populations, particularly those from rural environments, the obligation to provide for kin is overriding. This accounts for much of the stability of American ethnic communities.

Anthropologist Larissa Lomnitz (1971) who has studied the shanty towns around Mexico City, has found an assemblage of closely-knit networks based on kinship. Only 10% of the migrants she studied came on their own; the rest had been attracted by relatives who already lived there. They created a reciprocal economy of exchange and mutual assistance. For instance, the pioneer member of one group obtained a job as a carpet layer. Of the 17 adult males in this group, she reports, all but two are carpet layers. The reciprocal economy is set up quite distinct from the larger market economy; it includes loans of money or material goods, aid in caring for children, the old and the ill, reinforced by very close and more or less continuous contact. Two of Lomnitz' observations are particularly relevant here. One is that the member of the network community who seems to be getting ahead is immediately suspect as a renegade, so that the very upgrading influence which Downs and others see as desirable in mixing lower class with middle class households would, under these conditions, be subversive of community identity. In her words, "The norms or rules of reciprocity presuppose a long-term relationship among equals, in which the exchange is part of social life and is related to social distance and social expectations." Negative pressure is often felt by American blacks who have "made it" in the white community and suffer from being called Uncle Toms. Lomnitz' other relevant observation is that the members of the kinship networks tend to be uninterested in a larger community (conceptual space) beyong their groups even on the local level, and particularly on the national level. Disinterest with the larger world also tends to be true of the lower classes in the United States and presumably other countries.

But involvement with a larger community is precisely the principal characteristic of the business and professional middle classes into which suburb opening will transplant the poor. This is not to suggest that preservation of kinship networks is always crucial or even desirable in industrial societies. Lomnitz notes that in the Mexican shanty towns this form of community organization is not a carry-over of the rural economy; it is neither rural nor urban, but a way of surviving for large human groups on the threshold of the modern industrial world. Individuals can and do leave it to enter that world. My point is that if we really want to develop a plan for community design that will facilitate that transition with the least amount of human misery and danger, in the U.S. or anywhere else, we must examine these characteristics of social-physical organization at a much finer grain than most policy-planning pursues. One of the overlooked variables which is extremely critical in population mixing is the degree to which different individuals within any population can adapt to both new social and new physical environments.

In my own work and in my university courses in planning, I have found it useful to start off with two lists for every problem. The first list contains those elements in the situation which are not to be changed, but preserved or even enhanced. The other contains a list of those elements which are to be changed. The plan, among other things, is the synthesis of these opposites. Toffler has suggested that the only antidote to "future shock" is that some aspects of the individual's experiential environment be held constant. For reasons I have elaborated in this book, proxemic needs must rate high among the most desirable constants for most people. Thus, in any program for suburb opening, or any other kind of planned transplant of populations, the "no change" list must include, in my opinion, some provision for preservation of psychological (as compared with economic) territory, for proprietory social-physical relationships. In short, "squatter's rights" must be considered high among other rights (as they often implicitly are in Mexico and elsewhere). The "change" list will include those spatial rearrangements necessary to the proxemic integrity of the in-migrating group, whatever it is. A plan for population redistribution must somehow find a way to reconcile constructively what may often be highly conflicting needs in these respects.

I have suggested that the fewer conceptual resources people have, the more, rather than less, dependent they will be on relationships which are defined by geographical space. A reminder of the caveat is needed here: formal education does not guarantee a wide conceptual world; in any case, what is considered "educated" is itself a function of class and culture. Nevertheless formal education increases conceptual opportunity. For sophisticated urban man, conceptual territories may be provided by professions, hobbies, religious or political organizations, which can substitute for physical territory. Such people may be relatively indifferent to physical design and location. The poor and cultural minorities will be most likely to need secure physical-cultural boundaries. To intrude them heedlessly into territories, the residents of which have more conceptual, as well as physical, resources, in the name of improving their lot, can be expected to benefit only the most able and conceptually agile among them. On the other hand, they will be well received only by those whose conceptual territories, or self-images, are in one way or another secure from invasion.

We who propose, devise, and administer laws and institutions are very likely to come out of the professional middle class. We may in some cases be people of little formal education, but who nevertheless have had tremendous conceptual resources of some sort. We will be most likely to organize space and events in abstract, conceptual, intellectual terms. We will continually model environments on our own needs for intellectual complexity, projecting as a universal good what is in fact a minority point of view, even if a most important one. We can afford to be relatively indifferent to other peoples' needs for secure physical-cultural territory, because we have other resources. We can moralize about the "greed" of affluent groups whose security depends on material welfare, because we have other symbolic ways of maintaining status and power. Still our problem is, like that of everybody else, how to bring about environments which will enable all of us to survive, let alone life happily together.

Wherever mass migrations occur, the interests of two opposing parties must be considered and constructively provided for; the proxemic integrity of the incoming people and the territorial integrity of the proprietory group. The law and its institutions can provide a structure for compromise, but the negotiation and arbitration will have to be personal and particular in each case.

Since legal and institutional mechanisms cannot create these by edict, but can only discover them, changes in laws and institutions must be preceded by what might be called current anthropology, or better, human ethology.

Designing for diversity requires that one accept the very difficult and painful task of trying to come to terms with other groups' concept systems. This is painful precisely because of Cassel's syndrome — when we enter another's proxemic space we are intruders in an alien world, literally emissaries bearing a flag of truce, with no guarantee at all that it will be understood or accepted.

In my final chapter I will attempt to outline a strategy for applying my model to this immensely difficult task. But before doing so I would like to explore one more set of relationships which are implicit in the model and which I believe underlie all the environmental and population problems of our time.

Chapter 11

Social evolution

The phrase "survival of the fittest" never means that it would be impossible to imagine something fitter.

Paul Leyhausen

In a study of migration patterns among Argentine peasants, geographer R.W. Wilkie (1972) found that a peasant community, which in a typical sociological view would be considered "lower class," actually was stratified not only with a lower, middle, and upper class, but with two kinds of middle class. Wilkie found that at the poles of upper and lower class, people tend to be conservative for different reasons (as shown in Fig. 31); in the upper classes because they are oriented to peer group expectations, and in the lower ones because of lack of confidence in their ability to cope with the environment. In addition, a portion of the middle class also resembled these groups. It was out of a segment of the middle class that the most adventuresome and dynamic migrants appeared, and presumably it is in this group also that creativity and innovative behavior will be most likely to be found.

One of Wilkie's conclusions is that dynamic behavior corresponds to trust in the environment, and that this presumably comes from the security of feeling that one can cope with it successfully. By contrast, dependence on authority, especially the authority of tradition and group norms, correlates with mistrust of the environment. This led Wilkie to find support for Riesman's concept of "inner directed" and "other directed" individuals in his Argentine village. But Wilkie's studies also suggest that such individuals can appear in any "class," including what may appear by normative standards to be the "lowest."

Wilkie developed this theory by combining what are essentially ethological observations with extensive interviews and a multi-variate statistical technique. He is not at this point ready to extend his theory beyond the Argentine villagers he has been studying. But since almost everything I am presenting here is offered only as hypothesis, I will have the temerity to do so. In any case, one part of it can be supported by general observation: we can well expect to find the greatest conservatism at both the upper and lower poles, at the upper because the establishment has — or thinks it has — little to gain and much to lose by change, and at the lower because people tend to have little experience with successful control of events and are unwilling to risk

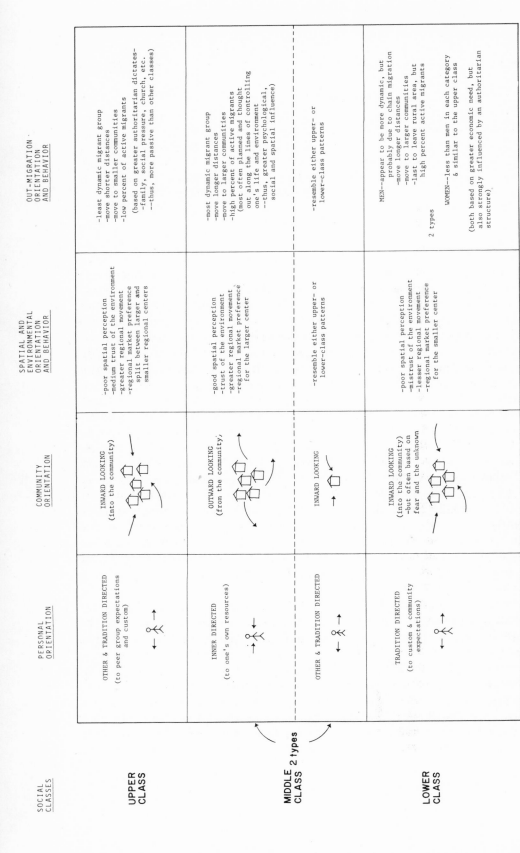

Fig. 31. A typology of peasant types of orientation and behavior by social class: Aldea, San Francisco, Entre Rios, Argentina. This is a generalized typology that ignores the diversity of sub-groups within each social class, although it does represent the composite statement of the internal behavioral processes at each level in the community. (From Wilkie, 1972, reproduced with the author's permission.)

what little they have. In both cases security may be expected to take priority over opportunity.

The dynamic element will be likely to appear in the middle (and in Wilkie's analysis only in a portion of the middle class at that), and it is composed of those individuals whose life experience leads them to believe they can cope with change successfully. Their first priority is not security, but opportunity. It is the dynamic portion of the middle class that in Wilkie's studies has proved to be most ready to migrate, and to remain in the new environment having done so. This conforms to what Cassel has found in his studies of disease which I discussed in Chapter 7. It also confirms what is observed in many ethological studies of animal behavior, some of which we have examined.

What offers so much promise in Wilkie's theory, in my judgement, is that this distribution of characteristics may be expected to be found in any class, even the lowest. Thus in locating or relocating populations across class or ethnic lines, it would be important on each level to find the most dynamic members for the highest degree of integration, and to provide territorial buffers between the most conservative elements in all groups. A first objective in humane strategy for dispersing anybody anywhere would seem to be to develop some way of determining who will be likely to benefit from a change in social, as well as physical, milieu, and under what conditions.

I think looking at relocation in terms of providing a better life, rather than merely access to economic resources, calls for a double strategy, which treats territorial security as a psychological need quite separately from economic needs, even though ultimately meeting the former is dependent on at least minimal satisfaction of the latter. The "insecure rich" and the "insecure poor," which may well include people from the entire range of income groups, should have proxemic territories located so as to prevent them from threatening each other, commensurate with a workable economic and ecological framework. On the other hand, the more mobile citizens, socially and conceptually, require, in addition to proxemic home environments, ready access to opportunities in distemic space of whatever kind is important to them, with employment, and commercial and cultural centers presumably at the top of the list. If the theory holds up, such dynamic individuals may be expected to appear in all social strata, and it is these individuals among the poor who may be expected to benefit from social mixing, and to benefit those with whom they mix.

Of course, this raises another problem which has already been of great concern to urban sociologists, that selecting out the most dynamic elements of a slum population may depress it even further. The only answer to that is to maintain the proxemic relationships in a form which will entice some of the most vital segments of its population to stay and upgrade the rest, which is essentially a policy advocated by Jacobs (1961) which she called unslumming. But this is a case against scattering. If relocation is to serve such a purpose, entire populations would have to be moved more or less intact with the agreement and cooperation of all concerned. That certainly cannot be accomplished on a piecemeal re-zoning or laissez-faire basis.

Pursuit of this logic from either direction risks invoking the nature—nurture controversy which has so bedevilled attempts to relate human and non-human animal activities. We can assume that migratory dynamism (whether of an intellectual or geographical nature) will be partly the result of cultural experience, partly of opportunities in the physical environment, and partly the result of individual characteristics, including health and basic vitality. A serious fault of planners in general is failure to distinguish between the characteristics of a given population and the relative capacities of individuals within it. This is important not only for real justice, but to the continued evolution of societies as well as species. In biological evolution, changes in species take place only in populations, but the individual is always the agent for change. I will argue — and it is the strongest point I want to make in this book — that social evolution is what real equality of opportunity is all about, that territorial spacing performs this function for human cultures as it does in nature for the development of species, and that the individual plays very much the same role in this process.

Perhaps the most virulent version of the nature—nurture controversy has emerged around the assertions of Richard Herrnstein (1971). Herrnstein has outraged egalitarians by citing evidence that IQ is inherited, arguing that because of the increasing reliance of modern societies on technology, for which relative intelligence is essential, we are sorting ourselves out into inherited castes of employables and unemployables, and that the more affluent and socially mobile a society becomes, the more likely is this to occur. Herrnstein's critics, recoiling at this vision of the future, stand on the still-orthodox social science doctrine which asserts that intelligence is entirely, or largely, the result of environmental influences. But the British psychologist Eysenck (1973a, 1973b) frames the whole question quite differently. He says that the hard evidence is that IQ is mostly determined genetically but also observes that the assertion that it is wholly determined by heredity is "a position not maintained by any serious psychologist who has studied the literature." His main argument, however, is that the laws of genetics do not point to the rigid stratification Herrnstein sees, but in exactly the opposite direction. Eysenck consideres inherited IQ in terms of the theory of genetic regression, based on the mechanism of segregation and recombination of genes. He cites numerous studies which show that the effect on the intelligence of children in technological cultures is to average out the extreme IQ's, reducing those of children from professional and semi-professional classes, and raising those of offspring from less-skilled parents. Children of both groups regress toward the mean IQ for the population as a whole. Neither economic upgrading nor social mobility are likely, according to Eysenck, to result in castes. Neither is the reverse likely. Regression theory does not predict that maintenance of sharp class cleavages maintains the intelligence of the aristocrats. Eysenck (1973a) observes: "A caste system prohibiting intermarriage between members of different castes and precluding social mobility would within six to eight generations equalize IQ's between castes, however, unequal the original distribution . . . it has in fact been shown that Brahmins and Untouchables in India have very similar IQ's."

In biological evolution two complementary processes appear to be essential for the creation of new forms of life, including behavioral innovation. One of these is the breeding isolation of a population. The other is the opportunity for interbreeding which allows the recombining of different genes. New species develop in isolation usually in relatively small populations because special characteristics of individuals adaptive in a particular local environment are likely to be swamped in larger and more fluid populations. This process is partly a function of the mathematics of the transmission of dominant and recessive genes. While some characteristics tend to become dominant because they are adaptive in a stable environment, when there are significant changes, other previous characteristics or mutations which have been less useful or even harmful may now become beneficial. If the isolated population is too small, genetic "minorities" may be lost through predation or some environmental catastrophe, since there are so few of them. The random loss of potentially adaptive genes in small populations is called "genetic drift," and has been referred to by geneticists as "random sampling error." In larger populations, even though the potentially useful characteristics are carried only by a minority, it may be numerically large enough that some are likely to survive. However, if the population is too large, the swamping effect will take over, and minority characteristics will not be likely to prove useful in the behavior of the group even if they continue to be passed on. Thus we have the optimum evolutionary situation where there are partially, or temporarily, isolated populations which are neither very small nor very large.

Theories of genetic evolution are meaningful in the context of the subject of this book more as analogies which suggest underlying processes than as predictive models. Genetic changes usually take many generations. Even the six to eight generations which Eysenck says can equalize IQ's between castes in a rigidly stratified population represents more than a century of human development. This is a much longer time span than is the first concern of those to whom this book is primarily directed. Many of the social and cultural characteristics which concern public policy of the kind I have been discussing appear, disappear, or change form in one or two generations; in any case planners and designers face many problems we dare not wait even one generation to solve if we can do anything about them.

On the other hand, there are forms of evolution that are not genetic, but which, often in obscure ways one can only guess at, seem to follow very similar principles. Perhaps the great advantage to our species has been that cultural behavior can change form much more rapidly than genetically programmed behavior, even within the lifetime of individuals. Nevertheless, it seems to follow an essentially evolutionary course, through continual recombination of advantageous characteristics, and my conclusion is that it too requires partially or at least periodically isolated populations which have varying degrees of opportunity for interaction with other populations, and that these will best facilitate the evolution of culture when they are neither too big nor too small. This would appear to follow the course of urban history from tribes through city states to nations and a world community, in which the older forms are incorporated within, not obliterated by, the later ones. Village culture, which does tend to foster individual resourcefulness within limits, is very vulnerable in the face of radical changes in the economic and technical environment. Conversely, massive urban populations, polarized into grossly and sharply divided social classes, may very well facilitate the kind of intellectual mediocrity suggested by Eysenk's theory, and at the same time mitigate against any possibility that individuals with useful capacities that deviate from that norm will point the culture toward new and adaptive ways of dealing with the environment.

This seems to me a far more significant basis for the right kind of suburb opening and other kinds of population-mixing than the moralistic arguments so often advanced by the anti-exclusionists. One does not have to take sides in the controversy over intelligence or its degree of inheritability to apply the basic principles in this context. Eysenck's argument combined with Wilkie's observations suggests that social mobility results in the interaction within the middle class of those who rise from below and fall from above. Restricting movement to one class can on the one hand, up to a point, lead to useful specialization, but cannot ultimately retain whatever superiority that class may start with, but will simply level everyone out within it. Similarly ghettoization of the lowest classes inhibits development of their most able members and reduces the potential adaptability of the whole ghetto population, especially when combined with effects of real environmental deprivation.

Our exclusive suburbs, to the extent that they are actually walled off from cross-cultural intercourse, may be expected to be also subject to this kind of deterioration. So indeed may be the conceptual territories, expressed in the bureaucracies of corporate business, government, academia, and the professional military. In our physically mobile world, where even many of the very poor migrate frequently and over considerable distances, the highest walls of modern ghettos are possibly cultural and conceptual, rather than geographical. In some cases these walls seem to be rising around middle class suburbs, where physical mobility is likely to be highest, and therefore, if Hypothesis V in Chapter 8 is correct, people may be conceptually very circumscribed. It is the very absence of the security of proxemic physical territory lost in excessive motion over the landscape that can lead some people first to territorialize, and then to ghettoize, ideas. But not all; there seem to be Marco Polos in every population who thrive on change.

Throughout history, fortress walls have crumbled with the declining energy of their builders before the assaults of barbarians with greater conceptual and physical vigor. Various social organisms have become extinct or emerged in new hybrids as a consequence. Some barbarians merely destroy, others assimilate, and some, thanks presumably to the infusion of new genes and "higher IQ's," reinvigorate the indigenous culture and raise it to a higher order. The classic function of cities, the object of historic urban design, in my view has been to offer a safer, more continuous vehicle for the recombination of both genes and cultural systems by organizing physical space within and between the fortress walls so as to enable distinct and diverse groups to interact. Traditionally these have been centered around the market places. But in neo-technic societies the traditional urban scale market, with its person-to-person relationships, is no longer the main medium for the distribution of basic economic resources. Modern technology requires a different scale. Yet the psychological function of the market remains; presumably encoded in the human brain somewhere between the limbic system and the neo-cortex. Some new post-industrial equivalent of the old market place must be evolved. I have no clear vision of what it will be like. But I believe I know what its function must be, and that is to provide for the free movement and safe conduct of individuals into, out of and between groups. This cannot occur between ghettos, whether they be of the poor or the affluent, whether on the ground or in the mind.

It is the capacity to interact in diverse ways that enabled man to break out of the instinctual prisons (and also safeguards) that rule other species. Hugh Iltis (1970) notes, "Ecologists have a basis hypothesis — that the more complex and diverse a community of living things, the greater its stability." My own lesson from ethology is that this hypothesis applies to cultural systems as well. Thus, diversification of our population is not only essential to the middle class qua middle class, but even to the most conservative among the upper classes, to all classes if they wish to maintain any portion of whatever affluence they have. This means that a purely territorial approach to the use of space and other resources must doom its own advocates.

All establishments attempt to remain closed populations, and therefore, whether they consciously desire it or not, strive for mediocrity by opposing any deviation from the norms that established them in the first place. They tend to coalesce a small proxemic group around a given symbolic system. In the modern bureaucracies and technocracies of government and industry, technological and scientific concepts often become customs which serve as a symbol of membership in the small group, and thus the organization achieves a territorial interest in an established way not only of doing things, but of thinking about things. (Of course this is true of all culture.) Distemic organization provides for two necessities which can counteract this. On the one hand, it provides an open arena for behavior and thought which deviate from group norms, and on the other it makes such deviance safe for all concerned by settings constraints on how it may be expressed. Thus it combines the safety of limited conformity with the freedom of diversity from all other kinds of conformity, very much as obeying traffic rules provides an individual the freedom offered by an automobile. In turn, diversity provides that essential concomitant of real technical progress, invention.

Not all deviants are innovators, of course — probably most are not. But all innovators are deviants; at the very least they deviate from the accepted way of solving problems. All inventors, real scientists, and real artists are deviants in conceptual space. In Chapter 4, I reported Calhoun's observations that among rats innovation occurs only among the marginal members of a society, but it will show up even in optimum environments. Among many simpler animals, deviant behavior, whether caused by physical disability or functional circumstance, will often be attacked. Tinbergen (1961) observed that a gull whose nesting behavior was momentarily changed by his intervention was immediately assaulted by other gulls. Among mammals with their capacity for more complex behavior, deviance seems frequently to be ignored, unless it actually threatens an individual or group. Only man, however, puts deviance to use, largely through specialized roles that allow exceptional and normative behavior to coexist.

The voluntarily walled-off suburbanite and the involuntarily walled-off ghetto resident have at least a common interest in keeping conceptual deviance free. As we are becoming increasingly aware, all industrial societies are utterly helpless when any major national or international technical problem becomes defined only in proxemic terms. In the current "energy crisis," the affluent may temporarily have some short range edge over the poor in that they can better cope with inflation, and have better opportunity for hoarding and bribery, but a really massive electrical power failure is not likely to respect suburban zoning ordinances. Without fuel, a split-level colonial ranch can be as cold as a slum. People who have access to healthy donkeys are more mobile than people with two cars and no gas. The environmental crisis has already projected the handwriting on the wall of the proxemic cave. Air pollution does not recognize air rights, and water pollution ignores riparian ones. The growing international economic crisis underscores the same unity in adversity, which only the innovations which distemic relations make possible can cope with. We are, all of us, rich and poor alike, running out of just about everything that can be defined only in proxemic terms. We can survive only by distemics: formalized relationships in both physical and conceptual space which permit interactions by socially diverse elements. But the price of allowing deviance is that it must be circumscribed. Since, in their essential purpose, distemic spaces are designed for cultural diversity, they cannot be self-policed in the same way as defensible proxemic spaces. Small-scale proxemic space, defined by Newman as defensible space, requires instant recognition of strangers, who are presumed unsafe until proved otherwise. Distemic space, like the urban streets Jane Jacobs advocates, must be safe for strangers as strangers; which is to say the strangers must be kept safe, whether they intend to be or not, as the ticket for being in that space. One method advocated by Jacobs is to assure a sufficiently high proportion of proxemic residents, ready to police it for their own interests, who indirectly protect others. But in many kinds of distemic space this is not practical.

Distemics require danger to be recognized, not from personal knowledge of the character of the individual, but on the basis of objective behavior. They require restraint on some kinds of deviance. Most importantly they require objective authority, which, as Newman notes, must be imposed. On the other hand, the bureaucratization of objective authority on too large a scale becomes inflexible so that the multiple expressions of deviance which give meaning to distemic space and are the reason for its existence are also likely to be circumscribed. Thus distemic space must be policed on the one hand by authorities who have sufficient status and force to exert control, and on the other the conventional rules must be appropriate for the primary groups who will use that space. Cops will (or should) exert different kinds and degrees of control over behavior at a rock festival, a garden club show, and a Presidential inauguration.

Public, or distemic, space requires control of behavior on the part of people as individuals, because here their behavior is least likely to be controlled by group norms, or public opinion. One is far more likely to value the opinion of those one knows personally than of those one would not recognize on the street. The problem becomes quite complex, because, in distemic space, law enforcement authorities will also be less concerned with local opinion than they are in proxemic space where they can be called to account personally. They will tend to replace loyalty to a local public with loyalty to their own professional in-group, and in conflict situations may look upon those they are supposed to protect as aliens and enemies. This difference between the policing of proxemic and distemic space is well illustrated by the comment of the retiring police chief of my own community which has in a decade grown from a small Ivy League college town to a large university one. In the past, he said, "you had to watch out who you kicked in the ass; he might be the next secretary of state!" (Blossom, 1973.)

It is because proxemic and distemic spaces require different kinds of behavioral control, among other things, that they must be defined clearly, that is they must have recognizable boundaries between them. Only when Rome is small and occupied mostly by Romans must you do as the Romans do. Whereas proxemic space must be under the clear proprietorship and obvious surveillance of its residents, distemic boundaries must be permeable membranes, rather like chemical, electrical or mechanical valves which allow free flow in one direction but only controlled flow in the other. Because it cannot be internally controlled, distemic space requires objective, as compared with subjective, policing. Distemic space requires rather arbitrary conventions applied with absolute impartiality. On the other hand, large law-enforcement bureaucracies, even the best-intentioned, will have great difficulty policing any large public area without the cooperation of the people who use it most frequently. Thus, while it is not defensible space in the Newman sense, the primary proxemic groups who have access to a distemic area must feel sufficient responsibility for it to agree among themselves how and to what extent it must be policed. Even distemic law-enforcement requires a hierarchical territorial structure. In practice, of course, if often does follow such a structure; but in theory the functional relationships are often ignored in pursuit of the oversimplified "discontinuous continuum" between private and public which I set forth in Chapter 8.

I see two great dangers in the current course of attack on zoning as exclusionary. The first is that it makes no provision for the different degrees and kinds of exclusion appropriate to these different kinds of space. The other is that it proposes to abolish or limit one kind of behavioral control (for that is what zoning ultimately is) without a clear and workable set of substitute controls. Without agreement on control of those spaces which do not belong clearly to one group or another, voluntarism can lead to the most brutal kind of control by the most brutal or irresponsible elements in the population. The anonymous thug, the mere threat of whose presence on my street deters me from taking a walk, very effectively controls my behavior. Under such conditions distemic space becomes impossible. A park which one dares not use because of fear of mugging is not, in any social sense, a park at all. This is where one kind of self-interest in population redistribution can involve the walled suburbanite. Not only are his walls a precarious defense, the net effect is that they keep him in prison.

The poor are special victims of crime, not only because they live where most of the street variety of criminals live, but because their communities are so often too fluid or too fragmented to offer defensible proxemic spaces on the one hand, and policeable distemic spaces on the other. Thus they spawn the crime which spills over into areas that might normally be both defensible and policeable. Police, whether brutal or humane, cannot cope with crime under such conditions, because authority is concentrated in the hands of people who are considered to be territorial invaders by criminals and victims alike. Proxemic relationships must be difficult and distemic ones impossible where firemen — to say nothing of cops — are shot at when they attempt to control the consequences of arson. Rene Wagler was burned to death in broad daylight on a well-used street in the Roxbury section of Boston, and yet no witnesses could be found to identify the murderers. It is inconceivable that any whole population, no matter how poor and how bitter, could have condoned such a crime; what this suggests is that no part of that population felt that any good would come of bringing the law into the case.

Among mice and rats the behavioral sink that comes with the breakdown of social organization as a consequence of lost territorial control only begins with the low in status. It eventually reaches even the most-dominant. The human behavioral sink is no longer confined to the ghettos and slums; at least in the United States it extends to the drug scene of middle class cities and suburbs and to the predominantly middle class universities where sofa pillows are "ripped off" student lounges, where books are ripped off libraries, where equipment is ripped out of laboratories, and vandalism is becoming a way of life. This is becoming increasingly intolerable, and now demands for better police protection are coming from students, who in the yesterday of the late sixties, looked upon all cops as "fascist pigs." As black leaders develop more effective constituencies, thereby bringing some order to the social chaos of their environments, they too indicate an increasing interest in better police protection. Some groups, like the Black Muslims, for example, appear to be far more puritanical than most of the prevailing middle and upper classes. Indeed the danger is not so much that there will be complete social breakdown — although this is a real possibility — as that the most repressive kinds of authority will be voluntarily invoked on all sides to put matters straight. In his impassioned plea for the cooperation of individuals in "The Social Contract," which has been so strangely ignored by egalitarian critics of his "Territorial Imperative," Robert Ardrey quotes Theodore White, "If men cannot agree on how to rule themselves, someone else must rule them."

The law is and always was — once it evolved from tribal proxemic law — a bargain. As such the bargainers must know each other even if those they bargain for do not. This necessitates rules of conduct, formalized by contract, which are arbitrary simply because they don't come "naturally," that is out of the draco-limbic system, and which are adhered to not because people are ethically responsible, or love each other, or believe in justice, but because the cost of breaking the contract will cost all parties more than it will gain. Breaking the law makes distemic space unusable, as is the case now in so many urban parks. Distemic space is space where every one can "do his own thing" with a diversity of expression not possible in proxemic space, but nevertheless within constraints set, and enforced with the cooperation of at least two and usually many proxemic groups.

Suburban zoning laws, in their crude way, define not only proxemic neighborhoods, but distemic relations between them. It is precisely the regional bargains between local territorial groups which make the policing of such communities possible. Laws designed and administered by bureaucrats who have no personal connection with or interest in the groups they are to affect, tend to be viewed as alien by all those groups. The same is true for those commercial bureaucracies, the large corporations. People who will cheerfully steal from the telephone company would walk with Abraham Lincoln through a stormy night to return a penny to the neighborhood grocer.

The increasing impotence of large agencies created to assist small groups, such as many housing authorities, bears this out. Large bureaucracies are essential for some purposes, of course; much of what they do cannot be done otherwise. It is a matter of the scale of the problems to be solved. For example, in determining whether resort hotels or wilderness trails for back-packers are going to go into a national park, spokesmen for powerful nation-wide interest groups like the Sierra Club and the ski industry must slug it out as representatives of broad constituencies. At some point each will have to settle on a common interest in policing the area, and will support official and usually quite impersonal methods of insuring this, such as registering visitors, and marking and patrolling trails. Regardless of the degree of citizen partici-pation these will be incorporated into policy set and administered by a large bureaucracy, such as the Park Service, more or less in accordance with general values that are recognized nationally. But at the other end of the scale, a neighborhood park may be quite viable as a park for specific groups, even though it permits pot smoking on its benches, nude bathing in its foun-tains, and sexual intercourse on the lawn, things which are considered by the larger population to be both illegal and immoral. The cloisters of a church may also function as a viable public space even though the overseers put con-straints on behavior which would properly be considered repressive on the Boston Common. In all three cases, laws against murder, robbery, and rape must be enforced, and they can be effectively enforced only in two ways: (a) admission is carefully limited to those with the proper credentials or (b) the area is patrolled by consent of a majority of the patrollees with clear agree-ment as to who does what, and with which, and to whom. Small residential neighborhoods governed in either way still exist on both ends of the socio-economic spectrum, as well as in the middle, and they are often much safer and more satisfactory places to be than those policed according to national codes by extra-territorial authorities.

In my view, the only workable alternative to "fortress suburbia" is some modern equivalent of what has always been the alternative to fortresses in the past — those highways to diversity: open markets, the political forums, the athletic arenas, all policed by conventions. Our dispersed neo-technic cities, now sprawling in polluted chaos, are quite capable of order, if we are willing to look for it. The key to both spatial order and its correlate, social order, as with all other forms of order in nature, is a hierarchy of zones. The administrative authority for such hierarchy must, as I have said, in itself re-main hierarchical, in essential form not so different, if hopefully much more logical, than the various orders of municipal and regional governments that now exist. These are the very orders that planners most detest, because, of course, they are so hard to generalize. The usual substitute for current sub-urban zoning boards, recommended by Downs, among others, is the typical solution of the regional planner: establish a comprehensive bureaucracy which will somehow be "above" the conflicts of local interests. But only rational local interest, on a rising scale of complexity, can organize distemic space meaningfully, and therefore safely. The problem is to rationalize local authorities, not replace them with larger authorities which tend to encapsulate, and thereby fortify, the proxemic systems of their administrators in proportion to the square of the distance from their constituencies. I think zoning boards should generally remain right where they are now, but should be forced into some very hard bargaining with other agencies governing present or potential territories on their own scale. The right kind of court action could certainly facilitate this process, but it would have to be designed to establish new boundaries and not merely batter down old ones.

The essential difference between control of behavior in homogeneous groups and in heterogeneous ones is well summed up by Perin: "Homogeneous groups are not conflict-free, but they are free of conflicting rules for resolving conflicts." (1975, p. 51.) An unsentimental view of closed communities takes note that the advantages of behavioral predictability in such groups is balanced by the disadvantages of quite rigid limitations on behavioral choice. On the other hand, freedom of life-style leads to uncertainties that many find too taxing or too frightening, and most of us need some social predictability at some times. If I understand the concept correctly, Suttles' view of the "community of limited liability" offers security for people who thrive on social diversity during much of their daily life.

If I am right that the modern suburb is also largely a community of limited liability, it differs from the self-contained village precisely in that its function for its residents is so limited. It provides a proxemic home base for people whose life interests are to a great extent elsewhere. For this reason it is most satisfactory for businessmen, professionals, or skilled workers, whose days are full of activity in all sorts of other places and associations, who can return home in the evening for rest and the proxemic security of a family. It is least satisfactory for people of both sexes who do not have families, especially nuclear families, for young people of all ages and sexes who seek new experiences in which to try their capacities, and for energetic wives and mothers who are bored with the limited conceptual horizons of home, school, and local charities. In short, a suburb is a meaningful place for most of its residents only if there is some sort of city to go to for part of the time.

Suburbs which are actual fortresses are untenable for middle class society, not only because they are unjust, not only because their defenses are not fail-safe, but because they put the middle class in ghettos along with the lower classes, because they make middle class life impossible. Real middle class life thrives in social and physical diversity by its very nature. Distemic space, not proxemic space, defines the real city. The city is not only a physical space, a geographical place, but also an intricate hierarchy of conceptual spaces which vary greatly in the minds of its dissimilar citizens.

Perhaps the modern city is not even primarily a physical or geographical phenomenon. Yet we must come to terms with the relationship between conceptual and physical space. This relationship proceeds from two essential requirements. The first is clear physical structure which provides the proxemic security without which, if only in the memory of childhood, no one dares to venture far into conceptual space. The second is the opportunity to seek diversity of experience in various combinations of physical and conceptual space. For some, conceptual space offers adventure enough, and can be comprised in a very small area, as for Thoreau who "travelled a good deal in Concord," taking with him through the ensuing years a veritable metropolis of readers into the vast conceptual areas of that village and its nearby pond. But probably for most mental Marco Polos a change of physical milieu is essential for stimulation of the conceptual brain. In any case, trade in conventional tokens, whether of science, industry, commerce, or art, cannot take place without centers where diverse human beings, both culturally and individually, can interact.

The polarization of classes, races, and various subcultures along crude economic lines clearly interferes with such possibilities for interaction, and for this reason alone there are grounds for serious concern among all who espouse any form of democracy, however defined. There is no question that much of the present suburban pattern of development is moving in that direction, and that the direction is retrogressive from almost any point of view other than the most primitive kind of territorial self-interest. But in my view, reversal of this trend cannot be accomplished by thinking in suburban terms, and certainly not in zoning terms. The objectives are new town objectives and no other approach can begin to encompass the problems, let alone the solutions. In the next and final chapter I shall attempt to suggest how my proxemic—distemic model of human territoriality might be added to the already rich stock of theory and practice in the new town concept.

Chapter 12

A new look at new towns

Let not our town be large, remembering
That little Athens was the Muse's home,
That Oxford rules the heart of London still,
That Florence gave the Renaissance to Rome.
Vachel Lindsay

The essence of the new town idea, especially in its classic formulation by Ebenezer Howard (1946), is the clear structuring of urban space where residential neighborhoods on varying socio-economic levels are functionally organized around centers of employment, commerce, recreation, transportation, and more or less natural open space. Often overlooked in the discussions of new towns, pro and con, is that in theory they are not isolated rural villages, but satellites, each an entity in its own right with efficient linkages, not only to their metropolitan center, but to each other as well. Ideally, new towns provide the advantages both of cities and of suburbs without many of the liabilities of either.

While new towns certainly have not turned out to be a panacea, the concept has proved to be as successful as any urban planning theory in this century. Like so many useful inventions, Howard's embodiment was merely a reformulation of an ancient principle, as old as urbanization itself. Related to both centrality and boundary is the concept of optimal size, of critical mass, for each element in the hierarchy.

The new town model seems to me to be the only one which will make it possible to relocate populations with simultaneous regard for territorial, economic, technical, and ecological needs on all sides. Instead of following Downs' suggestion that middle-class communities be assured of retaining dominance (a promise which has questionable moral validity and might be very hard to keep in any case), it would relocate new populations without invading anyone's territory per se, by incorporating both resident and new populations into new regional communities. Conceivably, governance and essential form in the original suburb do in many cases stay intact, even while geographical boundaries are adjusted. A new hierarchical government, firmly based in the newly urbanized region, ideally incorporates these into itself without obliterating them on a sort of mini-federal basis. Most importantly, both old and new populations meet on a more or less equal footing on relatively neutral ground, and at least as far as the distemic spaces between them are concerned, both are pioneers.

155

New towns incorporating existing suburbs can theoretically offer very real economic as well as functional and cultural benefits to the indigenous middle class in place of the dubious feeling of responsibility which is really all that suburb-openers can offer them. In England, for example, the new towns, complete with capital improvements, including school and housing subsidies, have been self-financing over a period of fifteen or twenty years, a benefit which was built into Howard's original concept.

The new town efforts in America have not followed the English model as closely as, for example, they have in Scandinavia, and as a result have tended to become merely more comprehensive and better organized suburbs or subdivisions. One of the hurdles here has been the problem of public acquisition of land, which has been so central to the British version, and without which real economies are not possible. Failure to deal with the economic problems has greatly hindered attempts at providing a social mix. Outstanding in this regard is Columbia, Maryland, where some of the essential relationships I have attempted to define in this book have been considered, apparently with mixed success. Floyd McKissick's black new town Soul City, while planned to be largely homogeneous racially, also was planned to set up a neighborhood pattern which calls for a hierarchy of private-public spaces.

The main rationale of most programs to open up the suburbs, i.e. to relate centers of residence to centers of employment, is a central principle of the new town concept. Davidoff and Gold (1970) have focussed the new community sponsored by their Suburban Action Institute around the Ford plant in Mahway, New Jersey. Downs (1973), offering a more general and more comprehensive strategy, proposes three levels on which suburbs would be restructured. Downs' largest scale relates to job opportunities. For this he recommends the division of each metropolitan area into "commuting zones" within a specified rush-hour commuting time by public transportation to "all jobs" (not defined) in the zone, with a sufficient range in type and cost of housing to accommodate all employed within the zone. The logistical problems in this are horrendous, and their solution would seem to lead to de facto new towns in any case. But conceptually, this aspect of both the Downs and Davidoff proposals is sound in that it would relate residence to an important form of distemic space, industry, and commerce.

Downs' second level would arrange residential units around schools in a manner to assure integration, using a model not unlike Clarence Perry's "neighborhood unit," but much more heterogeneous socially. Schools, in my theory, may indeed form an important kind of distemic space. But I suspect it would be well to distinguish between elementary schools and secondary schools. Up to puberty the child's world is a widening extension of the family. It is in adolescence that the development of the social side of the child's personality begins to take increasing precedence over the individual personality, although this is a complicated subject which is both beyond the scope of this book and my competence to discuss in detail. I wish only to suggest that the high school level is more distemic than the grade school level. Among the young of both human and other species the generation gap is at its most acute between adults and the maturing juveniles, especially males, and it is among these young that social behavior tends to be most communal. It seems to me no coincidence that territorial behavior is most prominent among other animals when they are mating and breeding and that, among neo-technic humans, suburbs tend to be populated mostly by families in the child-bearing years. At the same time, of all the segments of the population for whom suburbia is less than satisfactory, the adolescents are typically the most unhappy. I think, therefore, residential patterns designed to facilitate secondary school integration are much more important than for the earlier grades, and of course this is often the case with regional high schools. Integration may not be desirable at all for some younger children and their families. In the long controversy over bussing, rarely is integration examined carefully from the child's point of view. The difficulty with this argument, of course, is that tolerance for diversity is most easily acquired by the very young. Adolescence may already be too late. Here again, it may be well to invoke Wilkie's theory in combination with Cassel's; those children who are most intelligent and healthy, and above all whose parents support them through emotional uncertainty and conflict on both sides, may be expected to benefit most from integration; those who lack what Cassel calls social assets may well be harmed more than helped by the well known, but little noted, ebullient cruelties of draco-limbic competition in the school yard.

Downs' third level of social integration (he stresses economic, rather than racial integration) is on the residential level. He declares, "In all cases, *some residential mixing of deprived households with non-deprived households, with the latter exerting a dominant influence, is necessary to achieve a significant upgrading of the former.*" (Original italics) (1973, p. 31). For reasons I have dwelt on throughout this book, such a proposal should be severely qualified before it is plugged into planning policy. In my theory, such interaction requires, at least for many people, a careful measure of buffered space. I would back off any plan which proposes to integrate anybody with anybody on the block level unless it is absolutely voluntary on both sides, or unless the planners know more than they are likely to be able to know, and probably have a right to know, about the lives of the people involved. For many groups the block level may be far too small for this purpose.

Any really integrated, comprehensive, and reasonably detailed plan which attempted to encompass these factors on a scale sufficient to make any real difference to the urban poor would be in almost any conceivable sense a new town, and would require a new municipal identity with new administrative mechanisms. To plan this on any other basis would seem to be the most regressive kind of piecemeal folly. A logical starting point in the United States would certainly appear to be better use of Title VII of the 1970 Housing Act, despite the fact that at the time of writing current projects under it are in financial trouble. Traditionally, zoning and other land-use controls have been tied to the existence of a plan. My own belief is that any court-ordered modifications of local land-use law involving significant changes in population or economic structure should be tied to a new town plan. This would be at least as much in the interests of newcomers as the territory-holders. Most importantly, it will create a vehicle for raising questions which otherwise may never get a public airing, and would not otherwise be faced until it is too late. I am suggesting that such planning be specifically labeled new town rather than regional, since there are regional matters that do not involve coordinated urban concentrations, and others which for a variety of excellent reasons require planned non-growth, in other words "exclusion."

For example, Davidoff and Gold have prepared a unified plan for their proposed Ramapo Mountain development, in Mahwah, through their architecture and planning consultants, Callister and Payne. This scheme does attempt to deal with various functional problems and certainly appears to be very sensitive ecologically and esthetically. But in the attempt to amend the local zoning ordinance to allow it to be implemented, there is no guarantee that others who enter the breach will follow such precedents, even assuming the plan is right for the people it proposes to serve, which seems far from certain. In any case, the planning involves an area of only 720 acres, little more than a square mile of land. Although some brief and very general consideration to outside linkages has been given, the plan is essentially no more than an elegantly conceived subdivision. It deals with few of the regional (as well as local) problems that both the old and new populations will face if the proposal is implemented, especially when it is considered that the proposed new community will nearly triple the population of the present one. The political implications of that, among other things, can hardly be lost on the voters of Mahwah.

There are a great many complex factors that enter into new town planning which are beyond the scope of this book, but which I think will underscore the necessity of taking this approach rather than a piecemeal assault on suburban structure as such. I have raised the new town subject mainly because it seems to me the best (if not the only) way to try out and test the proxemic—distemic model I have developed.

Ebenezer Howard's garden city model, and most new towns which have followed it, have been concerned largely with the physical structuring of space. The underlying philosophy is one of the desirability of a democratic mix of social classes, but this is generally sought through economic mechanisms; physical distinctions such as densities and house form are made in this regard largely on the basis of cost. With sufficient physical diversity offered in a general sort of way, and economic problems accounted for, the theory is that various groups will sort themselves out into workable neighborhoods. Under the right conditions this undoubtedly can occur, but I strongly suspect that it is most likely to occur where populations are relatively homogeneous culturally, even if not socially and economically. At the very least, the planners and designers must have a very clear picture of what the cultural needs are. There are reports, for instance, that Le Corbusier's Chandigarh in India has not worked well, because its physical design did not correspond to local traditions and proxemic needs. To my knowledge new towns have been most satisfactory in Scandinavia, where there tends to be a culturally very unified population.

A major problem facing planners in the United States is one of cultural pluralism, and there is some reason to believe that there will be a tendency for all post-industrial societies to fragment into small subcultures as a necessary psychological defense against the standardizations imposed by technology, as suggested by Toffler. I offer my model of a proxemic—distemic dichotomy, or, better, continuum, in order to try to make cultural pluralism possible within a framework of rational comprehensive planning. In other words I hope it will enable planners to make culturally determined social relationships, especially territorial ones, much more explicit than a vague, essentially laissez-faire view of "diversity of opportunity" permits, without, it must be said, imposing them on anyone.

In Fig. 32 I have tried to illustrate the relationship between proxemic and distemic form, using Howard's basic satellite scheme, adding to, rather than replacing, the original characteristics of his physical hierarchies. Distemic spaces are ultimately defined by adjacent proxemic ones, but not confined by them. Where proxemic spaces become physically smaller as the city grows (densities increase), distemic spaces become larger as the city grows, and the opportunities for recombinations within them correspondingly greater, since they are bounded by a wider variety of proxemic ones. For example, at the center, the distemic space, which might be a neighborhood park or a street corner hangout, is bounded by four proxemic communities (the number is not significant, except that it is small).

Much of the literature on community structure, and especially on the "turf" of street gangs, suggests that neighborhood parks are often largely proxemic, and of course, where this is true, they would fit my diagram only within a proxemic community, not in the white space joining them. But it is important that a particular space may play a dual role in this regard, and the question for the planner and designer is to determine, insofar as possible, which is the primary role, and furthermore, in which direction a change in use is likely to occur if and as population changes or expands in the surrounding area, and to provide for secure boundaries and necessary substitutions if the movement is, as it is likely to be under conditions of rapid change, from proxemic to distemic. The literature on the turf of juvenile gangs certainly suggests that street corners and other hang-outs may be largely proxemic, but they will not necessarily be so, and may in fact be ways in which juveniles of ghetto areas who have little opportunity otherwise to explore distemic relationships may do so on their own level of under-

160

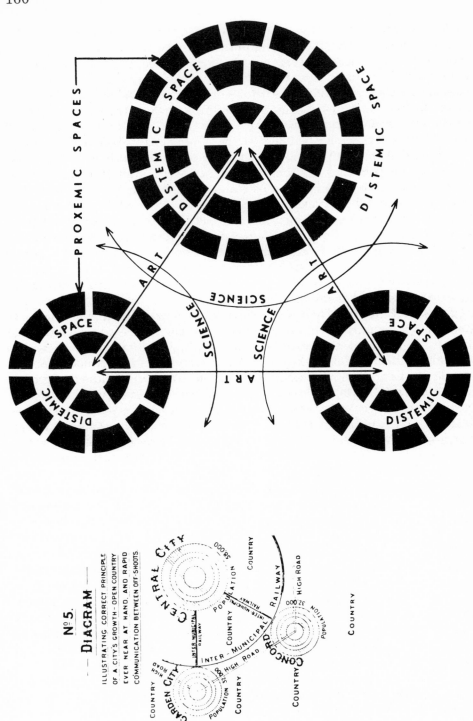

Fig. 32. The conceptual city, drawn analogously to the Garden City shown inset (Howard, 1946).

standing. For example, I recall a drug store near a socially mixed large-city high school which I attended in my youth. There was a general tendency for students to socialize within their own class and family or neighborhood associations, but this drug store was known as a place where those who wanted to experiment more widely could find new friends and "dates." It had a sort of permanent core, presumably proxemic in some form, but there was a considerable diverse floating population, of which I was a member, which came and went as motivations and moods changed. It was not a territory, and I do not remember ever feeling threatened by insiders; on the other hand, undoubtedly partly because of its physical size, it drew on only a fraction of the school population, a far smaller proportion than attended a football game or, what were then fashionable, the school proms.

The relationship between these kinds of space is first of all functional and should be viewed in terms of the degree to which social exclusion facilitates or inhibits that particular function. Proxemic spaces will tend to be fully bounded (although not necessarily always by physical barriers) whereas distemic spaces are open-endedly enclosed by a subset of proxemic ones. The distemic space may be defined by, and hopefully policed by, those proxemic populations that bound it. In the outer ring of my diagram, greatly extended distemic space is encompassed by a great variety of proxemic ones, until eventually the boundaries between the towns in themselves form distemic space defined by those towns. There are interstices, or alleys, between the proxemic territories, which are penetrable, but are nevertheless subject to surveillance from the defensible spaces they pass by. I have used this form simply to compare it with the Garden City model (Fig. 32). In essence it is a cell tissue model, as proposed by Saarinen (1943), who like Geddes (1915) and others chose a biological, rather than an economic viewpoint.

I certainly do not propose such a paradigm as a prescriptive formula, and must admit to some apprehension that it may be received that way. The possibilities for trouble in doing so must be obvious to any thoughtful reader, although I cannot see that it will be any more dangerous, even if certainly no less so, than blindly applying any other formula to human affairs, including the many that continually find their way into plans and policies.

I view this theory, like other environmental theories, primarily as a framework for asking questions. The answer to the questions, not the theory itself, should determine policy. So I will attempt to show how the theory might be used and tested by suggesting some of the questions which might be raised by it within a new town framework, taking as examples some of the proposals of those two most articulate of suburb-openers, Davidoff and Downs.

As noted, both of these advocates and most others on that track propose that housing for the ill-housed be related to job opportunities, particularly those kinds of industry which provide the jobs for which the poor can qualify or be trained to qualify. I should like to extend this argument (as in fact the new town pioneers did) to all classes and income groups, the skilled and educated as well as those without such conceptual resources, on the very grounds that one of the interests of the unskilled is opportunity to know the skilled without being unduly disadvantaged in the process. This, indeed, is also a consideration implicitly raised by Davidoff et al. (1970), and explicitly so by Downs (1973). Such a mix for the more dynamic members of the incoming group may well be beneficial as such, but for those less equipped for competition, it might be better to consider optimizing what assets they have so as not to further reduce them by comparison. In facing this, one would have to ask whether the industry contemplated will for any particular proxemic group be merely a source of income, interchangeable with almost any other employment opportunity, or whether the job it offers also has cultural and status meaning, or whether it represents some particular level of aspiration. In the former case, the employment focus may have relatively little significance in distemic terms, and the local ethnic proxemic one may be the main source of self-identity. On the other hand, for many skilled and semi-skilled workers, a particular place of employment (e.g. construction worker, machinist, longshoreman) or a union may be important both as proxemic norm and distemic meeting ground for people whose proxemic lives are more or less confined to ethnic relationships. Among businessmen or professionals the job may perform both proxemic and distemic roles, whereas for a retail merchant his particular enterprise may concern him merely in economic terms, that is, he may cheerfully exchange a hardware store for a supermarket, while his role in the chamber of commerce and various community affairs may unite both distemic and proxemic worlds for him.

For the housewife whose proxemic world places her main role in life as that of wife and mother, home and child-related matters may nevertheless have both proxemic and distemic meaning, especially if she considers the cultural and intellectual development of her family part of her responsibility. For such a woman the relationship of school or church to residential area may be of considerable importance, and a Perry (1929) neighborhood unit may in fact represent a satisfactory neighborhood. A job may be simply a means to augment the family income. But for a wife and mother in the professional middle class who has the same distemic interest in an independent job as her husband, a very different relationship to the center of employment may exist; she may either commute like her husband, in which case residential area is of importance as a place for rest and security, with distemic focus in a metropolitan center, or the local community may itself be a distemic center, as for the retail merchant whose distemic world centers in the chamber of commerce.

A population least considered by planners is that of working single people of both sexes. For some of these, especially the older ones, the place of employment may be an essential proxemic center of social life, with relatively little distemic meaning. For such people, the loss of a job may have the effect of the loss of a family. On the other hand, for many single people access to recreational and cultural activities after hours becomes paramount; both the small town and the suburb will be an intolerable bore. One of the restraints on the movement of some kinds of industry and of corporate headquarters out of the central city has been the difficulty they have experienced in obtaining qualified secretaries or younger technocrats of both sexes who are unwilling to live in what they consider the "boondocks." Libraries and schools in smaller areas have often experienced difficulties in recruiting top-notch personnel, even with a seriously depressed job market. The rising divorce rate and the increased interest of the popular media in the "singles" suggest that community planning should pay more attention to such groups, and consider carefully the possible very different proxemic—distemic relationships involved.

For many, the small scale proxemic relationship of family, relatives, and close friends is the main locus of interest and self-esteem, and the economic aspects of employment may be all that really matter. For both husband and wife, distemic as well as proxemic values may be tied to recreational activities (e.g. bowling clubs) which may be inter-ethnic and even inter-class, but strongly based on a nuclear family or extended family life style. In fact, it is probable that such recreation-focussed relationships are primary in some suburbs. Questions of this sort have been examined for a long time by sociologists and urban anthropologists in terms of a variety of theoretical constructs. I suggest that it may be useful to have them re-asked in terms of small-scale proxemic defensible spaces and in relation to the distemic functions of factory or commercial and cultural center. The skilled workman who owns a good car may spend a lifetime in one community, with a variety of jobs in shops or factories within a radius of one hundred miles. For people who spend their lives in mining villages, the proximity of the mine may have strong proxemic symbolic meaning, and distemic relations may be confined to membership in the union, if there are any at all. (The love—hate attraction of the mine for miners, as a community focal point, is vividly expressed in the poetry of Dylan Thomas and such novels as Llewellyn's classic, "How Green Was My Valley.") When miners must go to work in big city factories, we may well ask which if any of these symbolic spatial characteristics can be transplanted for them, and to what extent might doing so reduce the pathological consequences for these very people which have been identified by Cassel? On the other hand, to what extent is reluctance to leave such a proxemic social-physical environment responsible for the depressed economies of Appalachia?

There are two large questions in the application of any such theory as this. One is, who will do the applying? The other is, where does the right or obligation to apply any theory to anybody end? That is, at what point is it both practical and essential to let people make their own decisions. Much of what

I call proxemic space must be out of bounds to planners and all but do-it-yourself designers.

As regards the first, it appears to me both unfair and unrealistic to expect most working planners and designers either to ask questions of this kind in detail, or to adequately evaluate the answers. Not only are they harassed with more problems and complications than even the best disciplined conceptual brain can manage, but the mind-set that comes with their training makes it unlikely that they will be able to ask the right questions or see the answers when they appear. As a rule planning deals with generalities, and planners are taught to look for large-scale relationships, at least partly because if they don't, nobody else will. As a plan moves from concept to implementation, from long range to next year, it also moves from the general to the specific and at some point becomes design. Designers work best when all or most of the background information is given to them: good designers have strong minds of their own, and need strong constraints to keep them on target.

Thus people whose main business is to obtain information rather than devise solutions must be brought into the process. But I believe interdisciplinary teams often founder because they approach problems theoretically. Interdisciplinary projects are difficult enough among academic or "pure" scientists; they become doubly confounded when traditional scientists try to cooperate with applied practitioners on a theoretical basis. The pure scientist is somewhat in the position of the architect of a building: for him the elegance and integrated completeness of the theory are primary. The practitioner is more like the occupant of the building: elegance may contribute substantially to his esthetic satisfaction with the product, but his first interest is in how well it meets his functional objectives. I think the only way out of this dilemma is the interdisciplinary activity be problem-oriented. As such it may well include a variety of theories, even conflicting ones, so long as the result is information which at some point can be applied with reasonable reliability to some problem. But it also requires a willingness on the part of all concerned to accept the different theoretical vantage points: in other words the team itself must be the ultimate in distemic conceptual space.

For this purpose I see developing a new science of comparative human ethology, of which Hall is the foremost pioneer (see especially Hall, 1974). Undoubtedly animal ethologists, especially those who, like Calhoun, and Leyhausen, are also human psychologists, will be valuable and very willing recruits. Field-oriented psychologists like the Hutts and Roger Barker, together with sociologists like Herbert Gans, Gerald Suttles and Lee Rainwater, have already pointed the way. But I think that for the particular kinds of questions that need answering, perhaps the greatest help can come from applied anthropologists. Anthropology, as of now, appears to have contributed relatively little to contemporary urbanology, with the exception of Hall and his associates. To be useful in this context, anthropologists will have to surrender their preoccupation with exotica, and the understandable satisfactions of being neo-technic gods among the primitives. They must be willing to apply their investigative techniques to their own kind in the often dreary surroundings close to home. On the other hand, both by training and outlook, anthropologists should be ideally equipped, I would think, to provide exactly the sort of precise detailed social information which planners rarely, if ever, can afford to find, even if they were disposed to look for it. One of the more comparative among anthropologists, Clifford Geertz (1965), argues that perception of uniqueness in human culture is the primary role of anthropology. Certainly making uniqueness explicit is the chief requirement in this connection.

It goes without saying that funding agencies must be willing to budget for this sort of information as they are now, belatedly, providing for input from ecologists. The extent of such probing and the restraints that must be placed on its use have, however, raised a major ethical question in the social sciences. I can only reiterate that I view the protection of privacy in proxemic space, both for individuals and groups, as the primary function of such space, and that the first task of planning is to protect it from territorial invasion, even by planners. How to find out what needs to be learned to allow it to exist without invading it clearly is a major task for human ethology. One way, of course, is to act so that one will be invited. Another is to use the information in a way that will assure that one will be invited back.

In this connection, the twenty year ongoing studies by Barker and his associates of American and English towns, referred to in Chapter 2, set an admirable example. In these studies the observers worked with the full knowledge and cooperation of the peoples concerned, to the extent that they became largely unnoticed in the life of the community. Maintaining trust to this extent over a full generation of time must offer some sort of model for research integrity. There are two aspects of Barker's work which seem to me to have particular pertinence for the assessment of what I am calling distemic. One of these is that it measures objective activities in space, rather than subjective responses to which so much sociological and psychological research is directed. Secondly, in Barker's work only the public environments of the towns are investigated. Private and family settings, and home surrogates such as hotels, are not included. This helps to circumvent the problem of invasion of privacy, since public behavior is by definition not private. The work led by Barker has been cogently summarized by Bechtel (1974) who has applied it to larger urban environments.

Of particular interest in the present discussion is the application by Bechtel and his colleagues of Barker's theory of "undermanning" and "overmanning" (Bechtel, 1970, 1974; Lozar, 1974; Srivastava, 1974). This theory can be briefly summed up as follows: larger population groups create larger behavioral settings and smaller groups create smaller settings. However, it is not the absolute size of the setting area or of its population which is crucial in the theory, but the rate of participation in the behavior that is denoted. (We may recall here Calhoun's and Cassel's observations of mice and men respectively.) Smaller settings tend to be undermanned; that is, there are more demands by the environment on all members for activities than there are individuals to fulfill them. The larger settings tend to be overmanned; in other words there are more people available than tasks to be performed. The consequence for individuals is that in smaller settings each has to work harder, has a greater sense of importance and of a greater variety of activities, but a lower level of maximum performance and consequently less need to be concerned with individual differences. There are lower standards for admission of newcomers who are accepted more readily than in large settings. This suggests one basis for the "friendliness" and apparent informality of village life, as compared with city life, noted in Chapter 9. Also under such circumstances an important economic basis for xenophobia in industrial societies, fear of unemployment through job competition, is not likely to be a factor. However, Barker also observes that in the smaller undermanned settings there is greater insecurity, because there is a greater likelihood of failure as well as success.

In one study conducted by Bechtel (1970), the behavioral settings of two poor urban neighborhoods were compared with Barker's findings in small towns, using the latter's concept of "penetration" as a quantitative measure of participation in the activities in each case. Bechtel's hypothesis was that "one of the greatest sources of social problems in the city is the fact that the city as a large community simply has too many overmanned settings and the result is too many marginal non-involved people." But he also noted that "the city is so complex that one cannot tell whether this is a fact that touches all social strata of life there or whether this is only true at certain levels. In the midst of overcrowding there are many examples of undermanned settings such as professional services." (1970, p. 349.) Bechtel's data clearly confirmed his hypothesis. Barker's six-point penetration scale ranged from passive onlookers through active but low level participation, to individual leadership without which the activity could not take place. In Barker's small town, which he called "Midwest," the residents largely run the settings, with general participation and few activities directed by outsiders. In the city blocks examined by Bechtel the exact opposite occurred. The majority of activities were conducted by persons from outside the residential area, while the residents remained relatively passive onlookers. Bechtel summarizes his findings as follows: "although the kinds of behavior available to people in the city may be as much as three times greater than the kinds of behavior available to the townspeople, the striking contrast is that most of the people in the small town have control over their own activities while in the city most of the people are followers or onlookers." He also notes that in the small town there is a much higher proportion of settings of a "truly social nature," whereas in the city they are more of a service nature, such as street repair, deliveries, or police check.

This phenomenon is clearly apparent in the bureaucratic jargon of urban agencies such as "service delivery systems" where most attention is on the deliverer and little on the deliveree. One thinks of a semi-trailer truck backed up to a loading dock with cartons of brand name social goodies. This conceptual language contrasts with that of the agricultural extension services, for instance, where the emphasis is on providing information and advice to recipients who are expected to "do-it-yourself." In the early sixties when Harlem entered the long hot summers of rioting, the late Langston Hughes, surely no white racist, proposed in his New York Post column that black youths be paid to clean up their own streets, which he suggested would cost the city much less than sending in the sanitation men and would have the other advantages of providing the young people at once money, something to do, and some sense of responsibility for their own communities. It is a measure of the problem that, to my knowledge, no one took Hughes up on this suggestion to follow a practice which is a normal part of life in small towns, where the neighborhood kids are traditionally hired to rake leaves and mow lawns.

Bechtel concludes:

> The solution is to change the city from a low demand, overmanned environment to a high demand undermanned environment. The solution is simple to propose but not simple to enact. It means decentralization, fragmentation of many efforts, and a new value system that replaces mechanical efficiency or social structure as the highest goal with the necessity of participation of members as the highest good. (1970, p. 352.)

It might be added here, that currently fashionable "citizen participation" generally means participation in decision-making, not in decision-implementing. Advocates typically organize their constituencies for "action" aimed not directly at an environmental problem, but rather at "demanding" that somebody else do something. In Barker's small towns, decision-making and decision-following are done more or less jointly by the same people.

Because the city is complex, and many of its functions obviously must be carried on a large scale by professional cadres rather than residents, I believe the solution Bechtel proposes can be facilitated by structuring city form in terms of various scales of proxemic and distemic space, where on the smallest level of proxemic scale all activities which technically can be carried on by its members are conducted by them. For example, street cleaning and policing can be managed, I believe, on the block level, with only minimal direction from city agencies regarding collection points and fundamental laws. Garbage men cannot be expected to go through hallways with vacuum cleaners or into air shafts for refuse, anyway, and, as we have seen, the police are virtually impotent on the block level if there is no consensus between them and the residents as to what the law is. On the other hand, a multitude of inherently impersonal "behavioral settings," such as the installation and maintenance of utilities, cannot be planned or managed on the proxemic level at all.

Hall's methodology (1968, 1974), based on what he calls *situational frames* is similar in some respects to Barker's and Bechtel's, but purposely oriented to subjective rather than objective use of space. I suggest Hall's approach for proxemic and Barker's for distemic space. Field work from such disciplines as sociology and psychology might be integrated to a far greater extent than it usually is with cultural anthropology to order the complexities of proxemic specialization and diversity, while some sort of urban ethology, similar if not identical to Barker's "ecological psychology," especially as modified by Bechtel, can help to locate the kinds of essentially distemic settings where proxemic diversities can become synergistic for the larger urban organism.

As Bechtel notes, this is easier to propose than to carry out. It will obviously be expensive in manpower and time, but it should be possible to develop a cost—benefit scale, which I strongly suspect would show that after the price of crime, disease and vandalized public services is added to planning budgets which have lead to no solutions, such research would be a real bargain. That it is indeed a bargain is suggested by the Street Life Project being conducted by William H. Whyte, using time-lapse photography in conjunction with first hand observation of behavior on the plazas and sidewalks of central Manhattan (Whyte, 1974a,b). His studies strongly confirm conclusions of Jane Jacobs fifteen years earlier, on the crucial role of diverse and interesting activity centers in the public life of the city.

It is the objectivity of Barker's system which makes it possible, it seems to me, for human observers to achieve some of the detachment which is much easier for ethologists to maintain with non-human animals than for social scientists examining their own kind. Nevertheless, the subjective aspects are not obscured by objectivity, but rather become clearer. Calhoun, Leyhausen, and Fischer, among others, following Hediger's observations of animal path systems, all suggest directly or indirectly that territory and home range among animals comprise essentially a cognitive map (for a human survey of this field, see Hart and Moore, 1973), the coding of an assortment of sights, sounds, smells, and so forth by which the creature locates its nesting center, pathways, and outer boundaries, in accordance with its needs. These are highly selective, and do not encompass everything within the physical setting they define. In fact, we can assume this makes speciation possible. Animals which do not respond to the same environmental stimuli in the same way can co-mingle amiably in the same area because, presumably, as far as they are concerned they and the others are not in the same space. We can conclude that this is why territorial battles usually involve only members of the same species, or even sub-species, where spatial symbols are identical. As Kevin Lynch showed in his "Image of the City" (1960), human beings also perceive not an objective environment but a cognitive map. Both Hediger (1949) and the human psychologist Von Foerster (1973) show how it is only by acting on the environment in some way that any organism can perceive it.

This can help to explain much of the indifference to surroundings shown by many urban people.

Since proxemic and distemic spatial organization, then, are cognitive processes not immutably attached to external objects in the landscape, but only influenced by them, the kind of urban form I am advocating cannot be established only in physical terms. The hierarchy of private-public spaces I am suggesting is in, and of, itself hardly new. All good new town and community designs more or less follow some such structure. In fact, the difficulties with Perry's neighborhood unit concept, for example, have not arisen because it lacks formal structure and clear boundaries, but on the contrary because in its applications it has not provided for all the cognitive as well as functional variables that appear in plural societies. The proxemic—distemic model is intended to draw attention to some complexities that are not implicit in either a physical or a social view of urban behavior taken separately. One of these is the probability that different social groups will perceive different environments even while occupying the same space simultaneously, and that the same group will perceive different spatial relationships in the same area under different conditions. If one is driving through a commercial strip at the end of a day when tired and hungry, one will perceive both restaurants and motels which would remain unnoticed in the hodge-podge of signs on a Sunday afternoon ride. One would also not perceive an office building which might have leaped to attention at nine a.m. After a good meal, one is more likely to perceive motels (or the lack of them) than restaurants.

The complexities are illustrated in a small pilot study which attempted to explore the possibility of relating Cassel's findings discussed in Chapter 7 to perceived boundaries and the relative physical and social health of a community (Greenbie, Tuthill, and Brown, 1973). With very limited resources the study was methodologically inadequate and inconclusive regarding its main objectives, but despite limited data it illustrates well my proxemic—distemic thesis, even though originally that was not considered to be part of the project.

In order to try to get a working definition of "boundaries" we had selected four groups of boundary perceivers, the first of which was ourselves. Two of us who did not know our subject city (Springfield, Mass.) located on a map the obvious physical boundaries, such as highways, railroads, ravines, large industrial areas, and open spaces, which might be conceived as community boundaries, deliberately introducing a physical bias which might be expected to influence a planner. Our perceptions are shown in Fig. 33.

Our second study group consisted of eight taxi drivers in the downtown dispatcher's office, who were asked to identify neighborhoods with names, the center of those neighborhoods, principal streets and boundaries. Their perceptions of the city's main neighborhoods are shown in Fig. 34. The same process was repeated with eleven public health nurses. Their perception of neighborhood boundaries is shown in Fig. 35. We then interviewed, with the

170

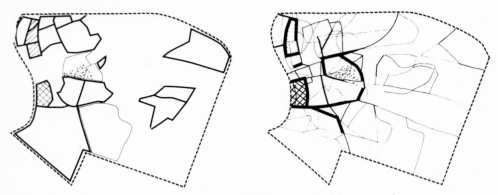

Fig. 33. Neighborhood boundaries in Springfield as perceived by researchers.

Fig. 34. Neighborhood boundaries in Springfield as perceived by taxi drivers.

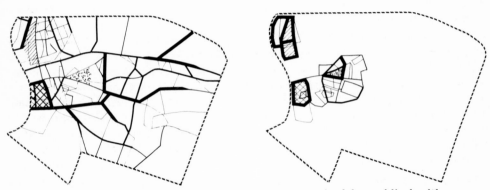

Fig. 35. Neighborhood boundaries in Springfield as perceived by public health nurses.

Fig. 36. Neighborhood boundaries in three areas of Springfield as perceived by residents.

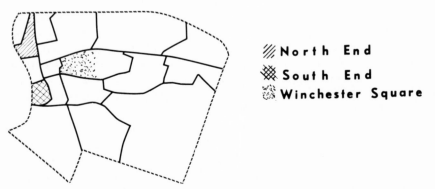

⬚ North End
⬚ South End
⬚ Winchester Square

Fig. 37. The officially recognized "planning districts" in Springfield. (Figs. 33—37 re-drawn by Margaret Kent from authors' originals.)

help of the public health nurses, approximately seventy-five residents of three areas which had appeared to be most clearly defined as neighborhoods. Their perceptions of community boundaries are shown in Fig. 36. The various line weights in Figs. 34—36 correspond to various levels of agreement, the finest line representing a single opinion, and the heaviest a majority one. Finally, we took the City Planning Department's "Planning District Map" to represent the local planners' view of city neighborhood structure. This is presented as Fig. 37.

A comparative view of these shows quite strikingly how varied the cognitive maps of neighborhood boundaries can be and underscores the well-known difficulties of defining "communities" solely in these terms. But two relationships are immediately suggested. One is that boundaries will be perceived in terms of the perceiver's purposes in looking at them. This is hardly a new discovery, but it is one worth rediscovering. The other is that the perceived areas become smaller and more detailed when boundaries are viewed in residential terms, in other words as they verge toward what I have been calling proxemic space. The taxi drivers, whose relation to the areas may be considered largely a distemic one, nevertheless expressed clear agreement only regarding the downtown area near their dispatcher's office, where most of the daily travels occurred. On the other hand, the public health nurses, whose relationship to the city was also primarily distemic, but whose work presumably includes a measure of proxemic empathy for various groups, had a much broader and more complex view of the city than any other group, including us, the researchers, and the city planners (as shown in their map, which, strictly speaking, is not really a cognitive map). Lynch (1960) looked at the various kinds of landscape features with which we started out, and found remarkable agreement concerning edges, barriers, nodes, and pathways (the same elements with which Hediger found animals to structure their territory). The consistency of the Lynch image can be attributed, not only to the cultural homogeneity of his sample, but I think also to the relatively neutral attitude his respondents had towards the subject. I suspect this is one basic shortcoming of most preference studies which do not make adequate allowance for various motivational attitudes. In other words, it is not merely what people will choose objectively when all other things are equal that counts most in their decision making, but rather what objectives they have and what problems they have to cope with in any given time and place. In our small study we deliberately selected groups with different motivational attitudes toward the area, including our own.

Of the three areas that emerged as having some sort of identity, the area due east of the center variously called "Winchester Square" or "Hill McKnight" had few consistently defined boundaries, although it was full of barriers which were also the least coherent set of physical edges in all the study areas. The area known variously as "The North End" or "Brightwood" was somewhat more consistently defined by all respondents, and it also was more coherently bounded physically, although it was badly lacerated by a railroad, interstate highways, and urban renewal, and was in the process of radical population change. However, the area called the "South End" was nearly unanimously identified as a neighborhood by all five subject groups, including the Planning District Map, and by that single name. This was also an area that was unmistakably bounded physically, especially in the predominantly residential parts of it which consist of a series of dead end streets running off a major commercial artery and terminating in steep bluffs (see Figs. 38 and 39). The "South End" is a traditionally Italian ethnic area. Some residents mentioned a small sub-area with particular enthusiasm as "a good place to live." It is an architecturally undistinctive but very cloistered area a few blocks square, called "Hollywood," which, as Figs. 40 and 41 suggest, is visually enclosed in all directions. It very closely fits Newman's description of a "defensible space," and its defensibility was brought home to us by the fact that while we had been conspicuously photographing all the other areas without drawing much interest, in this area our cameras attracted some inhospitable attention, as did we ourselves, and one proprietor angrily refused to let himself or his shop be photographed. Subsequent information confirms that the area is considered a good safe place to live, and that the residents are quite concerned that it remain so.

The fact that we found areas which were clearly bounded physically but which were not considered by anybody to be neighborhoods, even though they contained residences, underscores what should hardly be necessary to point out, that the mere existence of physical edges, or any other physical characteristic, will not in and of itself determine a neighborhood. However, the opposite conclusion, that such physical elements will not significantly influence behavior, which has been advanced by some urban theorists, including many "social" planners, does not follow at all, as well argued by Michelson (1970). Rapoport (1969) shows that the relation of cultural form to space in the case of house form is not deterministic, but nevertheless one expresses aspects of the other. In this case, I believe the evidence suggests that the availability of clearly bounded physical areas will increase the likelihood that homogeneous populations already predisposed toward social cohesion, such as ethnic groups, will seek them out in proportion to the degree to which ethnic or other proxemic community identity overrides other, possibly distemic, needs and objectives. I think this can be supported by a look at the environments of most traditional, stable ethnic communities in any of our cities. For instance, Boston's Italian North End and Irish South Boston are both essentially peninsulas, now separated from the rest of the city in the first instance by an elevated highway and in the second by a bridge. The same is true of Bayonne, New Jersey. There is some irony in the case of Boston's North End. Although the construction of such highways has been a major sore point among residents of so many low-income urban areas, and such isolation from the city is an anathema to urban designers, I have been

Fig. 38. The eastern residential side of Springfield's South End is clearly bounded by bluffs at which terminate dead end streets.

told by a Boston planner that the North Enders there expressed considerable concern at a public hearing over proposals that the raised highway be put underground. They were afraid that a major barrier to incursion from the re-developed area would be removed.

Fig. 39. All respondents agreed that the southern boundary of Springfield's South End is marked by this statue of Columbus, but one woman said it was "Kennedy." Perhaps a proxemic hero is a hero, whether he discovers America in 1492 or rediscovers it in 1960.

174

Fig. 40.

Fig. 41.

Figs. 40 and 41. Defensible space: the sub-community of Hollywood in Springfield's
South End is considered "a good place to live."

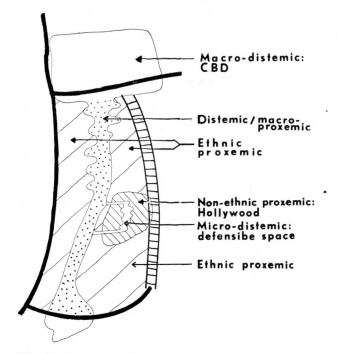

Fig. 42. Proxemic—distemic hierarchy in Springfield's South End.

But the other side of the proxemic—distemic relationship is also suggested by our study. The highly bounded, socially homogeneous, ethnic South End did not lack distemic spaces and relationships. On the contrary, it revealed these much more than the other two areas, both internally and externally. In Fig. 42 I have tried to illustrate my theory of the proxemic—distemic hierarchy as it appeared in the South End. This area has its own distemic space in the Main Street spine, which has a variety of commercial establishments and some industry. The proxemic aspects of this street are observable in its overall ethnic flavor, an Italian market, restaurants, bars, and lunch counters. This might be called *macro-proxemic*. But these are also patronized by outsiders, and the street is a minor arterial connecting directly with the CBD, which has been renovated through unusually successful and lively urban renewal projects. Thus, at the same time it can be considered distemic. In fact the distemic heart of the city is the northern boundary of this community, and the CBD can be called macro-distemic in this hierarchy. At the other end of the scale, the sub-community of Hollywood has its own main street, with some minor service type shops and a more or less micro-scale distemic center, the Hollywood Cafe. The proxemic character of this area has little visible ethnic quality, not nearly as much as some of the other residential cul-de-sacs, but rather the area appears to be a community of limited liability, as in Suttles' model. Taking the South End as a whole, the

Fig. 43. In contrast to the South End, neither older residents in the French Canadian section of Springfield's North End nor newer residents in the Puerto Rican section of the North End mentioned this statue at an obvious physical center. (Ironically, it is a Spanish-American War Memorial.) But several mentioned the Greek church behind it. The church maintains an active congregation, but one that is for the most part no longer resident in the area.

Fig. 44. Some French Canadians expressed some bitterness at the fate of a former library near the church, but the Puerto Ricans seemed unaware of it as a landmark.

hierarchical relationship of bounded areas with distemic spaces for increasing levels of trans-cultural interaction are suggested by Fig. 42.

The North End apparently had at one time a somewhat similar set of relationships. Memorial Square had constituted a social and cultural, rather than commercial, distemic center for the community, with its church and library, and a nodal arterial intersection, with North Main Street linking it too with the CBD. That link has now been interrupted by an east—west expressway that constitutes a visual barrier on the one hand, and deflects traffic away from the area on the other. Memorial Square is no longer a center, and its cultural symbols, to the extent that they survive at all, belong to a community population now isolated from it to the north. The church maintains an active congregation, but most of the parishioners now live elsewhere. The new and/or transient population in the immediate area have so little to do with this group that the church plays no distemic role for them.

In the Winchester Square area, distemic as well as proxemic relationships are fragmented by strong barriers that are neither socially nor physically functional and, therefore, are not seen as boundaries. The Square itself has remained a somewhat marginal commercial industrial node, but for a number of reasons, including heavy through traffic on State Street, it is more of a barrier than a distemic center. Since our study was conducted, a change in traffic routing has aggravated this problem, forcing some of the remaining establishments out of business, even though the area has been a target for Model Cities and other rehabilitation efforts which in some sections of the area have been more or less successful.

It is tempting to try to lay out a hypothetical town, city, or neighborhood using my proxemic—distemic model, but I shall limit my illustrations of it to diagrams for the same reason that Ebenezer Howard did. It is rarely useful to illustrate one generality with another; one can only move from the general to the particular or vice versa. This model must be applied in a way that is highly specific to the people and places involved, and be tested on that basis to be worth pursuing further. In any case, it is easier to recognize these relationships where they have emerged over time than to design them from scratch. If human social behavior is an evolutionary process with a history which is both phylogenetic and ontogenetic, as I believe it is, the urban designer-planner, like the landscape architect, must approach his problem like a gardener who can select, prune, and direct his organic raw material, but cannot manipulate it to the same extent as the architect who creates out of inorganic steel or stone. It is a humbler process than is the work of building architects and engineers. But like building architecture, the creation of human communities is still primarily art, requiring above of all an empathetic as well as an intellectual understanding of the building material, which in this case includes other human beings. For environments to serve experientially-whole human beings, they must be designed by people able to use a whole brain; not merely their logical forebrains, but also their draco-limbic brains. Such professionals approach their task with the view that the art of creating cities is inseparable from the art of living in them.

In my diagram of a proxemic—distemic version of Howard's Garden City, I have shown "science" as circular vectors concentric with distemic space. But I have shown "art" as radials, cutting across both proxemic and distemic space on all levels. Science, in its pursuit of general principles and properties, is, as we have seen, the child of the conceptual, peculiarly human, brain. The function of art, in my view, is to bridge MacLean's phylogenetic generation gap by integrating what rational man sees with what draco-limbic man knows. Such art is the only means we have to give primal, territorial man an emotional home without violating distemic space, and to enable him to explore conceptual space without violating natural space.

Explicitly in the classic new town model, and implicitly, if often unsuccessfully, in the suburban ones, natural space has been presented as having something of the same meaning urban parks once had for all classes. This is not always true, but natural space has another transcendent urban function. If there is one "instinct" in human beings that must have universal expression, surely it is that which ties us to the larger cosmic space we share. Colin Turnbull (1972) has found that even the powerful human propensity for group cooperation, which both sides in the nature—nurture controversy will concede is a most persistent human characteristic, will not show itself when the environment ceases to permit its expression. Nevertheless, his "Mountain People," who let old and young die without a sign of human compassion, who could not cooperate sufficiently even to copulate, and who, like Calhoun's mice, faced extinction, retained a last flicker of humanity in their wordless love for their mountain. The final component of my model is that distemic relations can not only hold our split brains together, but also tie us to the gravitational center of the earth from which we came and must return, and the skies into which we seem to be genetically programmed to peer.

As a final word I must reiterate that I do not offer this hypothetical design for diversity as a solution to our problems, but rather as a frame of reference for coming to grips with the prerequisites for solving them. This model certainly cannot assure anybody equality and justice. There have been, and are now, urban environments which are well-defined proxemically and distemically in which some go hungry, or may starve, while others live in luxury. I merely suggest that such structuring is a precondition for any viable society, just or unjust, and that a theoretically just system which will not work is something short of real justice. Neither the cultural diversity that makes life interesting nor the technical cooperation that makes it possible in our time can be accomplished by isolated subcultures confronting each other across a no-man's land between class barriers. The only choice we have is to structure the environment so as to protect distemic space from the incursions of tribal warriors out of adjacent proxemia, while recognizing that on an important level of experience we all remain tribal warriors. Most of us do not wish, and few of us could if we did wish, to be otherwise. We must do something with that.

An "intellectual deviant" who has made some contribution to the re-thinking of neo-technic man on the subject of waste, John Sheaffer (Bauer, 1969), defines pollution as a *resource out of place.* I think many of our socio-spatial ills are a consequence of cultural and conceptual resources out of place, which leads to Esser's "social pollution." Territorial aggressiveness is an important source of energy, which, like other forms of energy, can be useful or dangerous depending on how it is released. Like all energy in nature it can be converted, diverted, or regulated and conserved, but cannot be destroyed.

Territory was originally designed, or at least used, by evolution as a means of resource management relative to population size. But *Homo sapiens* transforms his instincts as he does everything around him. Man must still control his numbers, and very soon; but this has become a technological problem, since without technology our numbers would have been limited long ago. That problem cannot be solved on a territorial basis, even if that was the way our vertebrate ancestors solved it. For cultural man, territorial and status-ranking impulses are now no more limited to population control than sexual impulses are to population expansion. Like sex, to which it is so closely related, draco-limbic social-territoriality underlies our most noble and humane impulses as well as our meaner ones. It finds its expression in love and devotion to mate and progeny, and it provides energy and motivation for art, invention, statesmanship, revolutionary zeal, patriotism, religious fervor, and idealism of every sort. To assert that territorial impulses can only generate hostility, exploitation, and war, is like suggesting that sex must lead to rape. Normal uncrowded animals, as we have seen, commit neither war nor rape. Looking to art, we find in the songs, stories, and pictures which have recorded the history of ordinary people that the two most persistent themes are love and longing for union with the opposite sex, and love for homeland, for territory.

To recognize this is not to overlook that much of the human race lacks economic necessities, or to ignore that millions more may lack them soon, but to confirm what so many these days are proclaiming, that this too is partly a result of misdirected values. I do not believe a fairer distribution of resources (which can become technically possible only if population is controlled) is dependent on eliminating the urge for territory, dominance, and the excitement of competition. It can only come, it seems to me, if at all, by taking a lesson from the rest of nature where, according to the theories we have discussed, other animals compete not directly for resources, but for conventional tokens. Only in a world where excessive numbers lead to scarcity need the tokens represent necessity.

On the other hand, the profound attachments to home places that motivate us along with our fellow beings do not suggest that such a wandering mongrel as *Homo sapiens* can be understood only in terms of physical territories. My conclusion is that where there must be a choice, probably most people will choose *social cohesion in terms of proxemic space over distemic opportunity, but when the two combine in complementary ways the most creative force in life will come into play.* As planners and designers of the human habitat our first responsibility is to protect the group identity. Our second is to keep it from being a prison.

Selected bibliography

Adams, R.M., 1960. The origins of cities. Sci. Am., September: 3—10.

Alland Jr., A., 1967. Evolution and Human Behavior. The Natural History Press, New York, N.Y.

Almond, R. and Esser, A.H., 1965. Tablemate choices of psychiatric patients: a technique for measuring social contact. J. Nerv. Ment. Dis., 141: 68—82.

Amato, P.W., 1970. Elitism and settlement patterns of the Latin American City. J. Am. Inst. Plann., 36: 96—105.

Anderson, M., 1964. The Federal Bulldozer. The MIT Press, Cambridge, Mass.

Ardrey, R., 1970. The Social Contract. Atheneum, New York, N.Y.

Ardrey, R., 1966. The Territorial Imperative. Atheneum, New York, N.Y.

Ardrey, R., 1961. African Genesis. Atheneum, New York, N.Y.

Bailey, T.P., 1899. Bibliographic references in ethology. Univ. Calif. Lib. Bull., No. 13.

Bailey, T.P., 1898—1899. Ethology: standpoint, method, tentative results. Univ. Calif. Chron., 1: 539—551, and (1899) 2: 30—34.

Barker, R.G., 1968. Ecological Psychology: Concepts and Methods for Studying the Environment of Human Behavior. Stanford Univ. Press, Stanford, Calif.

Barker, R.G., 1951. One Boy's Day. Harper and Row, New York, N.Y.

Barker, R.G. and Schoggen, P., 1973. Qualities of Community Life. Jossey-Bass, San Francisco, Calif.

Barnett, S.A., 1967. Instinct and Intelligence: Behavior of Animals and Man. Prentice-Hall, Englewood Cliffs, N.J.

Barth, F., 1969. Ethnic Groups and Boundaries: The Social Organization of Cultural Difference. Little, Brown and Co, Boston, Mass.

Bauer Engineering, Inc., 1969. Muskegon County Plan for Managing Waste Water. Muskegon, Mich.

Bechtel, R.B., 1974. The undermanned environment: a universal theory? Proc. Environ. Des. Res. Assoc., 5th Int. EDRA Conf., Milwaukee, Wis., in press.

Bechtel, R.B., 1970. A behavioral comparison of urban and small town environments. Proc. 2nd Ann. Environ. Des. Res. Assoc. Conf., Pittsburgh, Pa., p. 347.

Bell, G. and Tyrwhitt, J., 1972. Human Identity in the Urban Environment. Penguin, Baltimore, Md.

Bellush, J. and Hausknecht, M. (Editors), 1967. Urban Renewal: People, Politics and Planning. Doubleday Anchor, New York, N.Y.

Berger, B.H., 1960. Working Class Suburb. Univ. California Press, Berkeley, Calif.

Berger, M. (Editor), 1963. The New Metropolis in the Arab World. Allied Publishers, New Delhi.

Berkowitz, L., 1969. Simple views of aggression. Am. Sci., 57: 372—383.

Blossom, R., 1973. A colorful chief, Hart served Amherst for 38 years. Amherst Record, December 26th.

Brody, E.B. (Editor), 1970. Behavior in New Environments: Adaptation of Migrant Populations. Sage Publications, Beverly Hills, Calif.

Calhoun, J.B., 1973. What sort of box? Man Environ. Syst., 3: C1—C28.

Calhoun, J.B., 1971. Space and strategy of life. In: A.H. Esser (Editor), Behavior and Environment. Plenum Press, New York, N.Y., pp. 329—387.

Calhoun, J.B., 1970. Space and scale: insights from animal studies relating to the archi-
tecture and contents of housing for the aged. In: L.A. Pastalan and D.H. Carson
(Editors), Spatial Behavior of Older People. Inst. Gerontology, Univ. Mich., Ann Arbor,
Mich., Chapter 11.

Calhoun, J.B., 1969. Promotion of Man. Global Systems Dynamics. Int. Symp., Char-
lottesville, Va., pp. 36—58.

Calhoun, J.B., 1968a. Design for mammalian living. Archit. Assoc. Q., 1 : 3 : 1—12.

Calhoun, J.B., 1968b. Environmental control over four major paths of mammalian
evolution. In: J.M. Thoday and A.S. Parkes (Editors), Genetic and Environmental
Influences on Behavior. Oliver and Boyd, Edinburgh.

Calhoun, J.B., 1965—1966. A glance into the garden. Three Papers on Human Ecology.
Mills College Assembly Series, Oakland, Calif.

Calhoun, J.B., 1952. The social aspect of population dynamics. J. Mammal., 33: 139—159.

Callan, H., 1970. Ethology and Society; Towards an Anthropological View. Clarendon
Press, Oxford.

Canaday, J., 1972. A wasp's progress. N.Y. Times Mag., March 19th, p. 32.

Canty, D., 1969. A Single Society; Alternatives to Urban Apartheid, Praeger, New York,
N.Y.

Caplow, T. and Forman, R., 1950. Neighborhood interaction in a homogeneous community. Am. Sociol. Rev., 15: 357—366.

Carrel, A., 1935. Man the Unknown. Harper and Brothers, New York, N.Y.

Cassel, J., 1971. Health consequences of population density and crowding. Rapid Population Growth. Nat. Acad. Sci., Johns Hopkins Press, Baltimore, Md., Chapter 12.

Cassel, J., 1970a. An epidemiological perspective of psycho-social factors in disease
etiology. Paper presented at Am. Publ. Health Assoc. Meet., Houston, Texas, November 1970.

Cassel, J., 1970b. Physical illness in response to stress. In: S. Levine and N.A. Scotch
(Editors), Social Stress. Aldine-Atherton Press, Chicago, Ill.

Cassel, J. and Tyroler, H.A., 1961. Epidemiological studies of culture change. I. Health
status and recency of industrialization. Arch. Environ. Health, 3: 25.

Chermayeff, S. and Alexander, C., 1963. Community and Privacy. Doubleday, New York,
N.Y.

Chomsky, N., 1968. Language and Mind. Harcourt, Brace, and World, New York, N.Y.

Chomsky, N., 1965. Aspects of the Theory of Syntax. The MIT Press, Cambridge, Mass.

Christenson, W.N. and Hinkle Jr., L.E., 1961. Differences in illness and prognostic signs
in two groups of young men. J. Am. Med. Assoc., 177: 247—253.

Clark, S.D., 1966. The Suburban Society. Univ. Toronto Press, Toronto, Ont.

Clynes, M., 1971. Sentics: precision of direct emotion communication. Paper presented at
Am. Assoc. Adv. Sci. Symp., Sentics, Brain Function and Human Values, Philadelphia,
Pa.

Clynes, M., 1969. Toward a theory of Man: precision of essentic form in living communication. In: N. Leibovic and J.C. Eccles (Editors), Information Processing in the
Nervous System. Springer-Verlag, New York, N.Y., Chapter 10.

Cohen, Y.A. (Editor), 1968. Man in Adaptation: the Cultural Present. Aldine, Chicago,
Ill.

Commoner, B., 1971. The Closing Circle. A. Knopf, New York, N.Y.

Darling, F.F., 1937. A Herd of Red Deer; A Study in Animal Behavior. O.U.P., London.

Darwin, C., 1910. The Origin of Species. D. Appleton, New York, N.Y.

Darwin, C., 1872. The Expression of Emotions in Man and Animals. Univ. Chicago Press,
Chicago, Ill. (new edition 1965).

Davidoff, L. and Davidoff, P., 1971. The suburbs have to open their gates. N.Y. Times
Mag., November 7th.

Davidoff, L., Davidoff, P. and Newton Gold, N., 1970. Suburban action: advocate planning for an open society. J. Am. Inst. Plann., 36: 12—21.

De Jonge, D., 1967—68. Applied hodology. Landscape, Winter: 10—11.

De Jonge, D., 1967. Some Notes on Sociological Research in the Field of Housing (unpubl. ms.), Center Archit. Res., Technol. Univ. Delft.

DeLong, A.J., 1970. Coding behavior and levels of cultural integration. Proc. 2nd Ann. Environ. Des. Res. Assoc. Conf., Pittsburgh, Pa., pp. 354—365.

DeLong, A.J., 1970. Dominance-territorial relations in a small group. Environ. Behav., September: 171—199.

DeLong, A.J., 1970. Seating position and perceived characteristics of members of a small group. Cornell J. Soc. Relat., 5: 134—151.

DeVore, I. (Editor), 1965. Primate Behavior; Field Studies of Monkeys and Apes. Holt, Rinehart and Winston, New York, N.Y.

Dimond, S.J., 1970. The Social Behavior of Animals. Harper Colophon Books, New York, N.Y.

Dobriner, W.M., 1963. Class in Suburbia. Prentice-Hall, Englewood Cliffs, N.J.

Dobzhansky, T., 1964. Heredity and the Nature of Man. Harcourt, Brace and World, New York, N.Y.

Donaldson, S., 1969. The Suburbian Myth. Columbia Univ. Press. New York, N.Y.

Downs, A., 1973. Opening Up the Suburbs: An Urban Strategy for America. Yale Univ. Press, New Haven, Conn.

Dubos, R., 1968a. The human environment in technological societies. Rockefeller Rev., July—August.

Dubos, R., 1968b. So Human an Animal. Charles Scribner, New York, N.Y.

Dubos, R., 1965. Man Adapting. Yale University Press, New Haven, Conn.

Dunnet, G.M. (in press). A Field Study of Local Populations of the Brush-Tailed Possum Trichosurus Vulpecula in Eastern Australia. Taylor and Francis, London.

Durant, W., 1926. The Study of Philosophy. Simon and Schuster, New York, N.Y.

Eibl-Eibesfeldt, I., 1971. Transcultural patterns of ritualized contact behavior. In: A.H. Esser (Editor), Behavior and Environment. Plenum Press, New York, N.Y., pp. 238—246.

Eibl-Eibesfeldt, I., 1970. Ethology: The Biology of Behavior. Holt, New York, N.Y.

Eibl-Eibesfeldt, I., 1968. Ethology. In: D.L. Sills (Editor), International Encyclopedia of the Social Sciences, Vol. 5. Macmillan, New York, N.Y., pp. 186—193.

Erikson, E.H., 1974. Dimensions of a New Identity: The 1973 Jefferson Lectures in the Humanities. W.W. Norton, New York, N.Y.

Erikson, E.H., 1966. Ontogeny of ritualization. In: R.M. Lowenstein et al. (Editors), Psychoanalysis — A General Psychology: Essays in Honor of Heinz Hartmann. Int. Univ. Press, New York, N.Y., pp. 601—621.

Esser, A.H., 1973. Cottage fourteen: dominance and territoriality in a group of institutionalized boys. Small Group Behavior, 4: 131—146.

Esser, A.H., 1972a. Strategies for research in man—environment systems. In: W.M. Smith (Editor), Ecology of Human Living Environments. Green Bay, Univ. of Wisconsin.

Esser, A.H., 1972b. Environmental design needs empathy to combat social pollution. In: W. Preser (Editor), Environmental Design Perspectives. M-ES-FOCUS Series.

Esser, A.H., 1971a. Social pollution. Soc. Educ., 35: 10—18.

Esser, A.H., 1971b. The importance of defining of spatial behavior parameters. In: A.H. Esser (Editor), Behavior and Environment. Plenum Press, New York, N.Y., pp. 1—8.

Esser, A.H., 1971c. The psychopathology of crowding in institutions for the mentally ill and retarded. Proc. 5th World Congr. Psychiatry, Mexico City.

Esser, A.H., 1970a. Interactional hierarchy and power structure on a psychiatric ward: ethological studies on dominance behavior in a total institution. In: C. Hutt and S.J. Hutt (Editors), Behaviour Studies in Psychiatry. Pergamon Press, Oxford.

Esser, A.H., 1970b. Evolving neurologic substrates of essentic forms. In: M. Clynes (Editor), Am. Assoc. Adv. Sci. Symp., Biocybernetics of the Dynamic Communication of Emotions and Qualities, Chicago, Ill.

Esser, A.H., 1968. Dominance hierarchy and clinical course of psychiatrically hospitalized boys. Child Develop., 39: 147—157.

Esser, A.H. and Etter, T.L., 1966. Automated location recording on a psychiatric ward. Am. Zool., 6 : 4 : 251.

Esser, A.H. et al., 1965. Territoriality of patients on a research ward. In: J. Wortis (Editor), Recent Advances in Biological Psychiatry, Vol. VII. Plenum Press, New York, N.Y. Also in H.M. Proshansky et al. (Editors), Environmental Psychology, Holt, Rinehart and Winston, New York, N.Y., 1970.

Eysenck, H.J., 1973a. IQ, social class and educational policy. Change, September: 38—42.

Eysenck, H.J., 1973b. The Inequality of Man. Temple Smith, London.

Feshback, S. and Singer, R.D., 1971. Television and Aggression. Jossey-Bass, San Francisco, Calif.

Fischer, F., 1971. Ten phases of the animal path: behavior in familiar situations. In: A.H. Esser (Editor), Behavior and Environment. Plenum Press, New York, N.Y., pp. 9—21.

Fischer, F., 1965. Der Wohnraum. Verlag für Architektur im Artemis Verlag, Zurich. (English transl., The Living Space, mimeographed ms., 1967.)

Fischer, R., 1971. A cartography of the ecstatic and meditative states. Sci., 174: 897—904.

Fletcher, R., 1957. Instinct in Man. Int. Univ. Press, New York, N.Y.

Flynn, J.P. and Chungming Chi, C., 1971. Neural pathways associated with hypothalmically elicited attack behavior in cats. Sci., 171: 703—706.

Flynn, J.P. et al., 1971. Changes in sensory and motor systems during centrally elicited attack. Behav. Sci., 16: 1—19.

Flynn, J.P. et al., 1970. Neural mechanisms involved in a cat's attack on a rat. The Neural Control of Behavior. Academic Press, New York, N.Y.

Forde, C.D., 1943. Habitat, Economy, and Society. Harcourt, Brace and Co., New York, N.Y.

Fried, M., 1963. Grieving for a lost home. In: L.J. Duhl (Editor), The Urban Condition. Basic Books, New York, N.Y., pp. 151—171.

Fried, M. and Gleicher, P., 1961. Some sources of residential satisfaction. J. Am. Inst. Plann., 27: 305—315.

Galbraith, J.K., 1971. The unbelievable happens in Bengal. N.Y. Times Mag., October 31st, p. 13.

Galbraith, J.K., 1967, The New Industrial State. Houghton-Mifflin, Boston, Mass.

Gans, H.J., 1973. More Equality. Pantheon Books, New York, N.Y.

Gans, H.J., 1968. People and Plans: Essays on Urban Problems and Solutions. Basic Books, New York, N.Y.

Gans, H.J., 1967. The Levittowners. Random House, New York, N.Y.

Gans, H.J., 1962. The Urban Villagers. Macmillan, New York, N.Y.

Gans, H.J., 1961. Planning and social life. Friendship and neighbor relations in suburban communities. J. Am. Inst. Plann., 27: 134—140.

Gardner, R.A. and Gardner, B.T., 1965. Teaching sign language to a chimpanzee. Sci., 165: 664—672.

Geddes, P., 1915. Cities in Evolution; An Introduction to the Town Planning Movement and to the Study of Civics. Williams and Norgate, London (new and rev. ed. 1949).

Geertz, C., 1965. The impact of the concept of culture on the concept of Man. In: J.R. Platt (Editor), New Views of Man. Univ. Chicago Press, Chicago, Ill.

Glazer, N. and Moynihan, D., 1963. Beyond the Melting Pot. The MIT Press, Cambridge, Mass., 1970, preface to 2nd ed.

Golding, W., 1959. Lord of the Flies. G.P. Putnam, New York, N.Y.

Golfman, E., 1971. Relations in Public, Microstudies of the Public Order. Basic Books, New York, N.Y.

Goodall, J. Van L., 1971. In the Shadow of Man. Houghton-Mifflin, Boston, Mass.

Goodall, J. Van L., 1965. Chimpanzees of the Gombe Stream Reserve. In: I. DeVore (Editor), Primate Behavior. Holt, Reinhart and Winston, New York, N.Y., pp. 425—473.

Gordon, M.M., 1964. Assimilation in American Life: the Role of Race, Religion, and National Origins. O.U.P., New York, N.Y.

Greeley, A.M., 1971. Why Can't They Be Like Us? E.P. Dutton, New York, N.Y.

Greenbie, B.B., 1974. Social territory, community health, and urban planning. J. Am. Inst. Plann., 40: 74—82.

Greenbie, B.B., 1973. An ethological approach to community design. In: W.F.E. Preiser (Editor), Environmental Design Research, Vol. I, Selected Papaers, 4th Int. EDRA Conf. Dowden, Hutchinson and Ross, Stroudsburg, Pa., pp. 14—23.

Greenbie, B.B., 1971a. What can we learn from other animals? Behavioral biology and the ecology of cities. J. Am. Inst. Plann., 37: 162—168.

Greenbie, B.B., 1970. Some implications for urban design from studies of animal behavior. Proc. 2nd Ann. Environ. Des. Res. Assoc. Conf., Pittburgh, Pa., pp. 366—371.

Greenbie, B.B., 1969. New house or new neighborhood? A survey of priorities among home owners in Madison. Wis. Land Econ., 45: 359—364.

Greenbie, B.B., Tuthill, R.W. and Brown, M.A., 1973. Contrasting Cognitive Maps of City Neighborhoods by Diverse Segments of the Population (unpubl. ms.). A summary to appear in E. Zube, R.O. Brush and J.G. Fabos (Editors), Landscape Assessment: Values, Perceptions and Resources. Dowden, Hutchinson and Ross, Stroudsburg, Pa., in press.

Grouse Research in Scotland, 1969. 13th Progress Report. The Nature Conservancy, Blackhall Banchory, Kincardineshire.

Gump, P.V., 1971. The behavioral setting: a promising unit for environmental designers. Landscape Archit., 61: 130—134.

Gutman, R. (Editor), 1972. People and Buildings. Basic Books, New York, N.Y.

Hall, E.T., 1974. Handbook for Proxemic Research. Soc. Anthropol. Vis. Commun., Washington, D.C.

Hall, E.T., 1968. Proxemics. Curr. Anthropol., 9: 83—108.

Hall, E.T., 1966. The Hidden Dimension. Doubleday, New York, N.Y.

Hall, E.T., 1959. The Silent Language. Doubleday, New York, N.Y.

Hallowell, A.I., 1955. Culture and Experience. Schocken Books, New York, N.Y.

Harlow, H.F., 1962. The heterosexual affectional system in monkeys. Am. Psychologist, 17: 1—9.

Harlow, H.F., 1959. Love in infant monkeys. Psychobiology: Readings from Scientific American. Freeman, San Francisco, Calif., Part I, Chapter 7.

Hart, R.A. and Moore, G.T., 1973. The development of spatial cognition: a review. In: R.M. Downs and D. Stea (Editors), Image and Environment. Aldine, Chicago, Ill.

Havelock, E., 1971. War as a way of life among the Greeks. Lecture at the University of Massachusetts, Amherst, Classics Department, May 6th.

Hawley, A.N. (Editor), 1968. Roderick D. McKenzie on Human Ecology: Selected Readings. Univ. Chicago Press, Chicago, Ill.

Heckscher, A., 1962. The Public Happiness. Atheneum, New York, N.Y.

Hediger, H., 1949. Saugetier-Territorien und ihre Markierung. Bijd. Dierk., 28: 172—184.

Herrnstein, R., 1971. IQ. The Atlantic Monthly, 228: 43—58.

Herrnstein, R., 1967. Introduction to J.B. Watson, Behavior: An Introduction to Comparative Psychology. Holt, Rinehart and Winston, New York, N.Y., pp. xi—xxxi.

Hinde, R.A., 1966. Animal Behavior: A Synthesis of Ethology and Comparative Psychology. McGraw-Hill, New York, N.Y.

Howard, E., 1946. Garden Cities of Tomorrow. Faber and Faber, London. (First published in 1898 as Tomorrow: A Peaceful Path to Real Reform.)

Howard, E., 1948. Territory in Bird Life. Collins, London. (New ed. 1964 by Atheneum.)

Howell, F.C., 1965. Early Man. Time—Life Books, New York, N.Y.

Hoyt, H.R., 1939. The Structure and Growth of Residential Neighborhoods in Amercian Cities. U.S.G.P.O., Washington, D.C.

Hunter, F., 1953. Community Power Structure. Univ. N.C. Press, Chapel Hill, N.C.

Hutt, S.J. and Hutt, C., 1971. Direct Observation and Measurement of Behavior. Chas. C. Thomas, Springfield, Ill.

Hutt, S.J. and Hutt, C. (Editors), 1970. Behavior Studies in Psychiatry. Pergamon Press, Oxford.

Huxley, J., 1934. A natural experiment on the territorial instinct. Brit. Birds, 27: 270—277.

Huxley, J., 1914. Courtship of the Great-Crested Grebe. Proc. Zool. Soc.., London, pp. 491—562.

Iltis, H.H., 1972. Shepherds leading sheep to slaughter; the extinction of species and the destruction of ecosystems. Am. Biol. Teacher, 34: 201—205, 221.

Iltis, H.H., 1970. Corn and cows are not enough! The uses of diversity. Paper presented at the 1st Nat. Congr. Optimum Pop. Environ., Chicago, Ill., June 7th—11th, 1970.

Iltis, H.H., 1968. The optimum human environment and its relation to modern agricultural preoccupations. Biologist, 5: 114—125.

Iltis, H.H., Loucks, O.L. and Andrews, P., 1970. Criteria for an optimum human environment. Bull. Atom. Sci., 26: 2.

Jacobs, J., 1961. The Death and Life of Great American Cities. Random House, New York, N.Y.

Janowitz, M., 1967. The Community Press in an Urban Setting: The Social Elements of Urbanism. 2nd Ed., Univ. Chicago Press, Chicago, Ill.

Johnson, E.A.J., 1970. The Organization of Space in Developing Countries. Harvard Univ. Press, Cambridge, Mass.

Johnson, S.K., 1973. Growing old alone together. N.Y. Times Mag., November 11th.

Jung, C.G., 1964. Man and his Symbols. Pergamon Press, New York, N.Y.

Jung, C.G., 1958. The Undiscovered Self (transl. from the German by R.F.C. Hull). Little and Brown, Boston, Mass.

Kaplan, R., 1973. Predictors of environmental preference: designers and clients. In: W.F.E. Preiser (Editor), Environmental Design Research, Vol. I, Selected Papers, 4th Int. EDRA Conf. Dowden, Hutchinson and Ross, Stroudsburg, Pa., pp. 265—274.

Kaplan, S., 1973. Cognitive maps, human needs, and the designed environment. Environmental Design Research, Vol. I, Selected Papers, 4th Int. EDRA Conf. Dowden, Hutchinson and Ross, Stroudsburg, Pa., pp. 275—283.

Kawai, M., 1965. Newly acquired precultural behavior of the natural troop of Japanese monkeys on Koshima islet. Primates, 6: 1—30.

Keller, S., 1972. Neighborhood concepts in sociological perspective. In: G. Bell and J. Tyrwhitt (Editors), Identity in the Urban Environment. Penguin, Baltimore, Md.

Klausner, S.Z., 1971. On Man in His Environment. Jossey-Bass, San Francisco, Calif.

Kuhn, T.S., 1962. The Structure of Scientific Revolutions. Univ. Chicago Press, Chicago, Ill.

Kummer, H., 1968. Social Organization of Hamadryas Baboons. Univ. Chicago Press, Chicago, Ill.

Lansing, J.B., Marans, R.W. and Lehaner, R.B., 1970. Planned Residential Environments. Univ. Michigan Press, Ann Arbor, Mich.

Lashley, K.S., 1949. Persistent problems in the evolution of mind. Q. Rev. Biol., 24: 26.

Le Corbusier, 1935. La Ville Radieuse: Elements d'use Doctrine Urbanisme pour l'Equipement de la Civilisation Machiniste. Editions de l'Architecture d'Aujourdhui, Boulogne.

LeMasters, E.E., 1975. Blue-Collar Aristocrats: Life-Styles at a Working-Class Tavern. Univ. Wisconsin Press, Madison, Wis.

LeVine, R.A. and Campbell, D.T., 1972. Ethnocentrism. Wiley, New York, N.Y.

Levitt, R., 1971. In pursuit of freedom: women in America. ZPG Nat. Rep., 3 : 5.

Leyhausen, P., 1971. Dominance and territoriality as complemented in mammalian social structure. In: A.H. Esser (Editor), Behavior and Environment. Plenum Press, New York, N.Y.

Leyhausen, P., 1969. Human nature and modern society. Soc. Res., 36 : 410—519.

Leyhausen, P., 1965. The communal organization of solitary mammals. Symp. Zool. Soc. London, 14: 249. Reprinted in H.M. Proshansky et al. (Editors), Environmental Psychology. Holt, Rinehart and Winston, New York, 1970.

Lomnitz, L., 1973. Reciprocity of Assistance: The Survival of the Unfittest. Doctoral Dissertation, D.F. Universidad Iberoamericana, Mexico (unpubl. ms.).

Lorenz, K., 1967. The evolution of behavior. Psychobiology: Readings from Scientific American. Freeman, San Francisco, Calif., Part I, Chapter 5.

Lorenz, K., 1966. On Aggression. Harcourt, Brace and World, New York, N.Y.

Lorenz, K., 1952. King Solomon's Ring. Crowell, New York, N.Y.

Lorenz, K. and Leyhausen, P., 1973. Motivation of Human and Animal Behavior: An Ethological View. Van Nostrand Reinhold, New York, N.Y.

Lozar, C., 1974. Application of behavioral settings analysis and undermanning theory to supermarket design. Proc. Environ. Des. Res. Assoc., 5th Int. EDRA Conf., Milwaukee, Wis., in press.

Lynch, K., 1960. The Image of the City. The MIT Press, Cambridge, Mass.

McBride, G., 1971. Theories of animal spacing: the role of flight, fight and social distance. In: A.H. Esser (Editor), Behavior and Environment. Plenum Press, New York, N.Y. pp. 53—68.

McHarg, I.L., 1969. Design with Nature. The Natural History Press, Garden City, N.Y.

MacLean, P.D., 1973a. The brain's generation gap: some human implications. Zygon/J. Relig. Sci., 8: 113—127.

MacLean, P.D., 1973b. Special award lecture: new findings on brain function and socio-sexual behavior. In: J. Zubin and J. Money (Editors), Contemporary Sexual Behavior: Critical Issues in the 1970's. Johns Hopkins Univ. Press, Baltimore, Md., Chapter 4.

MacLean, P.D., 1973c. A Triune Concept of the Brain and Behavior. Univ. Toronto Press, Toronto.

MacLean, P.D., 1971. Invited lecture, 138th Meet. Am. Assoc. Adv. Sci., Philadelphia, Pa.

MacLean, P.D., 1970. The triune brain, emotion, and scientific bias. In: F.O. Schmitt (Editor), The Neurosciences: Second Study Program. Rockefeller Univ., New York, N.Y.

MacLean, P.D., 1967. The brain in relation to empathy and medical education. J. Nerv. Ment. Dis., 144: 374—382.

MacLean, P.D., 1958. Contrasting function of limbic and neocortical systems of the brain and their relevance to psychophysiological aspects of medicine. Am. J. Med., 25: 611—626.

Maier, E., 1975. Torah as Movable Territory. Ann. Assoc. Am. Geogr., 65 : 1: 18—23.

Marsden, H.M., 1970. Crowding and Animal Behavior. Mimeographed paper prepared for Nat. Inst. Neurol. Dis. Stroke, Bethesda, Md.

Maslow, A.H., 1971. The Farther Reaches of Human Nature. The Viking Press, New York, N.Y.

Mayer, R.R., 1972. Social Planning and Social Change. Prentice-Hall, Englewood Cliffs, N.J.

Michelson, W., 1970. Man and His Urban Environment: A Sociological Approach. Addison, Reading, Mass.

Mill, J.S., 1843. A System of Logic, Vol. 2. John W. Parker, London.

Miller, G.R., Watson, A. and Jenkins, D., 1970. Responses of Red Grouse populations to experimental improvement of their food. In: A. Watson (Editor), Animal Populations in Relation to Their Food Resources, 10th Symp. Brit. Ecol. Soc. Blackwell, Oxford.

Minar, D.W. and Greer, S., 1969. The Concept of Community; Readings with Interpretations. Aldine, Chicago, Ill.

Montagu, M.F.A. (Editor), 1968. Man and Aggression. Oxford Press, New York, N.Y.

Moore, G.T., 1973. Developmental differences in environmental cognition. In: W.F.E. Preiser (Editor), Environmental Design Research, Vol. II, Symposia and Workshops, 4th Int. EDRA Conf. Dowden, Hutchinson and Ross, Stroudsburg, Pa., pp. 232—246.

Moore, O.K., 1969. Divination — a new perspective. In: A.P. Vayda (Editor), Environment and Cultural Behavior. The Natural History Press, New York, N.Y., pp. 121—128.

Morgan, T., 1973. Remembering Rene. N.Y. Times Mag., November 11th.

Morrill, R.L., 1970. The Spatial Organization of Society. Wadsworth, Belmont, Calif.

Morris, D., 1969. The Human Zoo. McGraw-Hill, New York, N.Y.

Morris, D., 1967. The Naked Ape. McGraw-Hill, New York, N.Y.

Mowat, K.E., 1971. Never Cry Wolf. Dell, New York, N.Y.

Moyer, K.E., 1971. The Physiology of Hostility. Markham, Chicago, Ill.

Mumford, L., 1966. The Myth of the Machine. Harcourt, Brace and World, New York, N.Y.

Mumford, L., 1961. City in History. Harcourt, Brace and World, New York, N.Y.

Mumford, L., 1934. Technics and Civilization. Harcourt and Brace, New York, N.Y.

Newman, O., 1972. Defensible Space. Macmillan, New York, N.Y.

Newsweek, 1971. The Battle of the Suburb. Special report, November 15th, pp. 61—70.

North, D., 1974. Life in an American Prison (unpubl. ms.). Dept. Landscape Archit. Reg. Plann., Univ. Massachusetts, Amherst, Mass.

Novak, M., 1972. The Rise of the Unmeltable Ethnics: Politics and Culture in the Seventies. Macmillan, New York, N.Y.

Nuckolls, K.B. and Cassel, J. (in press). Psycho-social assets, life crises, and the prognosis of pregnancy. Am. J. Epidemiol.

Oakley, D., 1970. The Phenomenon of Architecture in Cultures in Change. 1st ed., Pergamon Press, Oxford.

Paluck, R.J., Lieff, J.D. and Esser, A.H., 1970. Formation and development of a group of juvenile Hylobates Iar. Primates, 11: 185—194.

Papaz, J.W., 1937. A proposed mechanism of emotion. Arch. Neurol. Psychiatry, 38: 725.

Patterson, I.J., 1965. Timing and spacing of broods in the Black-Headed Bull. Ibis, 107: 433—439.

Perin, C., 1975. Social governance and environmental design. In: B. Honkiman (Editor), Responding to Social Change. Dowden, Hutchinson and Ross, Stroudsburg, Pa.

Perry, C., 1929. Neighborhood and Community Planning. Regional Plan Association of New York and Its Environs, New York, N.Y.

Pike, K.L., 1966. Etic and emic standpoints for the description of behavior. In: A.G. Smith (Editor), Communication and Culture. Holt, Rinehart and Winston, New York, N.Y. pp. 152—163.

Piaget, J., 1971. Biology and Knowledge. Univ. Chicago Press, Chicago, Ill.

Ploog, D., 1970. Neurological aspects of social behavior. In: J. Eisenberg and W. Dillon (Editors), Man and Beast. Smithsonian Institution Press, Washington, D.C.

Ploog, D. and Melnechuk, T., 1969. Primate communication. Neurosci. Res. Prog. Bull., 7: 419—509.

Popper, K., 1971. Conversations with philosophers — Sir Karl Popper talks about some of his basis ideas with Bryan Magee. The Listener, 85 : 2180 : 8—12.

Popper, K., 1935. Logik der Forschung. J. Springer Verlag, Vienna. (Transl. as The Logic of Scientific Discovery. Hutchinson, London, 1958.)

Rainwater, L., 1971. Poverty, race and urban housing. The Social Impact of Urban Design. Univ. Chicago Center for Policy Study, Chicago, Ill.

Rainwater, L. 1966. Fear and the house-as-haven in the lower class. J. Am. Inst. Plann., 32: 23—31.

Rand, C.T., 1974. The arabian fantasy. Harpers, 248 : 1484 : 42.

Rapoport, A., 1969. House Form and Culture. Prentice-Hall, Englewood Cliffs, N.J.

Rapoport, A. and Hawkes, R., 1970. The perception of urban complexity. J. Am. Inst. Plann., 36: 106—111.

Reps, J.W., 1965. The Making of Urban America. Princeton Univ. Press, Princeton, N.J.

Riesman, D., 1961. The Lonely Crowd. Yale Univ. Press, New Haven, Conn.

Rossi, P.H. (Editor), 1973. Ghetto Revolts. 2nd ed., Transaction Books, Brunswick, N.J.

Rossi, P.H., 1955. Why Families Move: A Study in the Social Psychology of Urban Residential Mobility, The Free Press, Glencoe, Ill.

Rossi, P.H. and Boesel, D. (Editors), 1971. Cities Under Siege: Anatomy of the Ghetto Riot. Basic Books, New York, N.Y.

Saarinen, E., 1943. The City. The MIT Press, Cambridge, Mass.

Sax, J.L., 1971. Defending the Environment: A Strategy for Citizen Action. A. Knopf, New York, N.Y.

Schaller, G.B., 1973. Golden Shadows, Flying Hoofs. A. Knopf, New York, N.Y.

Science News, 1971. The biology of violence: focus on the brain, 100: 403—404.

Sennet, R., 1970. Uses of Disorder: Personal Identity and City Life. A. Knopf, New York, N.Y.

Shepherd, N., 1973. The imperfect Israeli assessment of the Arabs. It is distorted by a bitter past and a segregated present. N.Y. Times, January 13th, p. 3E.

Sinclair, U., 1906. The Jungle. Doubleday Page, New York, N.Y.

Skinner, B.F., 1971. Beyond Freedom and Dignity. A. Knopf, New York, N.Y.

Snow, C.P., 1959. The Two Cultures and the Scientific Revolution, Cambridge Univ. Press, New York, N.Y.

Sommer, R., 1971. Spatial parameters in naturalistic social research. In: A.H. Esser (Editor), Behavior and Environment. Plenum Press, New York, N.Y., pp. 281—290.

Sommer, R., 1969. Personal Space. Prentice-Hall, Englewood Cliffs, N.J.

Spiro, M.E., 1965. Children of Kibbutz. Schocken Books, New York, N.Y.

Spiro, M.E., 1963. Kibbutz. Schocken Books, New York, N.Y.

Srivastava, R.K., 1975. Undermanning theory in the context of mental health care environments. Proc. Environ. Des. Res. Assoc., 5th Int. EDRA Conf., Milwaukee, Wis. in press.

Stavis, B., 1948. Lamp at Midnight. Dramatists Play Service, New York, N.Y.

Stein, M.R., 1960. The Eclipse of Community. Princeton Univ. Press, Princeton, N.J.

Stipe, R.E. (Editor), 1966. Perception and Environment: Foundations of Urban Design, Univ. N.C. Inst. Govt., Chapel Hill, N.C.

Storr, A., 1968. Human Aggression. Atheneum, New York, N.Y.

Stouffer, S.A., 1940. Intervening opportunities: a theory relating to mobility and distance. Am. Sociol. Rev., 5: 845.

Strong, A.L., 1971. Planned Urban Environments: Sweden, Finland, Israel, Netherlands, France. John Hopkins Press, Baltimore, Md.

Sumner, W.G., 1906. Folkways. Ginn, New York, N.Y.

Suttles, G.D., 1972. The Social Construction of Communities. Univ. Chicago Press, Chicago, Ill.

Suttles, G.D., 1968. The Social Order of the Slum; Ethnicity and Territory in the Inner City. Univ. Chicago Press, Chicago, Ill.

Synge, J.M., 1911. The Playboy of the Western World. Maunsel, Dublin.

Tiger, L., 1970. Dominance in human societies. Ann. Rev. Ecol. Systemat., 1: 287—305.

Tiger, L., 1969. Men in Groups. Random House, New York, N.Y.

Tiger, L. and Fox, R., 1971. The Imperial Animal. Holt, Rinehart and Winston, New York, N.Y.

Tinbergen, N., 1967. The curious behavior of the Stickleback. Psychobiology: Readings from Scientific American, Freeman, San Francisco, Calif., Part I, Chapter 1.

Tinbergen, N., 1961. The Herring Gull's World (rev. ed.). Basic Books, New York, N.Y.

Tinbergen, N., 1953. Social Behavior in Animals; with Special Reference to Vertebrates. Wiley, New York, N.Y.

Tinbergen, N., 1951. The Study of Instinct. Oxford Press, New York, N.Y.

Toffler, A., 1970. Future Shock. Random House, New York, N.Y.

Trotter, R.J., 1972. When people migrate. Sci. News, 101: 395.

Tunnard, C. and Pushkarev, B., 1963. Man-Made America: Chaos or Control? Yale Univ. Press, New Haven, Conn.

Tunnard, C. and Reed, H.H., 1955. American Skyline; The Growth and Form of Our Cities and Towns. Houghton-Mifflin, Boston, Mass.

Turnbull, C.M., 1972. The Mountain People. Simon and Schuster, New York, N.Y.

Twain, M. (pseud.), 1886. The Adventures of Tom Sawyer, by Samuel Clemens. The American Publ. Co., Hartford, Conn.

Twentieth Century Fund, 1971. New Towns; Laboratories for Democracy. Twentieth Century Fund, New York, N.Y.

U.S. National Advisory Commission on Civil Disorders, 1968. Report, N.Y. Times Co., New York, N.Y.

U.S. National Commission on the Causes and Prevention of Violence, 1968. Report, U.S.G.P.O., Washington, D.C.

Vanegas, H., Foote, W.E. and Flynn, J.P., 1969. Hypothalmic influence upon activity units of the visual cortex. Yale J. Biol. Med., December 1969—February 1970.

Von Foerster, H., 1973. On constructing a reality. In: W.F.E. Preiser (Editor), Environmental Design Research, Vol. II, Symposia and Workshops, 4th Int. EDRA Conf. Dowden, Hutchinson and Ross, Stroudsburg, Pa., pp. 35—46.

Walter, W.G., 1953. The Living Brain. W.W. Norton, New York, N.Y.

Washburn, S.L. and De Vore, I., 1967. The social life of baboons. Psychobiology: Readings from Scientific American. Freeman, San Francisco, Calif., Part I, Chapter 2.

Watson, A. and Moss, R., 1971. Spacing as affected by territorial behavior, habitat and nutrition in Red Grouse (Lagopus I. Scoticus). In: A.H. Esser (Editor), Behavior and Environment. Plenum Press, New York, N.Y., pp. 92—111.

Watson, A. and Moss, R., 1970. Dominance, spacing behavior and aggression in relation to population limitation in vertebrates. Animal Populations in Relation to their Food Resources, Symp. No. 10, Brit. Ecol. Soc. Blackwell, Oxford.

Watson, J.D., 1968. The Double Helix. Atheneum, New York, N.Y.

Watson, J.B., 1925. Behaviorism. W.W. Norton, New York, N.Y.

Whitten, R. and Adams, T., 1931. Neighborhoods of Small Homes; Economic Density of Low-Cost Housing in America and England, Harvard City Planning Studies, Vol. III. Harvard Univ. Press, Cambridge, Mass.

Whyte, W.H., 1974a. The best street life in the world. N.Y. Mag., 7 : 28 : 26—33.

Whyte, W.H., 1974b. Narrative Report: The Street Life Project. The Street Life Project, 30 Rockefeller Plaza, New York, N.Y. (mimeographed ms.).

Wilkie, R.W., 1974. The process method versus the hypothesis method: a nonlinear example of peasant spatial perceptions and behavior. In: M. Yeats (Editor), Proc. 1972 Meet. Int. Geog. Un. Comm. Quant. Geog., McGill-Queen's Univ. Press, Montreal and London, pp. 1—31.

Wilkie, R.W., 1972. Toward a behavioral model of peasant migration: an Argentine case study of spatial behavior by social class level. Population Dynamics of Latin America: A Review and Bibliography.

Wood, R.C., 1963. The American suburb: boy's town in a man's world. In: E. Geen et al.

(Editors), Man and the Modern City. Univ. Pittsburgh Press, Pittsburgh, Pa., pp. 112—121.

Wood, R.C., 1959. Suburbia: Its People and Their Politics. Houghton-Mifflin, Boston, Mass.

Wynne-Edwards, V.O., 1971. Space use and the social community in animals and men. In: A.H. Esser (Editor), Behavior and Environment. Plenum Press, New York, N.Y., pp. 267—280.

Wynne-Edwards, V.O., 1962. Animal Dispersion in Relation to Social Behavior. Hafner, New York, N.Y.

Yancy, W.L., 1971. Architecture, interaction, and social control. The case of a large-scale public housing project. Environ. Behav., 3: 3—21.

Zube, E., Brush, R.O. and Fabos, J.G. (Editors) (in press). Landscape Assessment: Values, Perceptions and Resources. Dowden, Hutchinson and Ross, Stroudsburg, Pa.

Index